BIOSTATISTICS MANUAL FOR HEALTH RESEARCH

BIOSTATISTICS MANUAL FOR HEALTH RESEARCH
A Practical Guide to Data Analysis

NAFIS FAIZI

Assistant Professor, Jawaharlal Nehru Medical College,
Aligarh Muslim University, Aligarh, India

YASIR ALVI

Assistant Professor, Hamdard Institute of Medical Sciences and
Research, New Delhi, India

ELSEVIER

ACADEMIC PRESS

An imprint of Elsevier

Academic Press is an imprint of Elsevier
125 London Wall, London EC2Y 5AS, United Kingdom
525 B Street, Suite 1650, San Diego, CA 92101, United States
50 Hampshire Street, 5th Floor, Cambridge, MA 02139, United States
The Boulevard, Langford Lane, Kidlington, Oxford OX5 1GB, United Kingdom

Notices
Knowledge and best practice in this field are constantly changing. As new research and experience broaden our understanding, changes in research methods, professional practices, or medical treatment may become necessary.

Practitioners and researchers must always rely on their own experience and knowledge in evaluating and using any information, methods, compounds, or experiments described herein. In using such information or methods they should be mindful of their own safety and the safety of others, including parties for whom they have a professional responsibility.

To the fullest extent of the law, neither the Publisher nor the authors, contributors, or editors, assume any liability for any injury and/or damage to persons or property as a matter of products liability, negligence or otherwise, or from any use or operation of any methods, products, instructions, or ideas contained in the material herein.

ISBN: 978-0-443-18550-2

For information on all Academic Press publications visit our
website at https://www.elsevier.com/books-and-journals

Publisher: Stacy Masucci
Acquisitions Editor: Linda Versteeg-Buschman
Editorial Project Manager: Matthew Mapes
Production Project Manager: Fahmida Sultana
Cover Designer: Mark Rogers

Typeset by TNQ Technologies

Working together
to grow libraries in
developing countries

www.elsevier.com • www.bookaid.org

All the IBM® SPSS® Statistics software ("SPSS") screenshots are permitted for use in this book through "Reprint Courtesy of IBM Corporation ©".

MedCalc Software screenshots are permitted for use in the book by M Frank Schoonjans, MedCalc Software Ltd.

Contents

About the authors

Nafis Faizi

Dr. Nafis Faizi is an Assistant Professor and Epidemiologist at Jawaharlal Nehru Medical College, Aligarh Muslim University, India. He is currently a fellow of Health Policy and Systems Research (India HPSR Fellow) and an Academic Editor of *Plos Global Public Health*. He is also an active trainer for Epidemiological Research Unit and a member of Statistics Without Borders and Global Health Training Network. For the past 9 years, he has been conducting regular workshops and training in biostatistics, data analysis, and research writing. His primary qualifications are MBBS and MD in Community Medicine from India followed by master's in Public Health (MPH) from the United Kingdom besides multiple executive courses and trainings including those from JPAL, SPSS South Asia, and International Union against TB and Lung Diseases (Operational Research). He is also a faculty for International People's Health University and teaches epidemiology and biostatistics at Victoria University. Previously, he worked as Scientist E at the Indian Council of Medical Research-National Institute of Malaria Research (ICMR-NIMR). He is a member of multiple professional associations including Statistics Without Borders, International Epidemiological Association, Health Action International, IAPSM, and IPHA.

Yasir Alvi

Dr. Yasir Alvi is an Assistant Professor at Hamdard Institute of Medical Sciences and Research, New Delhi, India. An alumnus of Aligarh Muslim University, his primary qualifications are MBBS and MD in Community Medicine. He has more than 8 years of teaching and research experience and has published numerous academic articles in reputed journals focusing on public health, mental health, HIV, tuberculosis, and COVID-19. He has been the lead investigator and statistical consultant in more than a dozen projects funded by the WHO, UNICEF, ICMR, and various research institutions. He is regularly involved in training and human resource development of public health students and healthcare providers on data analysis, research writing, and biostatistics.

Preface

In 1937, Sir Austin Bradford Hill wrote, "Statistics are curious things. They afford one of the few examples in which the use, or abuse, of mathematical methods tends to induce a strong emotional reaction in non-mathematical minds. This is because statisticians apply, to problems in which we are interested, a technique which we do not understand. It is exasperating, when we have studied a problem by methods that we have spent laborious years mastering, to find our conclusions questioned, and perhaps refuted, by someone who could not have made the observations himself. It requires more equanimity than most of us possess to acknowledge that the fault is in ourselves."

Over the past decade, we have provided statistical consulting and training to health researchers and have encountered their difficulties in biostatistical application. We have also conducted numerous biostatistics workshops, primarily based on SPSS. The most recurrent feedback postworkshop was the need for a biostatistics book that could help in day-to-day research. Clinicians and public health researchers typically have dual roles in addition to research—both in the services sector as well as in teaching and/or administration. There are excellent books on biostatistics, but most are theory-laden and do not help with practical applications. We have attempted to write a book that bridges this gap, provides enough theory, and delves into the applications and interpretations of biostatistical tests. We have also provided boxes in each chapter to highlight the problems that arise from wrong application or choice of tests, which to our surprise is quite common.

Our aim is to equip health researchers with all the necessary tools they need to confidently apply biostatistics and interpret their meanings correctly. This book is written as an instruction manual for applying, comprehending, and interpreting biostatistics rather than delving deeply into the theoretical underpinnings and heavy statistical calculations. This book originally began as a design for a handbook in our workshops and training sessions on epidemiological research, but has evolved into its current shape thanks to contributions from training participants, peers, and students. The book has been designed for 12 sessions to be conducted over 3 intensive days (an agenda is provided in annexure). We provide hands-on data with details for practice. Ideally, such a three-day session would be most beneficial for researchers who are preparing to write their research protocols, dissertations, or scientific papers.

This book has been written as an aid to the few biostatistics enthusiasts who stand as troubleshooters for the entire medical college, hospital, or institute. The book would serve as a very helpful rapid reference guide for epidemiology units, research advisory committees, and medical education units/departments. We believe that an experienced epidemiologist or health researcher can also conduct a workshop based on this manual. If anyone plans to hold such a workshop, we ask that the book be provided as a part of the workshop kit so that all participants can benefit from it and refer to it in the future. We continue to conduct workshops on biostatistics based on this manual, and would love to help in conducting such sessions.

Please feel free to advise, suggest, comment, and criticize the contents as well as intents of this work. We would be especially grateful if you could point out any errors—inadvertent or otherwise—in the book. This book is devoted to encouraging students and scholars to conduct research with a sense of curiosity. It remains the most effective source of hope in these trying times.

Nafis Faizi and Yasir Alvi

List of abbreviations

ANCOVA	Analysis of Covariance
ANOVA	Analysis of Variance
ASA	American Statistical Association
AUC	Area Under Curve
BMI	Body Mass Index
COPE	Committee on Publication Ethics
DDS	Data Documentation Sheet
GIGO	Garbage In, Garbage Out
GRRAS	Guidelines for Reporting Reliability and Agreement Studies
ICC	Intra Class Correlation
ICMJE	International Committee of Medical Journal Editors
IEC	Institutional Ethics Committee
IQR	Interquartile Range
KS or K—S test	Kolmogorov—Smirnov test
LIMO	Linearity, Independence, Multicollinearity, and Outliers
LINE-M	Linearity, Independence, Normality, Equality of variances, and Multicollinearity
LR	Likelihood Ratio
LSD or Fisher's LSD	Least Significant Difference
MANOVA	Multivariate Analysis of Covariance
NHST	Null Hypothesis Significance Testing
NPV	Negative Predictive Value
OR	Odds Ratio
PCA	Principal Component Analysis
PPV	Positive Predictive Value
RMANOVA	Repeated Measures Analysis of Variance
ROC curve	Receiver Operating Characteristic Curve
SAMPL	Statistical Analyses and Methods in the Published Literature
SD	Standard Deviation
SE or SEM	Standard Error of the Mean
SPSS	Statistical Package for Social Sciences
STARD	Standards for Reporting of Diagnostic Accuracy
SW or S—W test	Shapiro—Wilk test
TSA	Time Series Analysis
Tukey's HSD	Tukey's Honestly Significant Difference test
VIF	Variance Inflation Factor
WHO	World Health Organization

CHAPTER 1

Introduction to biostatistics

Statistical thinking will one day be as necessary a qualification for efficient citizenship as the ability to read and write.

H.G. Wells

1. Background

In 2010, while reading a popular biostatistics book, we came across a statement by Professor Frederick Mosteller on statistics that struck a chord with us and continues to do so. He said, "*It is easy to lie with statistics, but it is easier to lie without them*" (Pagano & Gauvreau, 2000). In human health and medicine, statistics are vital to gauge uncertainties and variations to measure, interpret, and analyze them. This in turn helps to determine whether they are due to biological, genetic, behavioral, or environmental variability or simply due to chance (Indrayan & Malhotra, 2017).

However, the contribution of data and statistics in medical education and public health is sometimes taken for granted. Despite the importance of data, little efforts are made in many hospitals (both private and public) to analyze the data and calculate vital information such as average duration of stay of malaria patients in the hospital ward, analysis of the catchment area of different specialties, time taken by a patient to finally see a doctor in a government hospital, and other data. These data have an effect on everyday practice, decision-making, and the working of hospitals. Healthcare is knowledge-based, and knowledge is created through careful transformation and treatment of data, scientific temper, and available expertise. While times have changed, we still find Florence Nightingale's note on hospitals relevant—"*In attempting to arrive at the truth, I have applied everywhere for information, but in scarcely an instance have I been able to obtain hospital records fit for any purposes of comparison*" (Nightingale, 1863).

With digitalization and smart technologies, data is everywhere but not often converted to meaningful information and even lesser to beneficial knowledge. T.S. Eliot's the Rock had a great reminder- "..Where is the life we have lost in living, where is the wisdom we have lost in knowledge, where is the knowledge we have lost in information.." "***Poor data is worse than no data***", and observations based on experience and eminence alone are worse than poor data, as they are poorly recorded and often, biased (Faizi et al., 2018). Knowledge in the era of evidence-based medicine critically depends on carefully conducted research and its statistical analysis, rather than the Alice in

Wonderland saying, '*I'm older than you, and must know better*" (Carroll, 1991). However, even within these limitations, we have different statistical tools which help in understanding these uncertainties and limitations better. We must strive to "*become aware of the nature and extent of these imperfect informations*" instead of getting "*paralyzed by this lack of knowledge*" (Cohen et al., 1987).

Let us consider this very important example from the 1950s regarding the then considered treatment of coronary artery disease (CAD) (Belle et al., 2004). CAD is a widely prevalent disease in which the coronary arteries get occluded, leading to angina pectoris (pain in the chest). Further narrowing leads to deprivation of blood supply to heart muscles, which eventually leads to Myocardial Infarction (MI), commonly known as a Heart Attack. In the 1950s, it was widely believed that a large blood supply would be forced to the heart by ligating internal mammary arteries (which supplies blood to the chest). Not only was this considered promising, but it was also carried out with reasonably successful results. It gathered a fair amount of support till adequately designed studies were conducted. We reproduce the results of one such study to emphasize the importance of statistics (Dimond et al., 1960). This study took 18 patients randomly selected for internal mammary arteries (IMA) ligation or sham operation. The sham operation consisted of a similar incision with exposure of IMA but no ligation. Both the cardiologist and the patients were blind to the actual procedure. Table 1.1 shows the results of the study. Please note that the results in Table 1.1 are based on the research paper (Dimond et al., 1960), but the groups have been clubbed for the sake of illustration.

Even a preliminary look at the data indicates no real difference between the sham operation and ligation of IMA. Based on this observation alone, some may even be tempted to say that the sham operation was actually better, as every patient felt cured/benefitted after the operation. However, there is always an element of chance in our observations, which must be accounted for, before interpreting the results. Numerical observations alone could be simply due to chance. This is something we will discuss later in this book. For now, we apply Fisher's exact test on this table, and the p-value is 0.28. Such a p-value means that the difference between the effects is not significant and could be due to chance. This means that the perception of cure/benefit was not significantly different with the Sham operation. Therefore, such statistical inference is vital. With

Table 1.1 Surgical benefit postligation of internal mammary artery (patients' opinion).

Perception of surgical effects on symptoms	Ligation of internal mammary artery	Sham operation
Cured/benefitted	9	5
Disappointed/no long-term improvement	4	0
Total	13	5

the careful application of epidemiology and research, statistics has truly transformed modern medicine, saving millions of lives. So, the next time you feel that it is too difficult to attempt climbing this learning curve, ask yourself whether you would consent for such an operation that ligates your artery in a futile attempt to improve angina pectoris.

2. What is biostatistics?

Biostatistics (biostatistics) is defined as "*statistical processes and methods applied to the collection, analysis, and interpretation of biological data and especially data relating to human biology, health, and medicine*" (Merriam-Webster, n.d.). However, if biostatistics is limited to human biology, health, and medicine, one is tempted to ask why not learn statistics itself?

2.1 Why biostatistics rather than statistics?

There are three distinct reasons for the focus on biostatistics in health research, rather than statistics (Belle et al., 2004). The three reasons are methods, language, and application. The first reason is the statistical methods. Some statistical methods have a distinct and everyday use in biostatistics unlike in statistics, requiring due attention and concern—for example, survival life-table analyses. Second, every subject has its language and the language of biostatistics is closer to biomedical and healthcare areas. The steep language curve to bridge the language of both these disciplines is easier to scale with biostatistics rather than statistics. The third is the application of biostatistical analysis. Owing mainly to its directed and tailored language, biostatistical analysis is directly understood and applied in healthcare and related policies. The application of biostatistics is ubiquitous in healthcare and is easily understood and applied among healthcare workers.

2.2 Role of biostatistics

Biostatistics is an essential tool for health research and clinical decision-making as well as healthcare research. While this manual focuses on its role in data analysis and interpretation, it is essential to note that biostatistics has a significant role in the following steps of research:
1. Research planning and designing
2. Data collection
3. Data entry and management
4. Data analysis
5. Data interpretation and presentation.

   In health research, more often than not, the biostatistician is consulted during or after the data entry for further analysis. In many cases, this is too late. Often, even resuscitation attempts could be rendered futile at such a stage. The famous statistician Ronald Fisher aptly commented in the first session of the Indian Statistical Conference, in Calcutta in 1938, "*To call in the statistician after the experiment is done may be no more than asking him to perform a post-mortem examination: he may be able to say what the experiment died of.*"

3. Statistical inference

Our world often revolves around the careful recognition of patterns and associations. Sometimes, they are entirely wrong, such as the many conspiracy theories and disinformation campaigns circulating daily on social media. Statistical and epidemiological illiteracy aids in making such mistakes. Such progressions are even pathological, as we see in cases of paranoia. This extreme error of perception is called *apophenia*, a tendency to interpret random patterns as meaningful. If apophenia is one extreme, the other extreme is unofficially called *randomania*, which is a failure to recognize or appreciate meaningful patterns when they exist. In statistical inferential terms, apophenia is a bigger problem as it is a Type 1 error, whereas randomania is akin to a Type 2 error. We will discuss this more in Chapter 3.

Statistical inference or inferential statistics is the *"process through which inferences about a population are made based on certain statistics calculated from a sample of data drawn from that population"* (Johnson et al., 2012). How to draw statistical inferences is the primary purpose of this book. In simpler terms, it answers a simple question, whether the numerical or observational difference in the data is significant, or is it due to chance? Essentially there are three forms of such inferences:

1. **Point estimation**: In point estimation, we are interested in a single number for the target population from a sample. For example, What is the mean weight of infant boys in rural Delhi? Through a designed cross-sectional study, we find that the mean weight is 10 kg.
2. **Interval Estimation** is about estimating the unknown parameter of the population that lies within the two intervals, as calculated from the sample. For example, the 95% confidence interval of the mean weight of infant boys in Delhi was found from the sample to be 9.1—11.0. This means that there is a 95% chance that the values of the actual population will lie between these values.
3. **Hypothesis testing**: This starts with a claim/assumption about the data-null hypothesis, and we check through data whether the claim is true or false. We will learn more about this in Chapter 3.

In terms of logic and reasoning, we must be aware that the inferential process in statistics and most science is inductive and not deductive like mathematics. While we refrain from a detailed discussion on this, it is essential to clearly understand inductive and deductive reasoning. Taking full responsibility of oversimplification, we leave it to Sherlock Holmes and Aristotle to explain this further in Fig. 1.1.

In dire opposition to the norms of police investigations, Sherlock Holmes gathered evidence without proposing a theory. He clearly explains his process akin to statistical inferential reasoning, *"Let me run over the main steps. We approached the case, you remember, with an absolutely blank mind, which is always an advantage. We had formed no theories. We were simply there to observe and draw inferences from our observations"* (Doyle, 1893).

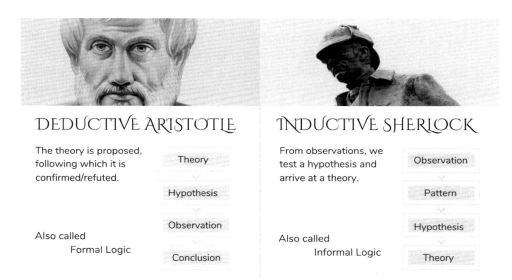

Figure 1.1 *The inductive Holmes and the deductive Aristotle.* Comparing deductive approach of Aristotle and inductive approach of Sherlock Holmes.

4. Aim of the book

This book is designed as a manual for doctors and health researchers, focusing on a practical understanding of applied biostatistics in health research. The book also deals with introductory biostatistics essential for any researcher. Over the years, we came across questions without satisfactory answers, such as the difference between association and correlation or the exact reason why we cannot apply multiple t-tests instead of ANOVA. We have tried to cover such questions in boxes. However, we have tried our best to refrain and restrict ourselves (sometimes with great difficulty) to only as much theory as is required to interpret, choose, and analyze statistical tests correctly. There is an abundance of theory-laden textbooks on biostatistics which are necessary to develop advanced skills in biostatistics. The contents of this book are as relevant and essential for understanding, reading, and writing papers, as it is for conducting research.

The book has been written in the form of a manual, as we believe that applied biostatistics can be best learned in a workshop-based environment. The book has been arranged accordingly so that each chapter is loosely based on a session (or atleast two in case of regression), and we also propose a workshop-based agenda should the medical education, and/or research units need to adopt a methodology that we have used for quite some time (see Annexures, Chapter 12). We use SPSS as the statistical software to perform the statistical calculations. In the next chapter, we introduce the SPSS software and provide screenshots of how to analyze the statistical tests under discussion in the following chapters. The second chapter also engages with relevant data management principles, including data entry, which is deprioritized to the level of deliberate and wilful neglect, despite its huge importance. The third chapter is essential to learn a few crucial concepts before analyzing any data and applying statistical tests. We are vehemently opposed to "garbage in and garbage out (GIGO)" practices where we commit gross injustice by playing with our data and submitting it to software to create sophisticated figures and statistics. At best, they contribute to creating a pile of rubbish research (along with noise pollution), and at worse, they find their way to better journals and affect guidelines and policy. The latter imperils human health and the former insults human mind. After the first three chapters, the rest of the chapters deal with statistical tests in different situations.

To summarize, the main objectives of this manual are to introduce biostatistics in a way that readers can:

1. Choose and apply appropriate statistical tests.
2. Interpret and present the findings of the statistical tests correctly.
3. Understand and review the results and statistical interpretations of most research published in medical journals.
4. Use SPSS for statistical analysis with ease and without anyone's help.

5. Two foundational concepts

There are two concepts that lay down the foundation for what we will learn later (they never fail to amaze us). The first is the law of large numbers, and the other is the central limit theorem (Box 1.1).

5.1 Law of large numbers

The law of large numbers is a probability concept that states, "*The more you sample, the truer your sample mean is to the average mean of the population.*" This means that as we increase the sample size of our research, the chances of our sample average being closer to the actual population average increase. This is extremely important for research as it establishes the consistency of the estimator and predicts the validity of the results in a wider population. In other words it helps in a strong internal and external validity as well as generalizability. Remember the story of the hare and the tortoise? The one in which

---

BOX 1.1 Central limit theorem and law of large numbers
Both these theorems are important theorems about the sample mean. The law of large numbers states that the sample mean approaches the population mean as n gets large. On the other hand, the central limit theorem states that multiple sample means approach a normal distribution as n gets large (n denotes sample size).

the slow and steady tortoise won the race? While the message could be true, the evidence behind it is not. The story lacks an adequate sample size for such a bold inference. Fiction and anecdotes can be helpful in highlighting messages but should not be a hindrance to evidence. A place for everything and everything in its place.

Another way to understand this is through the good old coin with two faces—head and tail. The probability of getting head is 50%, but this may not be evident when Mr. Lucky goes for a toss. Mr. Lucky has the habit of winning tosses. The law of large number states that Mr. Lucky has not been observed so much. If he participates in a "large" number of tosses and says head every time, the chances are that he would lose almost 50% of the time (Table 1.2). Gambler's fallacy is an interesting fallacy (Box 1.2).

Table 1.2 Law of large numbers in a coin toss.

Coin toss	Result		Probability of heads (out of 100 %)
Number of tosses	Heads	Tails	
1	1	0	1/1 = 100%
10	7	3	7/10 = 70%
100	65	35	65/100 = 65%
1000	601	399	601/1000 = 60.1%
10,000	5402	4598	5402/10,000 = 54.02%
100,000	50,100	49,900	50,100/100,000 = 50.10%

BOX 1.2 Gambler's fallacy

A common erroneous claim arises due to the belief that any number of the observed sample could represent a large population. Also known as the Monte Carlo fallacy, this is a famous story from the Monte Carlo casino in 1913. Gamblers mistakenly believe that if s/he is losing (or not getting the number) s/he expects, it would even out in the next turn, and they will win that turn. In Monte Carlo Casino, the ball fell on black 26 times in a row. As this was an extremely uncommon occurrence, the gamblers thought that the next will not be black. They lost millions putting a bet against black, believing that the streak was extremely unlikely and had to be followed by a streak of red.

This is due to their mistaken belief that if something is more frequent now, it will become less likely in the future. This is a fallacy as the next event or turn is "independent" of the previous event. This is similar to the joke on the poor deduction of surgical optimism. The surgeon proclaims—"Nine times out of 10, this operation is unsuccessful. This makes you a lucky patient as you are patient number 10."

5.2 Central limit theorem

The central limit theorem states that given certain conditions *if multiple samples are taken from a population, the means of the samples would be normally distributed, even if the population is not normally distributed.* Unlike the Law of Large Numbers, central limit theorem is a statistical theory, not a probability concept. In other words, if the means/averages of all the different studies from a population are plotted, we get a normally distributed curve. The mean/average of such a curve is the average of the population.

The normal distribution curve is also called the Gaussian curve after the name of Carl Friedrich Gauss who discovered it in 1809. Many scientists are of the opinion that Gaussian curve is a more appropriate name as the underlying distribution has both the so-called "normal" and "abnormal" values. In 1810, Marquis de Laplace proved the central limit theorem, validating and upholding its importance (Laplace, 1810).

As we would see later, the normal distribution curve is a bell-shaped curve with certain important properties that have profound implications for statistical tests (Fig. 1.2).

For now, it would suffice to know two of its properties:

1. The graph is symmetrical around its highest point. The highest point is the mean (μ, symbol for mean or average).
2. The distribution follows the 68—95-99.7 rule. This means that in a normally distributed data, 68% of the population has a value within mean $\pm$ 1 standard deviation ($\mu \pm 1$ SD), 95% have a value within mean $\pm$ 2 standard deviations ($\mu \pm 2$ SD), and 99.7% within a mean $\pm$ 3 standard deviations ($\mu \pm 3$ SD).

While discussing the 68-95-99.7 rule, another less important but interesting theorem is *Chebyshev's inequality theorem.* Chebyshev's inequality theorem states that regardless of

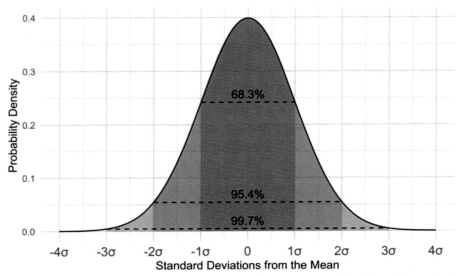

Figure 1.2 *The 68—95-99.7 rule.* Bell's curve showing the area covered by 1,2, and 3 standard deviations. *(From Wikipedia commons (CC-BY-4.0).)*

the probability distribution, at least $1 - 1/k^2$ of the distribution's values are always within k standard deviations of the mean. In other words, regardless of the distribution, at least 75% of the values will always lie within two standard deviations ($1 - 1/k^2$, with $k = 2$), and at least 88.8% of the values within three standard deviations ($1 - 1/k^2$, with $k = 3$).

6. Data and variables

6.1 Data

The word data refers to observations and measures often collected through research. When data are carefully arranged and analyzed, it becomes information. Data are classified as qualitative and quantitative. While qualitative data are nonnumeric, quantitative data are numeric. In statistical software and study questionnaires, we prefer entering data in numbers and assigning values for each number. For example, blood groups A, B, O, and AB could be coded as 1, 2, 3, and 4. This makes it more efficient as it is less prone to error while collecting and entering, as we will discover later. An important subclassification of data type is NOIR, that is, nominal, ordinal, interval, and ratio data. While nominal and ordinal data are qualitative, interval and ratio are quantitative (Table 1.3).

Table 1.3 Types of data.

Data type	Nominal	Ordinal	Scale
Nature	Qualitative	Qualitative	Quantitative
Assessment	Labels	Ordered/ranked	Countable/measurable
Expression	Proportions/percentages	Proportions/percentages	Average or mean
Measure of central tendency	Not applicable	Mode	Mean, median, mode
Examples	Normal, anemic	Mild, moderate and severe anemia	Hemoglobin levels (Hb g%)
	Obese, normal	Morbidly obese, obese, overweight	Body mass index (BMIs in kg/m^2)
	Normotensive, hypertensive	Mild, moderate, and severe hypertension	Blood pressure (mm g)
	Vaccine vial monitor (VVM): useable or unusable	4 stages of VVM	Not applicable
	Pediatric, adults, geriatric	Age groups: lowest, lower, higher, highest (0—10, 10—20, 20—30, 30—40)	Age

6.2 Qualitative data

Qualitative data are unmeasurable and uncountable data or attributes. It is categorical—described or labeled data into different categories or states. Quantitative data are either countable or measurable.

6.2.1 Nominal data

Nominal data are qualitative data with only names/labels/categories without comparable or intuitive order. Example: Blood Groups A, B, O, AB.

6.2.2 Ordinal data

Ordinal data are qualitative data with categories that could be ordered or ranked. However, the difference between the categories cannot be measured or is not known. For example, mild, moderate, and severe fever.

6.3 Quantitative data

6.3.1 Scale data: interval and ratio

Both interval and ratio are numerical data with little difference between them. In fact, many statistical software (including SPSS) consider no difference between them, as it considers both as scale data, the data that can be scaled. In interval data, as its meaning suggests (interval = gap = space in between), not only orders but exact differences are also known. Height, weight, blood pressure, etc. are all examples of scaled data.

The difference between interval and ratio is best appreciated when any attribute does not have an absolute or meaningful zero. For example, temperature is measured in degrees such as Celsius degrees. A temperature of $0°C$ is not "no" temperature as zero suggests. This is in stark opposition to the Kelvin scale, where $0 K$ actually means no temperature and is, therefore, a true zero (Table 1.4). Zero Kelvin is the lowest temperature limit of a thermodynamic scale. It is the temperature at the hypothetical point at which all molecular activity ceases, and the substance has no thermal energy. So, in ratio variables the zero has a meaningful role. For example, if your Car has an inside temperature of $12°C$ and the outside temperature is $24°C$, it would be wrong to say that the outside temperature is double than inside the car. This is because the reference point

Table 1.4 Temperature measures in Kelvin and Celsius.

Kelvin	Celsius	Fahrenheit
0 K	−273.15°	−459.67°
255.4 K	−17.8°	0°
273.15 K	0°	32°
373.15 K	100°	212°
Data type—ratio	Data type—interval	

to compare them needs 0 as a reference point, and the $0°$ on the celsius scale is meaningless. However, 24 K is double that of 12 K because it has a meaningful 0 as a reference point. The temperature in Kelvin is a ratio type data (Kelvin is also the standard unit (SI) of temperature measurement).

Both interval and ratio data actually measure an attribute, unlike nominal or ordinal data where the attribute cannot be measured but can only be labeled or ranked, respectively.

6.3.2 Discrete and continuous

Quantitative data are also classified into discrete and continuous data. Discrete data are countable, whereas continuous data are measurable. What does this mean? Discrete data are data that can take a restricted number of fixed specified values, for example, number of children born to a woman (can be 1, 2, etc. but not 1.5). Continuous data can take an unrestricted number of measurable values, although they may have an upper or lower limit. For example, weight cannot be <0 kg. Another essential point to note is that measures have units. For example, height can be measured in centimeters or inches. Countable data or discrete data do not have units of measurement. The ordinal (qualitative) and discrete (quantitative) data difference is explained in Box 1.3.

6.4 Cardinal and ordinal data

The term *Cardinal* measures answers the question of *how many,* whereas *Ordinal* measures *only rank* individuals or households, as explained before. So, cardinal measures are continuous measures such as age in years or weight in kilograms, etc.

6.5 Variable

Research use variables. Variables are any characteristics, numbers, or quantity that can be measured/counted, labeled, or ordered. In other words, variables are used as data items, and the term is used interchangeably with data. However, in health research, the term variable is strictly used to identify and describe the different characteristics of the sample.

BOX 1.3 Ordinal data versus discrete data

Whereas ordinal data are qualitative, the discrete data are quantitative data. In ordinal data, the ranking or order is only important (e.g., mild, moderate, or severe anemia), whereas in discrete data, both order and magnitude are important (e.g., number of children born to a woman). For discrete data, two points are important to note: (1) numbers in discrete data represent actual countable quantities rather than labels that can be ordered or arranged, and (2) in discrete data, a natural order exists among the possible values.

Table 1.5 Common terms, synonyms, and conventions for different variables.

Variable	Outcome variable	Exposure variable
Synonyms/alternative terms		
Dependence effect Questionnaire based Case-control design Interventional design Regressions	Dependent variable Response variable Case-control groups Outcomes Regressand	Independent variable Explanatory variable Risk factors Exposure/Treatment group Regressor Covariates (continuous) Factors (categorical)
Conventions		
Mathematical/Regression equations Tables Graphs	Left-hand side Columns y-variable Vertical	Right-hand side Rows x-variable Horizontal

In research, we describe variables as an outcome and exposure variables (Table 1.5). To test hypotheses, the outcome variables are also called dependent variables, whereas the exposure variables are called independent variables. Although, in the strict sense, "independent" means that the said variable independently affects the dependent variable. In regression and other mathematical models, the outcome variable is placed on the left-hand side of the equation and the predictors/exposures on the right-hand side. In tables, the independent variables are usually identified as rows and dependent as columns.

7. Measures of central tendency and dispersion

7.1 Introduction

Measures of central tendency describe the location of the middle of the data. It is a measure of the data average, a single value that could represent the whole data. Variability measures the spread of the data around its middle or central values. In other words, it is a measure of spread or dispersion.

7.2 Central tendency

The central tendency in inferential statistics is most commonly measured as arithmetic mean or mean. The mean is the mathematical average of the observations and is calculated by dividing the sum of the observations by the total number of observations (Table 1.6). In normally distributed data (or even nearly normal), the mean is the best representative measure of central tendency. However, since it is calculated

Table 1.6 Measures of central tendency.

Dataset (weight in kg)	Mean ($\bar{x} = \Sigma x_i/n$) (arithmetic mean)	Median (middle most value)	Mode (most commonly occurring value)
7,8,9,10,10,10,11,12.13	7 + 8+..+13/ 9 = 10	5th value = 10	10
7,8,9,10,10,10,11,12.13,30	7 + 8..+30/ 10 = 12	5th + 6th value/ 2 = 10	10
1,7,8,9,10,10,10,11,12.13	1 + 7+..+13/ 10 = 9.1	5th + 6th value/ 2 = 10	10

mathematically, it tends to be affected most by any one very large/very small value (outliers) in the dataset. Outliers also affect the normal distribution of the data. Mean is represented as (called x bar) and is calculated mathematically as follows: $= \Sigma x_i/n$, where Σ represents the summation of all individual values, that is, x_i and n represents the total number of values.

If the data are not normally distributed or have outliers, the median becomes a better representative measure of central tendency. This can be appreciated in the second and third datasets in Table 1.6. Usually median is not calculated mathematically but is simply the middlemost value when the data are arranged in an ascending or descending order. When the middlemost values (as in even number of data) are two, their average value is the median.

Sometimes, we need to know the most commonly occurring value to describe a phenomenon in health sciences. Such a measure is called mode. A dataset could be unimodal or bimodal, or even multimodal. The data in Table 1.6 show a unimodal presentation. However, diseases like Hodgkin's lymphoma have a bimodal presentation, with most common occurrence around age 15 and age 55 years.

Mean, median, and mode tend to overlap in a normally distributed data. However, the mean tends to be affected the most with the addition of even one outlier and reflects skewing (Fig. 1.3). One outlier toward the right (large value) moves the mean toward the right. This rightward shift or long right tail is called positive skewing, where mean becomes rightmost or higher than median and mode and is no longer the best representative of central tendency. Similarly, one outlier toward the left (small value) moves the mean toward the left. This leftward shift or long left tail is called negative skewing, where mean becomes leftmost or lower than median and mode and is no longer the best representative of central tendency.

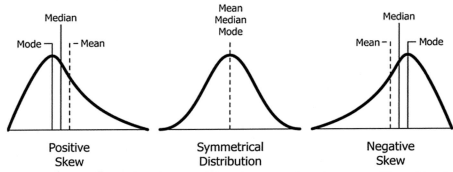

Figure 1.3 *Measures of central tendency and Gaussian curve.* Gaussian curve with positive skewing and negative skewing. *(From Wikipedia commons (CC-By-4.0).)*

7.3 Dispersion

Dispersion or variability is the measure of spread around the central tendency. There are many ways of measuring dispersion—range, interquartile range, standard deviation, and others. Standard deviation (s) is a mathematical measure of drift from the mean and is calculated mathematically as $s = \sqrt{\Sigma(x_i -)^2/n - 1}$, where the numerator is the sum of squares of individual data differences from mean $\Sigma(x_i -)^2$ and n is the total number of observations. The square root of the values is standard deviation, whereas, without the square root, it is called variance.

The reason standard deviation is measured by squaring the deviations at first and then taking the square root is to value the magnitude of difference from the mean, regardless of the direction of difference. Whether the values are shifted toward right or left from the mean, it is equally a measure of spread, and the magnitude is equal. For example, in Table 1.7, the difference between first and last observation from the mean is -3 $(7 - 10)$

Table 1.7 Calculating the standard deviation of a dataset.

Observations x_i	Mean ($\bar{x} = \Sigma x_i/n$)	Square of difference from mean $(x_i - \bar{x})^2$	Standard deviation $\sqrt{\Sigma(x_i - \bar{x})^2/n - 1}$
7	10	9	$= \sqrt{28/8} = 1.87$
8	10	4	
9	10	1	
10	10	0	
10	10	0	
10	10	0	
11	10	1	
12	10	4	
13	10	9	
Total	$7+..+13/9 = 10$	$\Sigma(x_i - \bar{x})^2 = 28$	

and 3 (13 − 10). Squaring them removes the impact of these signs. The other important feature is $n − 1$. In small samples such as the ones we use, $n − 1$ is a better mathematical measure than n. However, in population standard deviations, n should be used instead of $n − 1$. An example of standard deviation calculation is given in Table 1.7. In any case, most of these calculations are easily done through software, calculators, and websites such as easycalculation.com.

The range is the difference between the maximum and minimum values in the data set. The use of range as a measure of dispersion is very limited in biostatistics. Its most important usage is to signify if the range is quite large or relatively small. An interquartile range or interquartile range (IQR) is a better measure, especially in nonnormal distributions. The IQR is the range of the middle half of the values and does not get affected by extreme values or outliers like the other measures. It corresponds to the median as a measure of central tendency.

A quartile divides the dataset into three points which form four groups. The three points are Q_1 (lower quartile), Q_2 (median), and Q_3 (upper quartile). Each of the four groups represents 25% of the values (quarter = 1/4). Q_1 is the middle value of the lower half of the data (below median), and Q_3 is the middle value of the upper half of the data (above median). In the dataset in the first row of Table 1.8, the Q_2 (median) is 10. Q_1 is the middle value/median of the lower half, $8 + 9/2 = 8.5$ and Q_3 is the middle value/ median of the upper half, $11 + 12/2 = 11.5$. The interquartile range or IQR is $Q_3 − Q_1$. In this example, the IQR would be $11.5 − 8.5 = 3$.

If the data have outliers, IQR represents the dispersion better than the standard deviation. This can be appreciated in Table 1.8. Whenever the mean is presented in a dataset, it should be shown as mean ± standard deviation (± s.d.) or mean(s.d.). When there are outliers or the distribution is skewed, the median (Mdn) should be presented along with the IQR or Mdn(IQR).

Table 1.8 Measures of dispersion.

Dataset (weight in kgs.)	Standard deviation $(s = \sqrt{\Sigma(x_i − \bar{x})^2/n − 1})$	Range	Interquartile range
7,8,9,10,10,10,11,12.13	1.87	7−13	3 ($Q_1 = 8.5$, $Q_2 = 10$, $Q_3 = 11.5$)
7,8,9,10,10,10,11,12.13,30	6.56	7−30	3 ($Q_1 = 9$, $Q_2 = 10$, $Q_3 = 12$)
1,7,8,9,10,10,10,11,12.13	3.35	1−13	3 ($Q_1 = 8$, $Q_2 = 10$, $Q_3 = 11$)

References

Belle, Fisher, L. D., Heagerty, P. J., & Lumley, T. (2004). *Biostatistics: A methodology for the health sciences*. John Wiley & Sons.

Carroll, L. (1991). *Alice in Wonderland*. https://www.gutenberg.org/files/2344/2344-h/2344-h.htm.

Cohen, B. B., Pokras, R., Meads, M. S., & Krusha, W. M. (1987). How will diagnosis-related groups affect epidemiologic research? *American Journal of Epidemiology, 126*(1), 1—9. https://doi.org/10.1093/oxfordjournals.aje.a114639

Dimond, E. G., Kittle, C. F., & Crockett, J. E. (1960). Comparison of internal mammary artery ligation and sham operation for angina pectoris*. *The American Journal of Cardiology, 5*(4), 483—486. https://doi.org/10.1016/0002-9149(60)90105-3

Doyle, A. C. (1893). *The adventure of the cardboard Box*. Project Gutenberg. https://www.gutenberg.org/files/2344/2344-h/2344-h.htm.

Faizi, N., Kumar, A. M., & Kazmi, S. (2018). Omission of quality assurance during data entry in public health research from India: Is there an elephant in the room? *Indian Journal of Public Health, 62*(2), 150—152. https://doi.org/10.4103/ijph.IJPH_386_16

Indrayan, A., & Malhotra, R. K. (2017). *Medical biostatistics* (4th ed.). Chapman and Hall/CRC. https://doi.org/10.4324/9781315100265

Johnson, L. L., Borkowf, C. B., & Shaw, P. A. (2012). In I. John, J. I. Gallin, & F. P. Ognibene (Eds.), *Principles and practice of clinical research*. Academic Press.

Laplace, P. S. (1810). Mémoire sur les approximations des formules qui sont fonctions de tr'es grands nombres et sur leur application aux probabilités. *Memoires de l'Academie des Sciences* (pp. 353—415).

Merriam-Webster. (n.d.). *Biostatistics*. Retrieved March 18, 2022, from https://www.merriam-webster.com/dictionary/biostatistics.

Nightingale, F. (1863). *Notes on hospitals*.

Pagano, M., & Gauvreau, K. (2000). *Principles of biostatistics*.

CHAPTER 2

Data management and SPSS environment*

For every minute spent in organizing, an hour is earned

Benjamin Franklin.

1. Data management

1.1 Introduction

Data are central to quantitative research, and data management is integral for research. Data management is the *process of compiling, storing, organizing, and securing the data collected by the researchers*. The goal is to manage the data effectively with reliable strategy and methods such that it is retrievable when required. Data Management has become far more efficient, sensitive, and reliable in the smart world with improved access to smartphones, GPS, and the internet. However, poor data collection or management protocol can lead to misleading or even wrong results.

Research data management benefits researchers who conduct research and policy appraisals. Most senior researchers have some terrible memories of the research data they collected in past projects. Research data are not a one-time enterprise; researchers need the data themselves for future projects and even for institutional collaborations. Hence, data should be managed through an intuitive, reliable, reproducible, and reuseable method. Let us take an example of a senior's research on the MERS virus during their graduation or doctorate. Suppose we now want to test the correlations of MERS with COVID-19. This would be possible only if that data collected a decade ago had all the relevant details and could be retrievable with intuitive codes and values. The essence of open research data management is that data are retrievable, interpretable, and useable for any researcher. This can be possible if we give importance to data management and prepare a proper plan during protocol preparation and data collection.

Another reason why we advocate for data management is policy compliance. Usually, the Institutional Ethics Committees mandate that the project proposals explain their data management plan. Similarly, academic institutions, as well as regional and national research organizations, require statements on data management. Some organizations

---

*For datasets, please refer to companion site: https://www.elsevier.com/books-and-journals/book-companion/9780443185502

Biostatistics Manual for Health Research
ISBN 978-0-443-18550-2, https://doi.org/10.1016/B978-0-443-18550-2.00008-6

Figure 2.1 Data management cycle and characteristics.

such as Wellcome Trust and National Health and Medical Research Council need the data collected by the projects funded by them to be openly shared with other researchers. Data management and open data sharing are becoming common among research councils of a few countries, and others may and should follow suit. Additionally, while submitting the manuscript for consideration for publication, some publishers mandate declaring the data management and open data sharing plan.

Thus, we strongly encourage researchers to prepare the data management plan as a part of the protocol and follow it strictly during the entire study duration. This adds value to their work and supports data integrity. Fig. 2.1 shows the research data management lifecycle, which helps in keeping track of actions to take in data management.

1.2 Best practices for data management

- Data should be well *organized* on the data management platform. This helps in locating and transforming the data whenever required.
- The collected and organized data should be *stored* securely along with a backup. This helps in recovering lost data in the face of an unexpected event. We recommend keeping the data at three different places, and at least one of them be a cloud-based server.
- The stored data should be *accessible* to anyone with access. This accessibility should also be long-term and retrievable in the future.
- Ideally, people should be able to learn where the data are being used to support or help that project. A suggested citation for data use should be provided along with the necessary details of the user's project or research. Publishing the data is highly recommended unless it has sensitive information.
- The data should be anonymized wherever required.

1.3 Data management plan

The research data management plan should be prepared before the actual project starts as a part of the protocol explaining how the data will be managed during and after the project. We suggest checking for any existing data management format at your university or research council. A good data management plan and practices repository is available at the Global Health Training Network. The essential properties of a data management plan are shown in Box 2.1:

Every researcher should address in their data management plan the enlisted guiding points. They should describe the type of data they will collect, such as images, text, spreadsheets, audio and video files, patient records, blood or other specimens, reports, surveys, etc. It is also essential to determine who will collect and access the sensitive research data. Choosing the proper storage is critical for data management. Most researchers store the data locally on their personal or official computers. Although it serves the purpose, there are better tools with improved storage, access, retention, encryption, and data loss protection. Epicollect is one such platform that helps not only in data collection, but also with storage. When the data are stored digitally, it should have a predetermined naming pattern of files and folders. It should have sufficient details to sort and find them in the future. Being concise and consistent is the key to proper data storage and cleaning. Do pay due importance to version, date of creation, and creator in file naming. Table 2.1 is one such sample of a naming pattern.

BOX 2.1 Data management template should cover
- Background and Methodology, including Type of data collected
- Metadata or README file
- Plan on naming the files and folders (including updates and versions)
- Ethics and legal compliance
- People responsible and their role
- Data storage and backup, including long-term retention and encryption
- Sharing and public archiving
- Metadata or README file

Table 2.1 Naming a file.

File name	20220313_Ver1.1_COVIDreport_ HCWWHO_YSR.xlsx
20220313	Date of creation
Ver1.1	Version
COVIDreport	Content
HCWWHO	Standard acronym of the project
YSR	Creator initials

Note that we have used _ (underscore) in between the words rather than space as many software do not accept spaces.

We should also have a defined time period for data storage, including short-term and long-term. In a short-term plan, the data are stored until the research is completed and published, which is often the only concern of most researchers. A long-term data storage plan is gaining the interest of researchers, as it is helpful for self-use in the future or for other researchers. However, this is difficult and often costly as storing data or specimens from the research for a long period of time requires huge space. Moreover, the availability could be subject to the intellectual property associated with the data. Nevertheless, it is advisable to use a platform or storage option that facilitates sharing the data with others in all cases, unless restricted due to unavoidable reasons.

Disclosing how the data can be used by someone who has access to it from the public archives must be mentioned with suggested citation. Lastly, metadata describes the data you have collected in an easily understandable form. It is essential to explain a few data characteristics in a readme file. There may be one metadata file in a project describing all the variables and measurements as a data documentation sheet or multiple readme files in each folder you have saved electronically alongside the dataset.

2. Data documentation sheet

A data documentation sheet (DDS) is a 'codebook' containing the details of all the variables (like questions, variable names, input type, possible answers, and code for possible answers) to be entered. It is the first step in preparing a plan for data collection and entry. The DDS should be prepared before collecting data or at least before data entry in any software. In the proceeding exercise, we will try to prepare and understand the concept of DDS. While we provide this as an exercise, there is no right or wrong method for designing a codebook.

2.1 Template for DDS

As discussed above, metadata describes the data in an easily understandable form. This is done by detailing out characteristics of the data variables. In Table 2.2, we provide a template of DDS along with the essential attributes of each variable in the questionnaire.

The different components and attributes of a DDS is shown in Box 2.2.

Table 2.2 Data documentation sheet template.

Question	Name of variable	Variable type	Possible answer and value/code of them if applicable	Comments/missing

BOX 2.2 Attributes of a data documentation sheet

- **Question:** It describes the individual variable in the questionnaire. Try to keep it short and specific.
- **Variable name:** It is the shortened name for the question. It is highly advisable to keep it intuitive, unique single word, with small letters without spaces or special characters. Limit it to 8 words for better compatibility with different statistical software.
- **Input or variable type:** It describes the type of variable. It can be qualitative (categorical: nominal or ordinal) or quantitative (discrete or continuous), or any distinctive type (date, dollar, string, etc.)
- **Possible answers:** It includes all the responses a question may have. For categorical variables, all the categories become the possible answers. For a continuous variable, it is advisable to restrict them from minimum to maximum values.
- **Value/codes:** The numeric values assigned to each possible answer in categorical variables. It is instrumental in data entry and analysis.
- **Comments:** It can include any instruction or words for future purposes. What to do in case of missing data can be mentioned here.

2.2 Coding the dataset

A data documentation sheet or codebook contains the details of all the variables to be entered. Furthermore, it also has code for possible answers, often as Arabic numerals. This facilitates subsequent analysis of the categorical data as most of the software requires the data to be in Arabic numerals to perform statistical analysis. Data coding is done before the data collection, preferably during questionnaire development. The key is to prepare the unambiguous code. Apart from this, coding also reduces errors during data collection, entry, and even analysis.

The best practice for coding qualitative data is to start giving codes from 1 and go further. It is also recommended to use 0 for "negative" and "No" responses, while for "unknown," "not applicable," and/or missing values, we may use 9, 99, or 999.

Exercise 1: Prepare the DDS in the template (given in Table 2.2**) of the TB Patient Treatment card given in** Fig. 2.2. **The solution is given in** Table 2.3.

3. Data capture and cleaning

3.1 Data capture

Traditionally, researchers start their study with the data collection using a paper-based instrument, both for primary and secondary data. In most cases, after all the data have been collected, data from the completed paper-based forms is entered in a software such as excel, creating a master chart for further processing for analysis. This is often the weakest link that critically affects data quality (Faizi et al., 2018). Since data entry is often

TB Patient Treatment Card

Registration number: _____

Name: _____

Address: ____(Rural / Urban)_____

Age: _____   Sex: M ☐   F ☐

Treatment centre: _____   Date: _____

Bacteriologically confirmed TB case? Yes ☐ No ☐			
Date	Smear result (Neg/Scanty/1+/2+/3+)	Weight (kg)	Height (mt)
Molecular test: Positive ☐ Negative ☐ Not done ☐			

Figure 2.2 TB patient treatment card.

monotonous and uninspiring activity, it is often assigned to those with little knowledge of the importance of the research, which in turn, leads to potential errors.

As the saying "Garbage in, Garbage out" goes, we should exercise caution and concern during data entry to reduce errors at this integral step. Errors in data entry may lead to poor and misleading interpretations leading to erroneous decisions and flawed policies. Therefore, data quality is vital for data integrity and research findings. With the advancement of technology and better access to electronic devices, data collection and simultaneous data entry are possible nowadays. Data entry can be done on MS excel, Epidata, and other software after collecting data in a paper-based questionnaire. Mobile and electronic forms eliminate data entry as a separate step, saving resources for data entry and removing the possibility of errors during the process. This is termed data capture, as shown in Fig. 2.3.

Epicollect is one such mobile application that captures data efficiently and greatly facilitates subsequent handling of the data. Apart from the data capture, Epicollect is also an efficient data management tool as it assists in the secure storing of the data. It also improves data accessibility, storage, and archiving.

Advantages of Epicollect or other similar applications:
- It saves time, costs, and human resources by combining the process
- It produces more accurate data by preventing data collection and data entry errors
- Sharing of data is possible
- Helps to establish data validity processes by supervisors.

Table 2.3 Data documentation sheet: solution to Exercise 1.

Question	Name (variable)	Type (variable)	Possible answer and value labels	Comments/missing
Serial number	sn	Numeric		Unique field if missing/ nonunique enter 999
Registration number	r_no	String		If missing/ nonunique enter 99
Name of the patient	name	String		If missing/ nonunique enter 99
Address	address	Numeric	Rural: 1, Urban: 2	
Patient's gender	gender	Numeric	Male: 1, Female: 2, Transgender: 3, Not recorded: 9	
Patient's age in years	age	Numeric	0—125, 126	
Treatment center	tret_centr	Numeric		
Date of registration	reg_date	Date	01/01/2019 to 31/12/2019, 01/01/1800	Range of legal dates enter "01/01/1800" if date is missing
Bacteriological confirmed case	Bact_confir	Numeric	Yes: 1, No: 2	
Date of test	test_date	Date	01/01/2019 to 31/12/2019, 01/01/1800	Range of legal dates enter "01/01/1800" if date is missing
Smear results	smear	Numeric	Negative: 1, Scanty: 2, 1+ : 3, 2+ : 4, 3+ : 5	If missing/ nonunique enter
Weight in kg	weight	Numeric	1.0—200.0, 999	Enter "999" if missing
Height in meter	height	Numeric	0.50—3.00, 9	Enter "9" if missing
Molecular test	mol_test	Numeric	Positive: 1, Negative: 2, Not done: 3	If missing/ nonunique enter 9

Figure 2.3 Data capture.

- It can collect different kinds of data (pictures, audio, video, GPS coordinates)
- Epicollect is a free tool and can work offline

Apart from Epicollect, there are a few other data capture tools, such as EpiData, Google forms, SurveyMonkey, KoBo Toolbox, etc. But the mobile app and ability to capture data offline simultaneously by multiple field investigators make Epicollect an excellent tool.

3.2 Data checking and cleaning

As we discussed the concept of "garbage in, garbage out," we should observe every record form for completeness and errors in data collection and data entry if they are performed separately. Checking after the data collection may be feasible for a small sample, but periodic checking is a must for large datasets.

Many data entry software can be utilized to simultaneously perform data checking and data entry. Epicollect, EpiData, and KoBo Toolbox and, to some extent SPSS dataset can be coded to facilitate such operations. For example, restricting the cell to one digit will prevent an error of double typing the response. In some data-entry software, we can limit the data entry to only a few codes, and any other entry would be illegal. Such commands and checks prohibit wrong entries and typos. Thus, data checking can be done during data entry (interactive checking) and after data entry (batch checking). Although recommended as good research practices, double-entry, matching, and search for differences (validation of data) are often reserved for critical variables and often not performed at all (Faizi et al., 2018).

Data checking is followed by data cleaning, where the inaccurate records are corrected by screening, diagnosing, and subsequently editing by modifying, excluding, or replacing them (Fig. 2.4, modified from Van Den Broeck et al. (2005)).

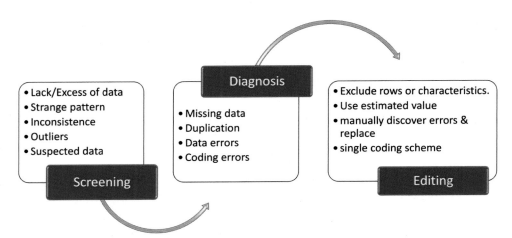

Figure 2.4 Data cleaning. *(Modified from Van Den Broeck, J., Cunningham, S. A., Eeckels, R., & Herbst, K. (2005). Data cleaning: Detecting, diagnosing, and editing data abnormalities. PLoS Medicine, 2(10), 0966–0970. https://doi.org/10.1371/journal.pmed.0020267)*

BOX 2.3 Important terminologies related to data management

Derived variables: Variables created from one or more variables in the original data by manipulating them. For example, Computing the new variable BMI from the original variable of weight and height.

   Recoded variable: Transforming one variable into a different variable by altering the variable's coding. For example, Creating a new categorical variable of "age group" with 5-year intervals from the continuous variable of "age."

   Data snooping: Analysing the relationship only after examining the findings, which was not planned before, to extract something meaningful from the study.

   Data imputation: Data imputation is the substitution of estimated values for missing or inconsistent data items/fields. The substituted values are intended to create a data record that does not fail edits (Organisation for Economic Co-operation and Development (OECD), 2008).

In this step, we take a closer look at the data for any issue it may have in the analysis. IBM SPSS software can help in data cleaning, which we delve further into in Section 6. Data transformation in SPSS. Nevertheless, whenever you perform data cleaning, it is recommended to describe it as a standard part of reporting statistical methods (Ethical Guidelines for Statistical Practice, 1999). The important terminologies related to data management are shown in Box 2.3.

4. SPSS environment

4.1 Introduction to the software

Statistical Package for the Social Sciences, or SPSS, is a popular software used by statisticians and researchers worldwide. It is easy-to-understand and user-friendly interface, minimal to no coding requirements, and a wide range of applicability makes it popular among health researchers. Given the time and resource constraints, SPSS provides an excellent platform for complex statistical analysis within a few clicks. In this section we will go through the SPSS environment and learn some basic commands.

   Statistical Package for the Social Sciences is owned by IBM Corporation (IBM) and is available under a trial version and licensed on a subscription basis. It is available for almost all operating systems, including Windows, macOS, Linux, and UNIX. A team of developers regularly works on its revision and updates, with the latest being 28.0. This book is based on version 26.0 running on a macOS. There are minor differences in different versions for health researchers unless they use advanced techniques.

4.2 The first thing you will see

When you open the SPSS software for the first time, you are greeted with a dialog box that prompts you to open a data file (Fig. 2.5). You may open an existing SPSS data file or a file in another format, including Excel and text containing data. The SPSS data file can also be opened directly from your computer. If you have the data or master chart as an MS Excel file, you have the option of "Open another type of file" and locate the file on your computer. We will be proceeding with a beginner in mind who is new to the SPSS environment and does not have a data file.

To create a new SPSS data file, you can dismiss the dialog box by clicking "Close." The best practice is to check "Don't show this dialog box in the future", so that you don't get disturbed by this dialog box. This takes us to the main window with two view modes: "Data View" and "Variable View" (Fig. 2.6).

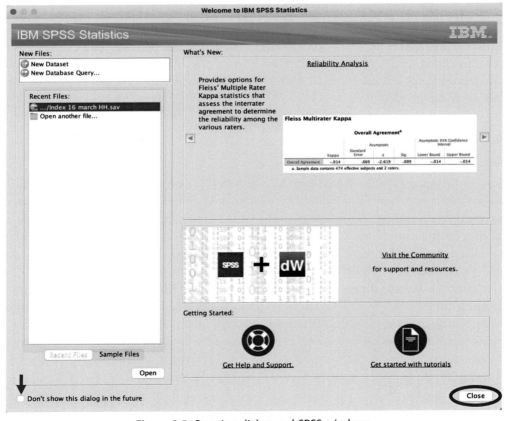

Figure 2.5 Opening dialog and SPSS windows.

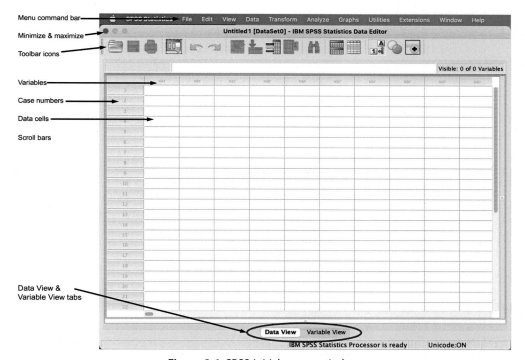

Figure 2.6 SPSS initial screen window.

4.2.1 Data View

The Data viewer is a spreadsheet-like interface with rows and columns where data can be viewed or entered. The subject/case/participant in the data are represented by individual horizontal rows, while each column contains variables of interest. The top of the Data View window you will find a drop-down menu and toolbar, while at the bottom, the user can toggle between Data View and Variable View.

4.2.2 Toolbar icons from left to right (Fig. 2.7)

The toolbar icons from left to right are as follows:

1. **File Open** (Folder) allows particular data files to be opened for analysis.
2. **File Save** (Floppy disk) saves the file in the active window.

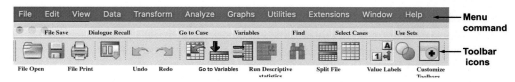

Figure 2.7 Toolbar and menu.

3. **File Print** prints the file in the active window.
4. **Dialog Recall** displays a list of recently opened dialog boxes, including recently performed analysis, any of which can be selected by clicking on their name.
5. **Undo**
6. **Redo**
7. **Go to Case** allows entering the number of the case you want to go to in the data file.
8. **Go to Variables** allows entering the number of the variable you want to go to in the data file.
9. **Variables** provide data definition information for all variables in the working data file.
10. **Run Descriptive statistics**
11. **Find** (binoculars) allows data to be found easily within the data editor.
12. **Split File** splits the data file into separate groups for analysis based on the values of one or more grouping variables.
13. **Select Cases** provides several methods for selecting a subgroup of cases based on criteria, including variables and complex expressions.
14. **Value Labels** allows toggling between actual values and value labels in the Data Editor.
15. **Use Sets** allows the selection of sets of variables to be displayed in the dialog boxes.
16. **Customize toolbar**

4.2.3 Variable View

The Variable viewer displays the properties of individual variables represented in columns (Fig. 2.8). The properties of variables in SPSS can be described in the following headings:

Name: This is a shortened, unique single word. It must not contain spaces or special characters or begin with numbers. The default variable name begins with VAR00001, which should be renamed by double-clicking. For practice, hover on to the first cell in Variable View, enter "ABC," and notice changes in other columns.

The best practice is to limit Name to 7−8 words for better compatibility with other statistical software and to have an intuitive name to find the variable easily.

Type: This shows the type of data attribute. As we saw in the first chapter, data are classified into two types: qualitative/categorical or quantitative/continuous. As shown in Fig. 2.8, a variable can be classified into nine different types. The default variable type in SPSS for data entry is numeric (can take numbers only), which is also the most used for analysis. The quantitative/continuous data in SPSS can be entered as "Numeric", while qualitative/categorical data can be entered as "Numeric" and "String" (can take any letters or numbers). We could also select the "Date," "Dollar," or "String" as the type of variable, wherever applicable.

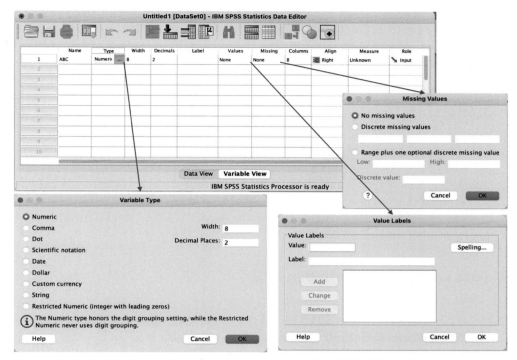

Figure 2.8 Variable View and properties of variables.

The best practice for qualitative and quantitative data entry is using the "Numeric" type. For qualitative data with finite/known number of possibilities, the "Numeric" type with value labels is used. Each numerical value is coded for possible answer. In the data where responses cannot be presumed, like the Name of the patients or Unique ID, we use "String" and, if required, data cleaning can be done later.

Width, decimal, and columns: *Width* provides words/digits count that can be entered in an individual variable, while *Column* is the size of a particular variable in Data View. The *Decimals* show how many decimals values can variable take (only for the numeric data type). As a best practice, reduce the width according to requirements.

Label: The label is an expanded option for the variable name. It does not have letter restrictions and can be used to describe the short variable name. The analysis outputs mention the label name. This should be used to define the clear and complete name of the variable.

Values: It is a beneficial tool for data entry. As described earlier, any type of study variable with multiple finite responses may be entered in SPSS as a numeric type, with each numeric value representing different responses of the dataset. These responses are added as values corresponding to different numbers. The *Value* label command may be activated by clicking "three dots" in the right corner of the value box. Although not essential, allotting a number to missing variables may be considered.

Missing: It is essential to inform SPSS that if some values are missing, what would they be coded as? A unique number should be provided that does not overlap with the actual value numbers/records. As a best practice, this should be mentioned in the DDS (Table 2.3).

Measure and role: *Measure* describes our variable's scale of measurement. Although we know that there are four scales; nominal, ordinal, interval, and ratio, the SPSS has only three, with interval and ratio merged into one and labeled as a scale. A *Role* describes what the variable will play in the analysis. "Input," the default assignment, is used for the independent variable (predictor), while "Target" is used for the dependent variable (outcome).

5. Data entry and importing in SPSS

5.1 Data entry in SPSS

Exercise 2—Prepare a New SPSS file of the dataset using data given in Table 2.4 **and its DDS along with their coding as shown in** Table 2.5.

Solution to Exercise 2:

We need to build the form in the Variable View for data entry before entering data in Data View.

- The first variable in DDS (Table 2.5) is Serial Number. Doubleclick on the first cell in the Variable View window, rename it to sn (variable name as in DDS), and press Enter. All the other properties of the "sn" variable will be assigned by default, as shown in Table 2.6. You have to change a few things according to DDS. By default, *Label* column is empty, and you may enter the actual variable name for your convenience. Under *Missing*, click on the cell corresponding to "sn" to activate it, and then click three dots on the rightmost part of the selected cell (Fig. 2.9). A dialog box will appear where you can enter "999" under discrete missing values as in DDS. Click OK to confirm. Finally, under *Measure*, change to "Scale" by selecting it from the dropdown. Your first variable is now ready to be entered into SPSS.

- Registration Number, Name, and Treatment Centre variables are categorical variables with no prediction of their possible answer. Such variables are labeled as "String" type with appropriate width as per requirements. Similar to the Serial Number variable, create these new variables, rename them as discribed in DDS and change the *Type* as String. Similarly, enter "99" under discrete *Missing* value and increase the *Width* according to your requirement.

Table 2.4 Dataset for data entry Exercise 2.

sn	r_no	Name	Address	Sex	Age	tret_centre	reg_date	bact_confir	test_date	Smear	Weight	Height	mol_test
1	J2391	NEERAJ SHARMA	1	1	50	RHTC	07/02/2019	2	07/02/2019	1	49	1.79	2
2	J2395	RANI	1	2	26	CHC-JAWAN	21/05/2019	1	21/05/2019	4	42	1.58	3
3	J2424	SAHIR ANJUM	1	1	42	RHTC	09/03/2019	1	09/03/2019	5	56	1.69	3
4	J2431	AZAM MEHRAJ	2	1	28	MEDICAL COLLEGE	14/11/2019	1	14/11/2019	2	48	1.73	1
5	J2440	SONVEER SINGH	1	1	65	RHTC	10/06/2019	1	10/06/2019	5	42	1.72	1
6	J2489	RIZWAN	1	1	36	CHC-JAWAN	03/08/2019	1	03/08/2019	3	53	1.65	1
7	J2491	SUNNY	1	1	52	CHC-JAWAN	15/04/2019	1	15/04/2019	4	46	1.63	1
8	J2499	PUSHPA	2	2	42	UHTC	11/02/2019	1	11/02/2019	5	38	1.48	3
9	J2539	ABDUL AHAD	2	1	20	MEDICAL COLLEGE	22/05/2019	2	22/05/2019	1	65	1.78	3
10	J2595	BAJRUDDIN	2	1	40	MEDICAL COLLEGE	03/08/2019	1	03/08/2019	5	43	1.59	3
11	J2610	Dr. SAIF KHAN	1	1	41	RHTC	28/05/2019	2	28/05/2019	1	69	1.64	2
12	J2621	RIDA PARVEEN	2	2	26	UHTC	30/12/2019	2	30/12/2019	1	53	1.69	2
13	J2629	GULAM RASUL	1	1	69	RHTC	28/11/2019	1	28/11/2019	5	44	1.73	3
14	J2649	PAWAN KUMAR	1	1	16	CHC-JAWAN	19/10/2019	1	19/10/2019	5	49	1.74	1

Continued

Table 2.4 Dataset for data entry Exercise 2.—cont'd

sn	r_no	Name	Address	Sex	Age	tret_centre	reg_date	bact_confir	test_date	Smear	Weight	Height	mol_test
15	U0283	ABDUL MOEED	1	1	26	RHTC	07/10/2019	2	07/10/2019	1	57	1.65	3
16	U0387	AHMAD DANISH	1	2	22	CHC-JAWAN	20/03/2019	1	20/03/2019	4	32	1.53	2
17	U0342	AREEBA	1	2	58	CHC-JAWAN	05/01/2019	1	05/01/2019	4	35	1.59	2
18	U0379	DHARMENDRA	2	1	34	UHTC	09/09/2019	1	09/09/2019	3	55	1.69	3
19	U0441	IRSHAD MALIK	2	1	49	UHTC	17/08/2019	2	17/08/2019	1	50	1.74	3
20	U0473	MD. HASAN KHAN	1	1	19	RHTC	09/05/2019	1	09/05/2019	3	46	1.75	3

Table 2.5 DDS for Exercise 2.

Question	Name (variable)	Type (variable)	Possible answer and value labels	Comments/missing
Serial number	sn	Numeric		Unique field If missing/ nonunique enter 999
Registration number	r_no	String		If missing/ nonunique enter 99
Name of the patient	name	String		If missing/ nonunique enter 99
Address	address	Numeric	Rural: 1, Urban: 2	
Patient's gender	gender	Numeric	Male: 1, Female: 2, Transgender: 3, Not recorded: 9	
Patient's age in years	age	Numeric	0–125, 126	
Treatment center	tret_centr	String		
Date of registration	reg_date	Date	01/01/2019 to 31/12/2019, 01/01/1800	Range of legal dates enter "01/01/1800" if date is missing
Bacteriological confirmed case	Bact_confir	Numeric	Yes: 1, No: 2	
Date of test	test_date	Date	01/01/2019 to 31/12/2019, 01/01/1800	Range of legal dates enter "01/01/1800" if date is missing
Smear results	smear	Numeric	Negative: 1, Scanty: 2, 1+ : 3, 2+ : 4, 3+ : 5	If missing/ nonunique enter
Weight in kg	weight	Numeric	1.0–200.0, 999	Enter "999" if missing
Height in meter	height	Numeric	0.50–3.00, 9	Enter "9" if missing
Molecular test	mol_test	Numeric	Positive: 1, Negative: 2, Not done: 3	If missing/ nonunique enter 9

- Address and Patient's Sex variables in DDS are categorical variables with a finite number of possible answers. We will enlist them as "Numeric" type with coding under *Value* labels. Add the new variable "address" under the *Name* variable by double-clicking and pressing enter. A new variable "address" would be Numeric

Table 2.6 Properties of Serial Number variable in SPSS.

		By default	You have to enter/change
Serial Number	Name		sn
	Type	Numeric	
	Width	8	3
	Decimals	2	0
	Label		Serial Number
	Value	None	
	Missing	None	999
	Column	8	
	Align	Right	
	Measure	Unknown	Scale
	Role	Input	

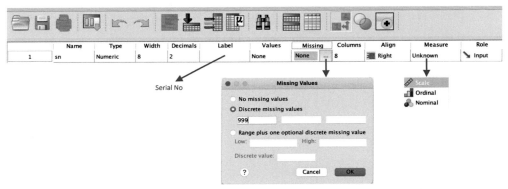

Figure 2.9 Variable properties of Serial Number in Variable View.

Table 2.7 Properties of address variable in SPSS.

		By default	You have to enter/change
Address	Name		Address
	Type	Numeric	
	Width	8	
	Decimals	2	0
	Label		Address
	Value	None	1: Rural, 2: Urban
	Missing	None	9
	Column	8	
	Align	Right	
	Measure	Unknown	Nominal
	Role	Input	

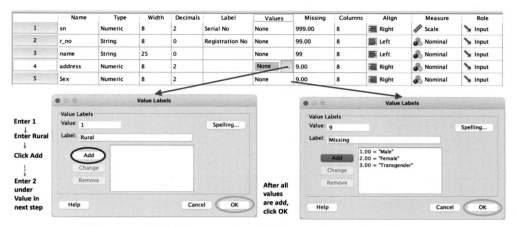

	Name	Type	Width	Decimals	Label	Values	Missing	Columns	Align	Measure	Role
1	sn	Numeric	8	2	Serial No	None	999.00	8	Right	Scale	Input
2	r_no	String	8	0	Registration No	None	99.00	8	Left	Nominal	Input
3	name	String	25	0		None	99	8	Left	Nominal	Input
4	address	Numeric	8	2		None	9.00	8	Right	Nominal	Input
5	Sex	Numeric	8	2		None	9.00	8	Right	Nominal	Input

Figure 2.10 Variable properties of address and sex in Variable View.

type, with width, decimals, and column as 8, 2, and 8, respectively, which needs to change according to DDS as explained in Tables 2.5 and 2.7. We need to inform SPSS that this variable has two probable answers. To use this feature, click on a cell in the *Value* column of the address variable row and click three dots on the right-most part of the selected cell (which appears only on clicking the rightmost part) (Fig. 2.10). A value label dialog box will appear where you have to assign a numerical to probable answers. As depicted in Fig. 2.10, Enter 1 in the box corresponding to Value, Rural under the Label, and click Add. Similarly, add the Urban label and then click OK.

- Other things which need to modify in default variable properties are reducing decimal to 0, adding missing value −9, and changing the Measure to Nominal. The address variable is ready for data entry. Similarly, the Patient's Sex, Bacteriologically confirmed TB case, Smear Result, and Molecular test variables could also be created as all are categorical variables with a finite number of possible answers.
- Patient's Age, Weight, and Height are continuous variables. They should be added as a Numeric type with the appropriate width and decimal place. As the age of the patient is recorded in years with no decimal place and 125 is maximum (DDS), we may change the width to 3 with 0 decimal. Similarly, weight can attain a value up to 200.0 kg; its characteristics need to be changed to width 4 with 1 decimal, to increase precision. Height is in meters with a maximum of 3.00 m, and its characteristics are changed to width 3 with 2 decimals to increase precision.
- Lastly, the Date of registration and the Date of test variables are added, changing their *Type* and *Missing* value according to DDS.
- You are ready to enter the provided data in Data View mode. The Variable view will look like the one in Fig. 2.11.

	Name	Type	Width	Decimals	Label	Values	Missing	Columns	Align	Measure	Role
1	sn	Numeric	8	0	Serial No	None	999	8	Right	Scale	Input
2	r_no	String	8	0	Registration no	None	99	8	Left	Nominal	Input
3	name	String	25	0		None	99	8	Left	Nominal	Input
4	address	Numeric	1	0		{1, Rural}...	9	8	Right	Nominal	Input
5	Sex	Numeric	1	0	Patient's gender	{1, Male}...	9	8	Right	Nominal	Input
6	age	Numeric	3	0	Patient's age i...	None	126	8	Right	Unknown	Input
7	tret_centre	String	15	0	Treatment Cen...	None	99	8	Left	Nominal	Input
8	reg_date	Date	10	0	Date of registr...	None	01.01.1800	8	Right	Scale	Input
9	bact_confir	Numeric	8	0	Bacteriological...	{1, Yes}...	9	8	Right	Nominal	Input
10	test_date	Date	10	0	Date of test	None	01.01.1800	8	Right	Scale	Input
11	smear	Numeric	1	0	Smear Result	{1, Negative...	9	8	Right	Unknown	Input
12	weight	Numeric	4	1	Weight in KG	None	999.0	8	Right	Unknown	Input
13	height	Numeric	3	2	Height in meter	None	9.00	8	Right	Unknown	Click
14	mol_test	Numeric	1	0	Molecular test	{1, Positive}...	9	8	Right	Unknown	Input

Figure 2.11 Variable form from the DDS in Exercise 2.

- In the Data View, start entering the data as given in Table 2.4. Entering Serial Number, Registration Number, Age, Weight, Height, and Dates is straightforward. In the categorical variable, we have given labels values that need to be entered. For example, in the Address variable, for entering Rural , we need to enter 1 (code for Rural). Type 1 in the first cell of the Address column, and you will see the magic. Similarly, do the data entry of all the 20 patients given in Table 2.4, with entering Labels codes instead of the exact character of the variables. Congratulations, you have learned the art of data entering in SPSS.

5.2 Data importing SPSS

Exercise 3: From the dataset provided along with this book, locate the file named "2.TB_reg_data.xlsx" and Import it into SPSS, clean the variables and save it as SPSS data file (.sav).

Solution to Exercise 3:

Steps:

1. SPSS can open Excel, CSV, STATA, SAS, or other database files. Download the excel file for importing. In SPSS, click the *File* menu, hover over *Open,* and Click *Data. Open Data dialog box will open* (Fig. 2.12).
2. For opening Excel file, you have to change the *Files of type* from SPSS Statistics (*.sav, *.zsav) to Excel (*.xls, *.xlsx, *.xlsm). Locate the file you want to open by changing the folder, select your file, and click *Open.*
3. This will open the Read Excel File dialog box with a few default settings, as shown in Fig. 2.12.
   - In the exercise file, you may not change any settings in the Read Excel File dialog box and click OK to import the Excel file to SPSS. If you are importing another excel file, you have to select the sheet that contains the data from the *Worksheet*

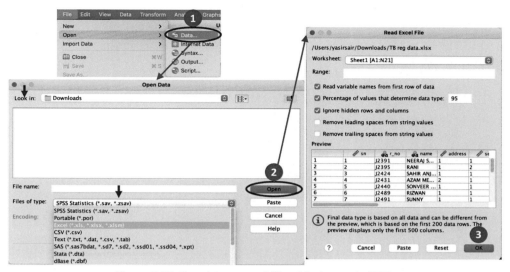

Figure 2.12 Opening an excel file with dataset in SPSS.

dropdown menu. In most cases, you will need to format an excel sheet before emporting. The variable names should be in the first row of the data.

- Another easier way to open an Excel file in SPSS is to go to the folder where it is located, drag it and drop oven SPSS window. The imported excel file into SPSS is the same as the SPSS file you just entered data in Exercise 2.

Note: The best practices for data management in SPSS is shown in Box 2.4.

6. Data transformation in SPSS

As discussed in Section 3.2. Data cleaning is a prerequisite for making the data ready for analysis. Data transformation helps in cleaning and refining the data. Most of these functions are available in the Transform menu, as shown in Fig. 2.13. The most useful ones are discussed below.

6.1 Compute variables

This function is extremely useful in creating a new variable after computing/calculating from existing variables in the dataset. We can use any arithmetic function between one or more variables. For example, we can calculate BMI if we have the weight and height of the patients.

BOX 2.4 Best practices for data management in SPSS

- Serial numbers should be additional to the unique id, registration code, or any other questionnaire number of the data. Serial numbers are helpful when we want to bring the order of the dataset to its original state. This can be done by right-clicking the Serial Number Column and selecting Sort Ascending.
- Modifying decimals and width to the minimum possible helps reduce data entry errors.
- Be very specific and do not categorize or group data while entering data into SPSS. For example, for entering the age of the patients, enter their exact age rather than assigning them into age groups, even if you want to analyze with age groups. Exact age entry increases the analytical options and can be transformed into any group later, but a grouped entry cannot be transformed later.
- Entered data should be the raw variables, not the composite variables. For example, for measuring the BMI, we should enter the weight and height separately. Later, when required, they can be transformed using "compute" option.
- If you want to change the entered variable/cases sequence, you can drag it horizontally from its original place to where you want it in the Data viewer. Similarly, it can be done in Variable viewer by dragging vertically.
- You may insert or delete extra cases (rows) and variables (columns) from your existing data file. You can do this by selecting the rows (for cases) or columns (for variables) and right-clicking the trackpad or mouse for the option Cut to delete or Insert Cases/Variable for adding extra Cases/Variable.
- You can save your data in other formats too. This can be done from the File menu. Hover over Export, and click on the type of file … to open the "Save Data As" dialog box. This is very useful to export data from SPSS to MS Excel and other statistical software.

Exercise 4: Calculate the BMI in the imported MS Excel file from Exercise 3.
Solution:

1. Under the *Transform* menu, click *Compute Variable* (Fig. 2.13). A Compute Variable dialog box will open up as shown in Fig. 2.14. The new computed variable name is to be given in the *Target variable* box. In our exercise, name it bmi.
2. The left side list all the variables in your dataset, which can be used to compute the new variable. They must be transferred to the *Numeric Expression* box by double-clicking, or clicking the arrow button, or simply dragging.
3. In our exercise, Weight and Height variables are transferred to the *Numeric Expression* box.
4. *The numeric expression* box uses many functions from the function box on the right. In most circumstances, we use the Arithmetic function only. In our exercise, BMI $=$ Weight/Height^2 can be calculated by dividing weight by the height * height in the bracket, as shown in Fig. 2.14. Click OK, and a new variable will be created at the last column in the dataset.

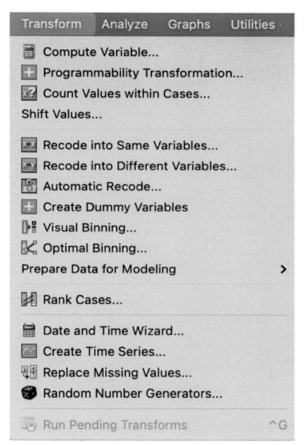

Figure 2.13 Transform menu and its functions.

6.2 Recode into same variables and different variables

There are conditions when we want to transform a single variable into a similar variable by combining its categories or values. For example, if we are going to create an age group variable from the age in year variable. In SPSS for recording, we have two options: Recode into the Same Variable and Recode into a different Variable. The difference lies in the output variable. *Recode into Same Variable* replaces the original variable data entry by the recoded values. *Recoding into a different variable* creates a new variable with recoded values at the end of the dataset without affecting the original variable. We suggest using *Recode into the same variable* sparingly and cautiously, as it overwrites the original variable data.

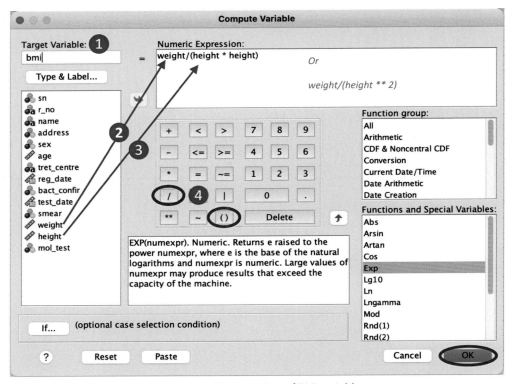

Figure 2.14 Computation of BMI variable.

Steps in Recoding into a different variable

1. After selecting *Recode into the Different Variables* in the *transform* tab (Fig. 2.13), you will see a dialog box (Fig. 2.15). All of the variables in the Numeric type in your dataset are listed on the left side. The variable of interest is transferred to the middle empty box under *Numeric variable - > Output variable*. Let us create an age group variable with three categories: Children <18, Adults 18–59, and Elderly ≥60. Transfer the age variable from the left list to the central box.

2. On the right side under Output Variable, give the name of the New variable as "age_gp," and click *Change*.

3. We need to give the codes for recording. This is done by clicking the *Old and New Value* tab, which opens a new dialog box.

4. In this dialog box, over left side, you can give the command to old values according to our interest, and on the right side, you give corresponding new value codes.

5. In our example of creating age groups from the age variable, select *Range* radio and add the age group you want to create; for example, for creating the Children <18 categories, click *Range, LOWEST through value,* and enter 17 under it while labeling

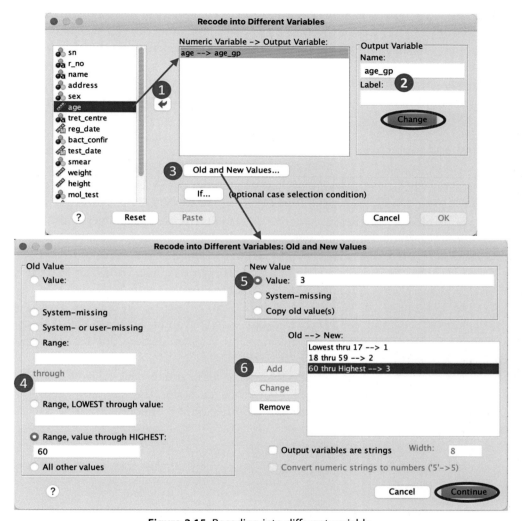

Figure 2.15 Recoding into different variable.

1 under *New Value* on the left side and then click *Add* button to add the new coded value.

6. Adult 18–59 category is added by selecting Range radio and entering 18 in the first box and 59 in the through box, while coding it as 2 in the value box under New Value on the right side, and then clicking the Add button. Similarly, you can add 60 years and above code either by selecting *All other values* radio or by selecting *Range, value through HIGHEST* on the left side. After giving all the codes, click *Continue*, give the new variable name in Name under Output Variable, and click *OK*. A new

variable, "age_gp," will be added at the end of columns. But before any meaningful analysis can be done, you need to assign values of numerical (1, 2, and 3 in our example of age group) under *Value* Labels as explained earlier in the Variable window.

Recoding into a different variable function can be used to create a variable based on the cut-off limit. Test results categorizing into positive and negative, or mild, moderate, and severe can be done.

6.3 Find and replace

- The find and replace option comes under the Edit tab as Replace. If the imported datasheet from Excel has entries in categorical values, for example, the Sex of the patients has been entered as MALE/FEMALE/NON-BINARY, it is better to change it to a numeric type with labeling 1 as MALE, 2 as FEMALE, and 3 as NON-BINARY. To do so, first select the row with the sex variable, then use Replace option in the Edit tab. This will open the Find and Replace dialog box (Fig. 2.16).

- In Find, write the variable quality to replace (in our example, MALE or FEMALE), and in Replace with, enter the value you want to replace it with (numerical value 1 or 2) and hit Replace all. This Find and replace can be used when the data have "Not Applicable" values in your excel spreadsheet, which must be changed to a unique value (99 or 999) to express the missing value as given in the Data documentation sheet.

Till now, we have covered an Introduction to SPSS and its basic skills. We hope by now you would have gained some confidence in performing all these steps. We encourage you to explore the other tabs and operations to understand SPSS and the data analysis better.

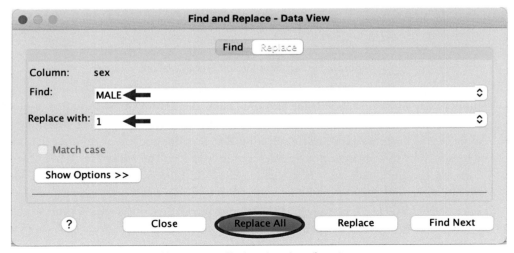

Figure 2.16 Find and replace function.

References

Ethical guidelines for statistical practice. (1999). American Statistical Association.

Faizi, N., Kumar, A. M., & Kazmi, S. (2018). Omission of quality assurance during data entry in public health research from India: Is there an elephant in the room? *Indian Journal of Public Health, 62*(2), 150–152. https://doi.org/10.4103/ijph.IJPH_386_16

Organisation for Economic Co-operation and Development (OECD). (2008). *OECD glossary of statistical terms.* https://stats.oecd.org/glossary/.

Van Den Broeck, J., Cunningham, S. A., Eeckels, R., & Herbst, K. (2005). Data cleaning: Detecting, diagnosing, and editing data abnormalities. *PLoS Medicine, 2*(10), 0966–0970. https://doi.org/10.1371/journal.pmed.0020267

CHAPTER 3

Statistical tests of significance*

The statistician cannot evade the responsibility for understanding the process (s)he applies or recommends.

Ronald Fisher

1. Hypothesis testing

A hypothesis is an assumption or a claim about the population parameter. The population parameter could be a population mean or proportion. Any research question that needs to be tested is expressed in terms of a statistical hypothesis.

1.1 Null and alternate hypothesis

The first hypothesis to be stated is the null hypothesis, which is expressed as H_o (pronounced as H naught). The null hypothesis is commonly known as the hypothesis of no difference. The research hypothesis or the hypothesis claimed is stated as the alternate hypothesis, expressed as H_a. The phenomenon of stating both the complementary hypothesis together was set forth by Neyman—Pearson Lemma (Lehmann, 1993). Let us consider the following examples as statements of null and alternate hypotheses (Table 3.1).

Before we proceed, please note that the statements of hypothesis statement stated earlier are shortened for understanding. Hypothesis should always be quantifiable, testable, and statistical in nature (Good & Hardin, 2012). For instance, the hypothesis—*Drug A reduces blood pressure* of *patients*—is wrong on all the three concerns. Ideally, it should be formulated as: *Drug A at a daily dose of 100 mg, reduces blood pressure by an average of 10 mm Hg in adult patients (18—60 years) suffering from primary mild hypertension.* The severity of diseases such as mild, moderate, or severe must be clearly mentioned. The null hypothesis should be stated first, by convention (Box 3.1).

1.2 Directional versus nondirectional hypothesis

In the directional hypothesis, the claim is about the difference from null in a particular direction. For instance, the third example in Table 3.1 claims a nondirectional association of depression with disease severity as compared to the fourth example, which states that

---

*For datasets, please refer to companion site: https://www.elsevier.com/books-and-journals/book-companion/9780443185502

Biostatistics Manual for Health Research
ISBN 978-0-443-18550-2, https://doi.org/10.1016/B978-0-443-18550-2.00009-8

Table 3.1 Null and alternate hypothesis.

	H_o = null hypothesis	H_a = alternate hypotheis
1.	Drug A causes no difference in blood pressure of patients. In scientific terms (μ stands for mean blood pressure): H_o: $\mu_{pre} = \mu_{post}$	Drug A reduces blood pressure in patients. In scientific terms (μ stands for mean blood pressure): H_a: $\mu_{pre} > \mu_{post}$
2.	Breakfast skipping has no association with obesity	Breakfast skipping is associated with obesity
3.	Depression is not associated with CD4 count in HIV/AIDS (disease severity). In other words, (μ = mean CD4): H_o: $\mu_{dep} = \mu_{non\text{-}dep}$	Depression is associated with CD4 count in HIV/AIDS (disease severity). In other words, (μ = mean CD4): H_a: $\mu_{dep} \neq \mu_{non\text{-}dep}$
4.	Depression is not associated with a CD4 count in HIV/AIDS (disease severity). In other words, (μ = mean CD4): H_o: $\mu_{dep} = \mu_{non\text{-}dep}$	Depression is associated with a lower CD4 count in HIV/AIDS (disease severity). In other words, (μ = mean CD4): H_a: $\mu_{dep} < \mu_{non\text{-}dep}$

BOX 3.1 Why should the null hypothesis be stated before the research/alternate hypothesis?

Although both the hypotheses are complementary, not stating the null hypothesis could imply bias from the start. The basis of the null hypothesis is similar to the presumption of innocence in the court. The burden of proof lies on the accuser, not the accused. According to the legal adage, "*Ei incumbit probatio qui dicit, non qui negat,*" the burden of the proof rests with the party who affirms, rather than the party who denies. The famous jurist William Blackstone said: "*Better that ten guilty persons escape, than that one innocent suffers*" (Blackstone, 1899; Bouvier, 1856; Volokh, 1997).

Thus, if the research hypothesis is that breakfast skipping is associated with obesity, one needs to start with an unbiased null hypothesis that breakfast skipping is not associated with obesity. Through research, we collect data and further analyze them statistically to determine whether the null hypothesis should be rejected or accepted. This depends on whether the differential result (in this case, more obesity present among breakfast skippers) is significantly different or could be due to chance.

disease is more severe in depression (severity measured through CD4). Thus, the former, H_o: $\mu_{dep} \neq \mu_{non\text{-}dep}$ is a nondirectional hypothesis, which does not say whether CD4 is lower or higher in depression patients. Whereas, H_o: $\mu_{dep} < \mu_{not\ dep}$ is a directional hypothesis claiming that depression is associated with a lower CD4 count (and not higher).

To make a directional hypothesis, some prior background research or rationale should be present in support. This also affects tails (from the normal distribution curve). For now, it is sufficient to understand that the directional hypothesis is one-tailed and the nondirectional hypothesis is two-tailed. However, by convention, most statistical tests in health research continue to be taken as two-tailed. For those interested, further discussions around them can be found in the literature (Bland & Altman, 1994; Enkin et al., 1994).

1.3 Steps in hypothesis testing

Hypothesis testing has six steps, which are essential to understand before applying and interpreting statistical tests. The steps are focused on the hypothesis and its claims and do not include actions related to data collection from the patients or study subjects. The six steps in hypothesis testing are shown in Fig. 3.1. One must realize that inferential statistics does not always involve hypothesis testing Box 3.2.

2. Statistical tests of significance

While there are data-based observations of the difference between the two groups, tests of significance help predict whether they could be due to chance. Based on the broad assumptions of statistical tests, they are divided into two major types. The first is parametric tests that are based on assumptions of normally distributed data or approximately so. The second is nonparametric tests, which hold no such assumption. It is essential to know the difference between the choice, nature, and application of these types of statistical tests.

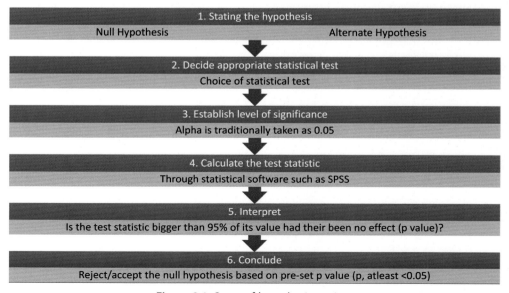

Figure 3.1 Steps of hypothesis testing.

> ## BOX 3.2 Tread Cautiously; not every inference is hypothesis testing
>
> Before proceeding to the next section, allow us to caution against the inappropriate use of hypothesis testing, especially frequent among P-value hunters. Statistical inference, as discussed in the first chapter is done for two other reasons than hypothesis testing-point estimation and interval estimation. For instance, the research question: What is the prevalence of intensive care unit patients needing reserve group of antibiotics such as Linezolid? In this case, you need to estimate the point/proportion and not frame a hypothesis. Similarly, what ratio of height to thyromental distance is a good predictor of difficult laryngoscopy? This can be answered through an interval estimation of ratios. One does not always need a hypothesis in statistical inference.
>
> We have seen the misappropriate use of hypothesis testing despite previous warnings in literature (Wasserman, 2004). As a practice, we should not test a hypothesis unless there is an epidemiological need and unless it is stated in the study protocol itself.

2.1 Parametric and nonparametric tests

In inferential statistics, if the data come from a population whose distribution is known (normal or near-normal) and only the values of *parameters* such as mean and standard deviation are unknown, we apply *parametric* tests (Pagano & Gauvreau, 2000). Essentially, it has certain assumptions of the distribution of the parameter (normal or near normal distribution). Parametric tests are tests of significance that are more powerful in detecting significance but are only applicable if three assumptions are fulfilled:

1. Normally distributed data or nearly normally distributed
2. Homogeneity of variance/homoscedasticity in the sample
3. Independence of the variable.

Nonparametric tests have no such assumptions but are less powerful than their parametric alternatives. Most of the nonparametric tests work on the principle of ranking of data rather than the data itself and are therefore less powerful. Sometimes, they are also called distribution-free tests (Table 3.2, Box 3.3).

Table 3.2 Parametric and nonparametric tests.

	Parametric tests	Nonparametric tests
Distinctive feature	More powerful *More chances of detecting a difference if it exists*	More robust *Applicable in wider situations (e.g., in non-normal distributions or to outliers)*
Assumptions	Normally distributed data	Distribution-free
Example	*t*-test ANOVA RMANOVA	Mann—Whitney U test Kruskal—Wallis test Friedman test

BOX 3.3 Are nonparametric tests assumption-free?
Contrary to the popular notion attached to with nonparametric tests, they are only distribution-free, not assumption-free. The assumption for population probability distribution such that the sample size is large enough for the central limit theorem leading to the normality of averages holds true. Also, randomness and independence of variable should be present as in any other tests. In other words, nonparametric tests cannot substitute for inadequate sampling numbers or poor sample selection.

2.2 Checking for assumptions of parametric tests

Parametric tests are the first choice for any statistical significance because they are more powerful. However, we need to check for its three assumptions before their application. This must also be mentioned clearly in the plan for statistical analysis, whenever parametric tests are used.

1. Normally distributed data or nearly normally distributed
2. Homogeneity of variance/homoscedasticity in the sample
3. Independence of the variable.

2.2.1 Normally distributed data

In general, there are higher chances of getting a normal distribution if the sample size is large. The best check for whether the normal distribution assumption is met can be done through a test in SPSS.

In SPSS, we apply the *Kolmogorov—Smirnov test* (*K—S test* or *KS test*) and the *Shapiro—Wilk test* to detect whether the data fulfill the normalcy assumption for parametric tests. If any of the test shows significance ($P < .05$), the assumption fails. We use two examples for the detection of normal distribution.

Application: Example 1

The first example is from a data on body mass index (BMI), diet, and lifestyle in adolescents (Data name—*3.Adolescents_BMI.sav*). The BMI for age Z score (BMIZ) is the exact measure of relative weight adjusted for age and sex. We want to check whether BMIZ follows normal distribution in SPSS. Applying *Kolmogorov—Smirnov test* and *Shapiro—Wilk test* helps in detecting this. The steps of the application are as follows:

The steps of the application are as follows:

1. Open file *3.Adolescents_BMI.sav* from the dataset provided with this book. Go to *Analyze*, hover over *Descriptive Statistics* and click *Explore* (Fig. 3.2)
2. In the Explore window, enter the desired variable for normality test (BMIZ) to the dependent list by either using arrow button or drag-drop. (Fig. 3.2)
3. To command SPSS to test normality, Click *Plots*
4. In Plots Box, Select *Normality plots with test*, leaving rest as default and click Continue

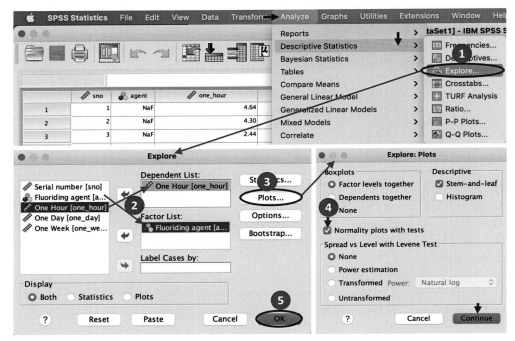

Figure 3.2 Applying normality tests.

Tests of Normality

	Kolmogorov–Smirnov[a]			Shapiro–Wilk		
	Statistic	df	Sig.	Statistic	df	Sig.
BMI for Age Z score	.044	1416	.000	.987	1416	.000

a. Lilliefors Significance Correction

Figure 3.3 Output: tests of normality.

5. In the main Explore window, click *OK* to get results in the output file. There would be three tables and three graphs, concentrate on the third table: *Tests of Normality* (Fig. 3.3).

Interpretation: Example 1

The interpretation of the test is easy (Fig. 3.3). We just have to look at the Tests of Normality table of Kolmogorov—Smirnov test and Shapiro—Wilk test results. The P-value or significance (sig. in the Figure) is 0.000. Whenever the sig is 0.000, it means that it is <0.001. For a significance test, the P-value should be <0.05. *If the test is significant, it indicates that the data violate the normality distribution and parametric tests should not be applied.*

In case of conflict between the test results, the more powerful test- Shapiro Wilk should be preferred for interpretation. Shapiro Wilk is not only more powerful, but also more specific measure of normality. Fortunately, SPSS (Version 21 onwards) gives a Lilliefors corrected value of the KS test which corrects for the small values at the tails of probability distributions. Thus, it is actually a Lilliefors corrected KS test as mentioned in the results at the footnote (Lilliefors, 1967). The chances of conflicting results between corrected KS and Shapiro—Wilk test are therefore, minimal. Kindly note that the Lilliefors corrected KS test are not available in older versions of SPSS (20 and below). However, it makes no difference to the researcher as one can safely prefer the Shapiro—Wilk test's significance in case of such conflicting significance.

Apart from this output, other outputs such as normality plots (P—P plots) are also available in SPSS. We do not need to discuss them at the moment. Further details on such plots and linearity are mentioned in detail in the chapter on regression.

Application: Example 2

The second example is from a research where the fluoride release after applying different fluoride agents on teeth was measured after 1 h (Data Name—*3. Fluorides_Dental.sav*). In this data, we want to check whether the fluoride release after 1 h (dependent/outcome variable) differs among the three different fluoride agents (independent/explanatory variable). To check whether we can apply the parametric test, we have to check for normal distribution in SPSS by applying *Kolmogorov—Smirnov test* and *Shapiro—Wilk test.* The steps of the application are as follows:

1. Open file *3.Fluorides_Dental* from the dataset provided with this book. Got to *Analyze*, hover over *Descriptive Statistics* and click *Explore* (Fig. 3.4).
2. A new dialogue box of Explore will open up. Transfer the desired variable for the normality test (1 h) to the *Dependent list* and factor variable (Fluoriding agent) under the *Factor list.* This can be done by either drag-drop or using arrow buttons.
3. To command SPSS to test normality, click *Plots.*
4. In the newly opened dialog box of Plots, check against *Normality plots with test* and click *Continue* to return to Explore dialogue box.
5. In the explore dialog box, click *OK* to get the results in the output window.
6. In the output file > concentrate on the third log—Tests of Normality (Fig. 3.5).

Interpretation: Example 2

The interpretation of the test is similar to the previous example (Fig. 3.5). The release of fluorides after applying each of the three fluoridating agents—NaF, SnF2, and APF, and the control group is mentioned. The *P*-value or significance (sig. in the figure) for NaF and SnF2 is not significant (>0.05) in both the tests. However, in the case of APF, there is a conflict. The KS is significant at 0.042 but Shapiro—Wilk is not. As mentioned in the first example, the results of Shapiro Wilk should be preferred and its non-significance indicates that the data fulfill the normality assumption for parametric tests (Box 3.4).

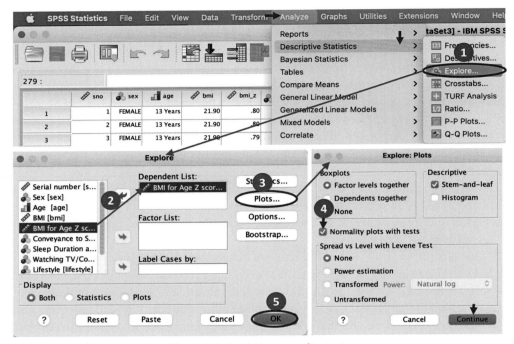

Figure 3.4 Applying normality tests.

Tests of Normality

	Fluoriding agent	Kolmogorov–Smirnov[a]			Shapiro–Wilk		
		Statistic	df	Sig.	Statistic	df	Sig.
One Hour	NaF	.183	10	.200[*]	.951	10	.681
	SnF2	.242	10	.099	.913	10	.299
	APF	.267	10	.042	.857	10	.070
	Control	.135	10	.200[*]	.940	10	.550

*. This is a lower bound of the true significance.

a. Lilliefors Significance Correction

Figure 3.5 Output: tests of normality.

2.2.2 Homogeneity of variance/homoscedasticity in the sample

Variance is a measure of the dispersion between numbers in data. Data from multiple groups should have the same variance. This means that the distribution or spread of scores around the mean is similar in different groups. The violation of this principle could lead

BOX 3.4 My data failed the normalcy assumption test. Is there any way to apply parametric tests?

A favourable (nonsignificant) result on Kolmogrov—Smirnov and Shapiro—Wilk test signals an approval for parametric test application. However, in some cases, even if these tests show a significant result, parametric tests are applicable as long as it has near normal distribution. More on this would be discussed in the next chapter on parametric tests.

to higher alpha error or type 1 sampling error (discussed later). However, commonly used parametric tests such as *t*-tests and ANOVA are generally robust if the compared groups have equal sample size. Even when they are unequal, as long as the ratio of largest to smallest group sample size is less than 1.5, this does not cause problem with the results. Homogeneity of variances can be checked with Levene's test, Bartlett's test, Box's M test, Brown—Forsyth test, and/or Hartley's Fmax test.

In SPSS, Levene's test for equality of variances is automatically performed while applying *t*-tests and it gives us clear results in the light of this assumption. Even when this assumption fails (Levene's test is significant), SPSS gives us an alternative result that we can use. We will see this in detail when we discuss *t*-tests. Violation of homogeneity of variance with unequal group sizes (difference >1.5) could lead to bias in parametric tests.

2.2.3 Independence of the variable

Independence of the variable means that there should be no inherent or natural connection with the outcome measure. For example, work hours and salary are not independent in settings where salary is directly dependent on work hours. On the other hand, eating or skipping lunch is independent of salary in most cases. Likewise, mean blood pressure cannot be an independent variable for systolic blood pressure as it is dependent on it. However, pulse rate could be independent to mean blood pressure. The independence of variables is directly related to a sound research design and choice of variables Box 3.5.

BOX 3.5 What will happen if I apply parametric tests even when the assumptions are violated?

The results could be misleading. Wrong application of parametric tests when assumptions are not met results in a high type 1 error/α error.

3. Choosing a statistical test

The choice of which statistical test to apply is made based on the outcome and exposure variable. This is elaborated more in Figs. 3.6–3.8 (Box 3.6).

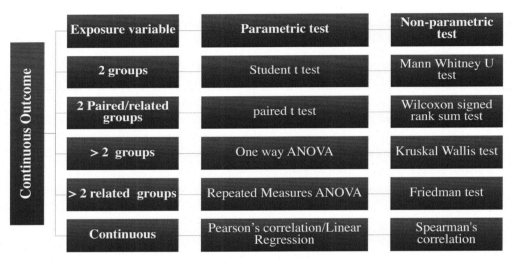

Figure 3.6 Choice of tests with continuous outcomes.

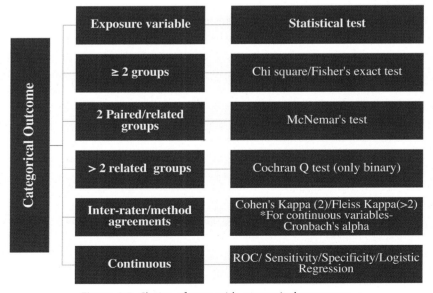

Figure 3.7 Choice of tests with categorical outcomes.

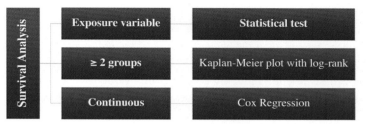

Figure 3.8 Choice of tests with survival outcomes.

BOX 3.6 Discrete variables: are continuous parametric tests applicable?

Discrete data are quantitative data that are countable but not measurable. They are different from ordinal/ranked categorical data as not only the rank but the magnitude is also important. A discrete measure example is the number of children born to a woman. As long as they obey the assumption of normal distribution in discrete data, we can safely apply parametric tests. In health research, visual analog scale (VAS) to measure pain and Likert scales are also used for assessment in an ordinal fashion. An interesting and contentious debate exists between *ordinalists* who argue that they are rank orders, and *intervalists* who argue they can be treated as interval data (Carifio & Perla, 2008). Intervalists argue that measures such as pain exist as a continuum and the measure, if appropriately applied is similar to a continuous measure. The debate per se is beyond the book's purview. However, if such pain scores are distributed normally, we agree with most experts that parametric tests, especially *t*-tests, can be safely employed (Carifio & Perla, 2008; de Winter & Dodou, 2010; Vieira, 2016).

To work with these figures, one needs to identify two things:

1. Outcome or dependent variable: whether continuous (scale data)/categorical/survival–related data.
2. Exposure or independent variable: whether categorical or continuous. Among categorical, whether two or more groups, which are either independent or paired/related and continuous.

4. Levels of significance and *P*-values

Generally, the level of significance (α, called as alpha) is set as 0.05. This α is the value that indicates how extreme observed results must be, in order to reject null hypothesis of a significance test. One can choose a more stringent level, such as 0.01 or even 0.001, but there is little incremental advantage. When α is set as 0.05, it means that we are trying to eliminate findings or differences that could have occurred by chance through a 95% level. It is important to understand the exact meaning of what this signifies, as both α and P values are confused with the use of the term significance and the value 0.05. α is a threshold value set before employing the statistical test, whereas P-values are computed with the statistical tests employed. For example, in the KS test above, we got a *P*-value. The *P*-value is a measure that tells us how extreme observed results must be in order to reject the null hypothesis. Technically, the *P value is the probability of obtaining a result as/more extreme than the observed results, if the null hypothesis is true.* So, if the *P* value is <0.05, it says that there is only a 5% probability of obtaining such results even if the null hypothesis is true. Thus, by convention a value lower than 0.05 is highly unlikely to be due to chance alone. It is important to reiterate that the level of significance (*α*, usually 0.05) should be set before the calculation of test statistic and should be mentioned in the statistical analysis section in the methods of the research protocol.

5. Errors in health research

Before discussing errors, we must recognize that errors are not synonymous with mistakes and are not necessarily deliberate. Moreover, we must realize that errors may be inevitable in scientific research will have errors, and a sound method acknowledges them and limits them through rigorous design and analysis. Errors in research are of two types—random and systematic.

Random errors are errors due to chance or random variation, predominantly affecting the precision or reproducibility of the research. Random errors are a part of the research and their impact is unpredictable. One of the sources of random error is sampling variability. A careful estimation of sample size and application of appropriate sampling methods reduces sampling errors.

Systematic errors or bias are predictable in the sense that they can affect some groups more than others, unlike random errors. In other words, they have a differential impact on different groups. They can occur due to selection or information biases. Poor epidemiological techniques such as flawed sampling method, biased or poorly framed questionnaire, overestimating/underestimating instruments, or even biological/behavioral effects such as higher blood pressures in the evening or during winters cause such systematic errors. Systematic errors can be reduced through the rigorous application of epidemiological methods and protocol. The epidemiological methods help reduce selection biases—nonrandom selection, selecting poor controls or poor blinding, etc. A strict protocol for measurements—where and when, training in the use of questionnaire, its validation, and regular calibration of measuring instruments also reduces such errors. Epidemiology and research textbooks deal extensively with such errors, and should be referred to, as this is beyond the scope of this book.

In terms of sources of error in health research, there are two types of errors—sampling and nonsampling errors (Fig. 3.9). Nonsampling errors arise due to poor methods of selecting samples or response errors, errors due to measurement and study tools errors, and other errors in data collection and processing.

5.1 Sampling errors

Sampling errors are important for hypothesis testing and need to be understood in detail. Sampling errors are a natural byproduct of the fact that we only take a sample for research instead of the population it represents. Sampling errors are of two types (Tables 3.3 and 3.4):

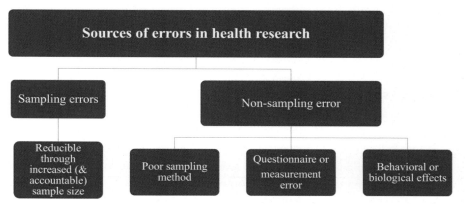

Figure 3.9 Sources of error in health research.

Table 3.3 Sampling errors.

Conclusion from sample observation	Truth in population	
	Effect/association	**No effect/association**
Effect/association	True positive/correct conclusion (power = 1 − β)	False positive α error (type 1 error)
No effect/association	False negative β (type 2 error)	True negative/correct conclusion (1 − α)

Table 3.4 Type 1 and type 2 errors.

	Type 1 error (α error)	**Type 2 error (β error)**
Also known as	Rejection error	Acceptance error
Definition	Wrongly rejecting null hypothesis	Wrongly accepting null hypothesis
Statistical implications	Significance level = α confidence Interval = (1 − α)	Power = 1 − β
By convention, the minimum acceptable value	α = 0.05 (95% confidence interval)	Power = 0.8

1. Type 1 error (Alpha (α) error): Alpha error is wrongly rejecting a null hypothesis.
2. Type 2 error (Beta (β) error): Beta error is wrongly accepting the null hypothesis.

5.2 Power and confidence interval

The power of the study is the ability to detect a true difference. In other words, it means rejecting the null hypothesis correctly when it is false (Table 3.4). Power is mathematically equivalent to $1 - \beta$. By convention, we should aim to have a power of at least 80%. The confidence interval is related to the level of significance $(1 - \alpha)$. By convention, the level of significance is 0.05 and thus the confidence level is 95% (1−0.05). This basically means that the probability of population parameters lying within the confidence levels is 95%.

5.3 Reducing sampling errors

The sampling errors can be minimized and controlled through adequate sampling. In probability sampling or random sampling which ensures an "equal probability of sampling," the sampling error is controlled by calculating and including an adequate sample size. Probability sampling could be simple random, stratified random, systematic random, and cluster sampling methods; whereas, nonprobability sampling methods are quota sampling, convenience sampling, purposive sampling, self-selection sampling, and snowball sampling. A discussion on details of sample size and sampling methods is beyond the scope of this book, but it is worth reiterating that sampling errors can be controlled to an acceptable level (generally at $\alpha = 0.05$ and Power $(1 - \beta) = 0.8$) by ensuring an adequate sample size based on those values, and using probability sampling methods. Inferences for larger populations are fairly powerful if probability sampling is done with due accounting of α and β errors.

5.3.1 Which sampling error is worse?

A pertinent question is which error is worse—α or β? The question is also crucial because there is a trade-off between α and β, which means that a more stringent α is frequently at the cost of a β value and vice versa. Well, the correct answer to the question is that both sampling errors have their implications and should be mitigated as much as possible, but by convention α error is considered worse.

This is due to two reasons:
1. It is akin to violating the principle of presumption of innocence (Table 3.5) as it would wrongly interpret that treatment X is effective. This has implications- 1. it raises false hopes, and 2. it delays the search for effective alternatives.
2. This could invite litigations based on treatment X's noneffectivity and the side effects it invites without any good reason.

Table 3.5 Which error is worse?.

Court verdict	Truth	
	Guilty	**Innocent**
Guilty	True positive/correct conclusion (power $= 1 - \beta$)	False positive α error (type 1 error)
Innocent	False negative β (type 2 error)	True negative/correct conclusion $(1 - \alpha)$

BOX 3.7 Data dredging and fishing expedition

The testing of hypothesis that is not mentioned in the protocol but is suggested by data is called data dredging (Abramson & Abramson, 2011). Proponents of data dredging consider it useful because it uncovers an existing association, calling its neglect as a *type 0 error*. However, data dredging is warned against by a majority of experts as it is an accidental association for which there was no pre-stated hypothesis. It could lead to fishing expeditions, where a large number of variables are studied in the hope that some will have a positive association (if the net is large enough, you will catch some fish).

What to do in such cases? Follow the advice of Altman (1991)- even if data dredging is used, it should be restricted *"to generating hypothesis for examination in further studies"* (Altman, 1991).

Remember apophenia from Chapter 1? Apophenia is a tendency to interpret random patterns as meaningful. Statistically, it is a type 1 error. Conspiracy theories, disinformation campaigns, and misleading hate-filled politics circulating daily on social media suffer from this error. Back to health research, the problem of sampling errors is best addressed by taking the conventional values of α and β. It must be ensured that α should never be >0.05 and power should preferably be at least 80% (Box 3.7).

5.4 Nonsampling errors

Nonsampling error is due to poor methods of selecting samples or eliciting responses, measurement and study tool errors, and other errors in data collection and processing. This error occurs during data collection and entry. A nonsampling error could be random or systematic and the latter is worse.

Nonsampling errors include poor sampling techniques, biased survey questions or interview techniques, measurement errors, data entry errors, high nonresponse rates, false information by respondents, wrong interpretation by interviewers, and inappropriate data analysis.

A strict protocol that defines the methods of random sampling, uses a validated questionnaire/measurement tool, ensures quality checks for data entry, and employs appropriate data analysis controls the nonrandom error. A good knowledge of epidemiological techniques is essential for this task.

6. *P*-values and effect sizes

In health research, whenever we study a sample and want to draw conclusions, there are two options: (1) statistical hypothesis test, and/or (2) confidence interval calculation (Pagano & Gauvreau, 2000). The statistical hypothesis testing has been discussed in the earlier sections. Null hypothesis significance testing (NHST) classifies into groups with significant effect or nonsignificant effect. Researchers often narrow down their research analysis and interpretation to whether they found the significance or not. Such judgemental value should not be accorded to P-values alone. Regardless, many researchers live their research life in pursuit of significant P-values. This psychological obsession is amusingly, yet appropriately called "significant-itis" (Chia, 1997). P-value never indicates the size or impact of the effect. It answers the fundamental question "*do you think there is an effect?*" (Hooper, 2011), and not whether it has clinical importance.

To know the impact and relevance, one needs to understand the strength or size of the effect. Effect size measures the relationship between variables or differences between the groups and has a practical significance for the outcome. If the effect is large, the finding could have a practical significance. However, if it is small, the practical implication is limited. Confidence interval is a measure of effect size as well as direction. A 95% confidence interval means that the chance of covering the true population value within it is 95%. Suppose the mean difference in weights of one-year-old boys in urban versus rural areas is 2.4 kg and the mean difference is statistically significant (P-value <.05). The 95% confidence interval of the mean difference is 1.2—3.6 kg. 95% confidence interval indicates that there is a 95% chance that the true weight difference between urban and rural population is within 1.2—3.6 kg. We can use confidence interval to know the significance as well. Suppose that a rural population is assumed to take more salt in food than the national average. Say the mean salt intake in the nation is 5 g and 10 g in the rural population. The 95% confidence interval of rural population's salt intake ranges from 4 to 15 g. As the confidence interval contains 5 g, there is no significant difference between this rural population and the national average. On the other hand, if the mean salt intake was 10 g, but the 95% confidence interval between 8 and 12 g, then it would be significant as 95% of the times the values of the rural population would be between 8 and 12, higher than 5 g (national average).

6.1 Basis of P-values and confidence intervals

Conceptually, both tests of significance and confidence intervals are computed from standard error. Standard error measures the accuracy of a sample distribution representing a population. It is calculated as standard deviation divided by the square root of sample size (SE = $\sigma/\sqrt{n}$, where σ = standard deviation and n = sample size). Naturally, as the sample size gets bigger, the standard error reduces. Confidence intervals are calculated directly from standard error. In contrast, the P-value is based on a summary/test statistic such as t value (in t-test) or F-value (in ANOVA). As the P-value is based on a summary measure, it is actually a composite measure of both effect size and sample size. Thus, sample size has a huge impact on P-values. A very small sample size can fail to find a difference, even if it exists; whereas, a very large sample size could lead to a significant P-value despite a minute difference. That is why confidence interval should accompany P values. If the P-value is not significant and confidence interval is very wide, it could be due to the small sample size. If the P-value is not significant and the confidence interval is very narrow then there truly maybe no difference.

6.2 ASA statement on *P*-values

Given the overt crisis in research due to significant-itis, the American Statistical Association (ASA) has set six principles on *P*-values that we briefly describe below (Wasserstein & Lazar, 2016):

1. **_P_-values can indicate how incompatible the data are with a specified statistical model.**

    Under the set of assumptions and null hypothesis, the *P*-value indicates incompatibility and evidence that the null hypothesis should be rejected, and the data invite deeper examination. The deeper examination is warranted because there may be an association or effect.

2. **_P_-values do not measure the probability that the studied hypothesis is true, or the probability that the data were produced by random chance alone.**

    Technically speaking, statistical significance only means that it is "statistically noticeable" or "statistically detectable" (Ellenberg, 2015). It is not a measure of probability.

3. **Scientific conclusions and business or policy decisions should not be based only on whether a _P_-value passes a specific threshold.**

    P-value, used alone is especially dangerous. A very small effect size with very little biological/clinical relevance could be statistically significant ($P < .05$). On the other hand a substantial effect size with probable biological/clinical relevance could be insignificant due to the small sample size ($P > .05$).

4. **Proper inference requires full reporting and transparency.**

    Significant-itis has become a global phenomenon with cherry-picking of significant data. The ASA statement advocates strict avoidance of "Data dredging, significance chasing, selective inference and *p*-hacking" for satisfying the significant threshold. Adherence to the protocol should be rigorous and transparent.

5. **A _P_-value, or statistical significance, does not measure the size of an effect or the importance of a result.**

    For effect size or biological/clinical relevance, a confidence interval should accompany the results along with *P*-values.

6. **By itself, a _P_-value does not provide a good measure of evidence regarding a model or hypothesis.**

    Instead of *P*-value alone, other appropriate and feasible approaches should also be mentioned.

6.3 Final word: best practices with *P*-values

Given the current backlash against *P*-value misuse, we should be well aware of the misuse and follow the steps in the protocol as discussed in this chapter. We reiterate the three critical points of concern in the use of *P*-values:

1. *P* values alone are likely to be misused as a measure of effect size. Some may consider that significance is an indicator for clinical or biological relevance, which it is not.

Therefore, all *P*-values should be accompanied by the confidence interval of the estimates. The confidence interval indicates effect size and relevance.

2. *P*-value is a gatekeeper, not a judge. It should not be used as a verdict in favor of a treatment/association but as a gatekeeper. A significant *P*-value like a gatekeeper or detective invites a more profound examination of the data within the context (Ellenberg, 2015; Gibson, 2021).

3. Despite their propensity for misuse, which could be true for any statistical concept including confidence intervals, properly used *P*-values are important in health research (Harrington et al., 2019).

References

Abramson, J., & Abramson, Z. H. (2011). *Research methods in community medicine: Surveys, epidemiological research, programme evaluation, clinical trials.* John Wiley & Sons.

Altman, D. G. (1991). *Practical statistics for medical research.* Chapman and Hall.

Blackstone, W. (1899). By T. M. Cooley. In *Commentaries on the laws of England in four books* (Vol. 1, p. 1753). Callaghan & Company.

Bland, J. M., & Altman, D. (1994). One and two sided tests of significance: Authors' reply. *British Medical Journal, 309*(6958).

Bouvier, J. (1856). *Dictionary of law.*

Carifio, J., & Perla, R. (2008). Resolving the 50-year debate around using and misusing Likert scales. *Medical Education, 42*(12), 1150−1152. https://doi.org/10.1111/j.1365-2923.2008.03172.x

Chia, K. S. (1997). "Significant-itis"—An obsession with the P-value. *Scandinavian Journal of Work, Environment and Health, 23*(2), 152−154. https://doi.org/10.5271/sjweh.193

Ellenberg, J. (2015). *How not to be wrong: The power of mathematical thinking.* Penguin.

Enkin, M. W., Bland, J. M., & Altman, D. G. (1994). One and two sided tests of significance. One sided tests should be used more often [13]. *British Medical Journal, 309*(6958), 874.

Gibson, E. W. (2021). The role of p-values in judging the strength of evidence and realistic replication expectations. *Statistics in Biopharmaceutical Research, 13*(1), 6−18. https://doi.org/10.1080/19466315.2020.1724560

Good, P. I., & Hardin, J. W. (2012). *Common errors in statistics (and How to avoid them).* John Wiley & Sons.

Harrington, D., D'Agostino, R. B., Gatsonis, C., Hogan, J. W., Hunter, D. J., Normand, S. L. T., Drazen, J. M., & Hamel, M. B. (2019). New guidelines for statistical reporting in the journal. *New England Journal of Medicine, 381*(3), 285−286. https://doi.org/10.1056/NEJMe1906559

Hooper, R. (2011). P-values are misunderstood, but do not confound. *Journal of Clinical Epidemiology, 64*(9), 1047. https://doi.org/10.1016/j.jclinepi.2011.03.003

Lehmann, E. L. (1993). The Fisher, Neyman−Pearson theories of testing hypotheses: One theory or two? *Journal of the American Statistical Association, 88*(424), 1242−1249. https://doi.org/10.1080/01621459.1993.10476404

Lilliefors, H. W. (1967). On the Kolmogorov−Smirnov test for normality with mean and variance unknown. *Journal of the American Statistical Association, 62*(318), 399−402. https://doi.org/10.1080/01621459.1967.10482916

Pagano, M., & Gauvreau, K. (2000). *Principles of biostatistics.* Brooks/Cole.

Vieira, P. C. (2016). T-test with likert scale variables. *SSRN Electronic Journal.* https://doi.org/10.2139/ssrn.2770035. https://papers.ssrn.com/sol3/papers.cfm?abstract_id=2770035

Volokh, A. (1997). N guilty men. *University of Pennsylvania Law Review, 146*(1), 173−216.

Wasserman, L. (2004). *All of statistics: A concise course in statistical inference.* Springer.

Wasserstein, R. L., & Lazar, N. A. (2016). The ASA's statement on p-values: Context, process, and purpose. *American Statistician, 70*(2), 129−133. https://doi.org/10.1080/00031305.2016.1154108

de Winter, J. C. F., & Dodou, D. (2010). Five-point likert items: T test versus Mann-Whitney-Wilcoxon. *Practical Assessment, Research and Evaluation, 15*(11). http://pareonline.net/pdf/v15n11.pdf.

CHAPTER 4

Parametric tests*

I couldn't claim that I was smarter than sixty-five other guys—but the average of sixty-five other guys, certainly!

Richard P. Feynman

1. Continuous outcomes

Continuous outcomes are outcomes with measurable data that can take an unrestricted number of measurable values. Some of them may have an upper or lower limit. For example, weight cannot be <0 kg. As the weight data are so mathematically precise, they can be subjected to further statistical calculations. Examples of such measures are hemoglobin levels (measured in Hb g%), body mass index/BMI (measured in kg/m^2), blood pressure (measured in mm Hg), height, weight, age, etc. As they are continuous in nature, it is possible to explore, analyze, and compare their mean, standard deviations, and confidence intervals meaningfully.

As discussed in Chapter 1, continuous outcome is a type of quantitative data, which can take an unrestricted number of measurable values, although they may have an upper or lower limit (for example, weight cannot be below 0 kg). Quantitative data can be interval and ratio, although SPSS does not consider any difference between them. For SPSS, all quantitative data are scale data.

2. Parametric tests

2.1 Introduction

As we recall from Chapter 3, parametric tests are powerful tests, which are applicable if outcome/dependent variable is continuous. The granularity of the data makes them useful and creates more options for further statistical treatments as compared to categorical data. The difference between parametric and nonparametric tests has been discussed in the last chapter. In summary, if the data distribution is assumed to be known (normal or near normal) and only the values of *parameters* such as mean and standard deviation are unknown, we apply *parametric* tests (Pagano & Gauvreau, 2000). Nonparametric tests have no such assumption for distribution (distribution-free tests). The nonparametric tests

---

*For datasets, please refer to companion site: https://www.elsevier.com/books-and-journals/book-companion/9780443185502

Biostatistics Manual for Health Research
ISBN 978-0-443-18550-2, https://doi.org/10.1016/B978-0-443-18550-2.00007-4

work on the principle of ranking of data rather than the exact magnitude of the data themselves, this loss of information makes them less powerful than their parametric alternatives. The parametric tests are shown in Fig. 4.1. As dependent/outcome variable must be continuous for the application of parametric test, the choice of parametric test depends on the nature of the exposure variable. Three factors in the exposure variable help us choose the right parametric tests.

1. The *outcome is continuous*. Is the *exposure variable also continuous*? If yes, **Pearson's correlation/Linear regression** can be applied.
2. The *outcome is continuous*, but *exposure is categorical* (in groups). Are there two groups or more? If two groups, *t*-test is applied, but if more than two **ANOVA** is applied.
3. Are the *categorical groups paired/related/follow-up measures*? If yes, **paired *t*-test** should be used for two groups, and **Repeated Measures ANOVA** - for more than two groups-.

2.2 Assumptions of a parametric test

Parametric tests are more powerful tests of significance but are only applicable if three assumptions are fulfilled:

1. *Normally distributed data or nearly normally distributed,*
2. *Homogeneity of variance/homoscedasticity in the sample,*
3. *Independence of the variable.*

A detailed discussion of the three assumptions is given in Chapter 3. We *apply Kolmogorov–Smirnov test* (K–S *test* or *KS test*) and the *Shapiro–Wilk test* to detect whether the data fulfill the normalcy assumption for parametric tests. If any test (especially *Shapiro–Wilk test*) shows significance ($P < .05$), the assumption fails. However, both *t*-test and ANOVA are fairly robust to such violations of normality, especially if the sample size is not too small. Levene's test of equality of variance is applied for homogeneity of

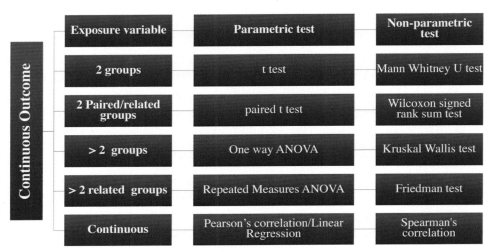

Figure 4.1 Choice of tests with continuous outcomes.

variance. Independence of the variable means that there should be no inherent connection with the outcome measure; for example, salary in many cases is related to work hours and cannot be considered independent. Wrong application of parametric tests when assumptions are not met could result in high Type 1 error/α error (Box 4.1).

> **BOX 4.1 If the assumption of homogeneity of variance is not fulfilled, can parametric tests be used?**
> Yes. Many statistical software, such as SPSS, check for homogeneity of variance and present results with the assumption as well as without the assumption. Such a t-test that does not assume homogeneity of variance is known as Welch's t-test and is clearly mentioned with the output of the t-test (Welch, 1947).

3. *t*-Tests: independent and paired

The t-tests are used to compare the means of two independent groups to determine whether there is a statistically significant difference between them (Box 4.2). When we test the difference between the means of two different groups, interventions, or change in measures/scores, it is known as independent or unpaired t-test. On the other hand, it is called a paired t-test and rarely, a dependent t-test or repeated measures t-test if it compares two means taken in the same group at two different times (e.g., pre- and postdrug intervention measures or fever temperature on day 0 and day 1). Thus, repeated measures on the same subjects are compared using paired t-test. However, paired t-test can also be applied in related samples, such as measuring alcoholism in twins or comparing the performance of the same students in anatomy and –physiology tests (The students, not the subjects, are the same, so don't misunderstand us!). Whenever a t-test is mentioned alone, it means an unpaired/independent t-test.

4. Independent *t*-test

4.1 Applying *t*-test

As we have already discussed, unpaired/independent t-test is used to test the difference between the means of two different groups, interventions, or change in measures/scores.

Before applying the test, one must ensure its applicability. The dependent/outcome variable is a scaled variable whose mean and standard deviation can be calculated and compared between the two groups. As discussed earlier, the three assumptions for applying the t-test are similar to other parametric tests:
1. Normally or nearly normally distributed data,
2. Homogeneity of variance/homoscedasticity in the sample,
3. Independence of the variable.

Among the three assumptions mentioned earlier, the one that needs to be checked is normal or near-normal distribution of data. It is important to note that even approximately normal data satisfy this criterion as *t*-test is significantly "robust" to violations of normality, especially if the sample size is not too small. If the data do not fulfill this criterion, they can be subjected to data transformations, randomization procedures, or nonparametric test (Mann—Whitney test) can be applied (Knief & Forstmeier, 2021). Homogeneity of variance, the second assumption, is automatically checked and resolved, as we discuss in the results.

Let us discuss the steps needed to perform the unpaired *t*-test. The data that we will use to understand the application of the unpaired *t*-test is named *3.Adolescents_BMI.sav*, which is based on our data set from a related paper (different data) on the association of sleep duration with obesity (Faizi et al., 2015).

The research question and hypothesis are as follows:

Research Question: Is inadequate sleep duration at night (IASDN) associated with a higher prevalence of overweight/obesity?

H_0: There is no difference in the mean BMI for age Z score of adolescents with IASDN as compared with those with adequate sleep duration at night (ASDN).

H_A: There is a difference in the mean BMI for age Z score of adolescents with IASDN compared with those with ASDN.

Steps in application of *t*-test is as follows:

1. Open data file (*3.Adolescents_BMI.sav*). Go to *Analyze > Compare Means > Independent-Samples T-test* (Fig. 4.2).
2. Select *Test Variable* (bmi_z) and *Grouping variable* (sleep_night) and transfer them to their respective boxes.

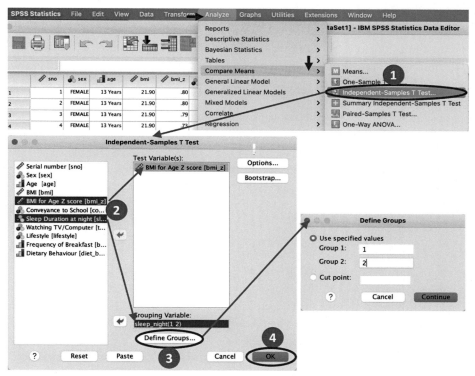

Figure 4.2 Applying independent samples *t*-test.

3. The question mark below the grouping variable will be activated as soon as we transfer any variable to it. To define two categories to be used, click *Define groups* and enter values of *Group 1 and 2* (IASDN is 1 and ASDN is 2) and click *Continue*. The important point is that in case there are multiple categories in the subgroup, one can choose to apply an independent *t*-test between any two groups whose codes are defined here.
4. After clicking *OK*, the results will be available in output window as two results tables are (1) group statistics and (2) independent samples test (Fig. 4.3).

Group Statistics

	Sleep Duration at night	N	Mean	Std. Deviation	Std. Error Mean
BMI for Age Z score	IASDN	334	.7694	.57105	.03125
	ASDN	1082	-.3064	.81259	.02470

Independent Samples Test

		Levene's Test for Equality of Variances		t-test for Equality of Means					95% Confidence Interval of the Difference	
		F	Sig.	t	df	Sig. (2-tailed)	Mean Difference	Std. Error Difference	Lower	Upper
BMI for Age Z score	Equal variances assumed	35.519	.000	22.537	1414	.000	1.07583	.04774	.98218	1.16947
	Equal variances not assumed			27.009	784.914	.000	1.07583	.03983	.99764	1.15402

Figure 4.3 Output: results of independent samples *t*-test.

4.2 Interpretation of results of *t*-test

The *t*-test compares the means of two groups for statistical significance. There are three important things to note from the results (Fig. 4.3):

1. The descriptive variables (Group Statistics): The mean BMI for age Z score of subjects with IASDN is 0.77 ± 0.57, which is higher in comparison-to those with ASDN -0.31 ± 0.81.

2. Choosing the *t*-test as per the assumption for equality of variance: SPSS uses Levene's test for equality of variances. If the significance of Levene's test is <0.05, then equal variances should not be assumed. In this case, the second line, that is, *t*-test with no assumption for equal variances, should be used.

3. The result of the *t*-test is thus the one with equal variances not assumed, $t = 27.01$ with df $= 784.91$ and *P*-value $<.001$ (Note that 0.000 is written in software results for *P* values beyond <0.001).

4. Thus, the null hypothesis is rejected, and the results can be written as follows.

The mean BMI for age Z score of adolescents with IASDN is 0.77 ± 0.57, which is significantly higher than those with ASDN −0.31 ± 0.81; t (784.91) = 27.01, P < .001. The mean difference in BMI for age Z score was found to be 1.07 (95% CI: 0.998−1.154). The 95% confidence intervals mean that there is a 95% chance that in the population, the difference in BMI for age Z score between adolescents with inadequate and adequate sleep duration will lie between 0.998 and 1.154.

Note: There are two types of *t*-test calculations-the traditional student *t*-test and Welch's *t*-test (Box 4.3).

BOX 4.3 Student *t*-test or Welch's *t*-test?

In research papers, we do not get to know which *t*-test was used. As discussed earlier, if the assumption of homogeneity of variance is fulfilled, the student's *t*-test is used; otherwise, Welch's *t*-test is used (Welch, 1947). Most statistical software such as SPSS automatically calculate the homogeneity of variance and give the results of Welch's *t*-test as well. Note that the degree of freedom (df) for calculating Welch's *t*-test differs from the normal df for *t*-tests, which is df $= n_1 + n_2 - 2$. In this case, the *t*-test has a df of 1414, but Welch's *t*-test df is 784.91. By looking at the df, one can know which t-test was applied.

---

5. Paired *t*-test

5.1 Applying paired *t*-test

As already discussed, paired *t*-test is used to test the difference between the means of the same or related subjects at two different times. Paired *t*-test is sometimes called dependent *t*-test or repeated measures *t*-test. Before applying the test, one must ensure its applicability. The two design–related features for applicability are the following:

1. The outcome measures are scaled variables (interval/ratio) whose mean and standard deviation can be calculated, and
2. These are paired/related variables (not independent).

The main assumption of a paired t-test is that the difference between the dependent variables should be normally distributed or nearly normally distributed. To test this assumption, one needs to compute a new variable, which is created by subtracting one variable from the other (difference = 1 h − 1 day). Computing a variable is explained in Chapter 2. (Transform > Compute Variable) and normality check in Chapter 3 (Analyze > Descriptive Statistics > Explore > Normality plots with tests). *Note that there is no assumption of homogeneity of variance in a paired t-test.*

The data for the paired t-test are from a research where the release of fluorides after the application of different fluoride agents on teeth was measured after 1 h and after 1 day (Data Name—*3.Fluorides_Dental.sav*). The researcher intends to measure whether the fluoride release has decreased significantly between 1 h and 1 day after application or not. The hypothesis is as follows:

H_0: There is no difference in the mean fluoride release between 1 h and 1 day.

H_A: There is a reduction in the mean fluoride release between 1 h and 1 day.

The steps in the application of paired t-test are as follows:

1. Open data file—*3.Fluorides_Dental.sav* and go to Go to *Analyze > Compare Means > Paired-Samples T-test*. A new dialogue box will open up (Fig. 4.4).

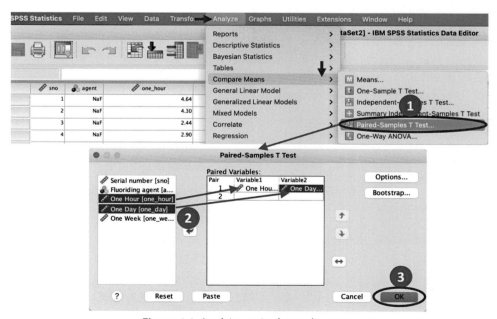

Figure 4.4 Applying paired samples *t*-test.

2. In Paired–Samples *T*-test box, transfer *Variable 1* (one_hour) and *Variable 2* (one_day) with the use of arrow button.
3. The *OK* button will activate. Click it to get the results in output window (Fig. 4.5). The three tables of results are- (1) Paired Samples Statistics, (2) Paired Samples Correlations, and (3) Paired Samples Test (Fig. 4.5).

5.2 Interpretation of results of paired *t*-test

1. The Paired Samples Statistics: The mean fluoride release after 1 h of application was 3.84 ± 2.70, which reduced to 0.64 ± 0.18 at 1 day (Fig. 4.5).
2. The second table is of paired samples correlations, and it gives an idea of how strongly the pre- and post-variables are correlated to each other. While we are interested in paired samples test, this Pearson's correlation signifies not only the significance of the correlation between 1 h and 1 day ($P < .001$) but also the strength of the correlation ($r < 0.862$). One can choose to report this in the results. We discuss correlation in detail in the next chapter.
3. The result of paired samples *t*-test is $t = 7.98$ with df = 39 and *P*-value $<.001$ (Note that 0.000 is written in software results after the *P*-value is <0.001). The degree of freedom of paired sample *t*-test is n-1, where n is the number of observations.
4. Thus, the null hypothesis is rejected, and the results can be written as follows.

The mean fluoride release at 1 h was 3.84 ± 2.70, which significantly reduced to 0.64 ± 0.18 after 1 day with t (39) = 8.14, P < .001. The correlation between fluoride release at 1 h and 1 day was very strong and positive (r = 0.862, P < .001). The mean difference in fluoride release at 1 h to 1 day was reduced by 3.20 (95% CI: 2.389–4.011).

Note: Reporting the mean difference between the two groups with their 95% Confidence interval is necessary, as it gives an idea about the strength/impact of the difference. Box 4.4 pertains to the wrong application of unpaired t-test instead of paired t-test.

Paired Samples Statistics

		Mean	N	Std. Deviation	Std. Error Mean
Pair 1	One Hour	3.8360	40	2.69508	.42613
	One Day	.6360	40	.18569	.02936

Paired Samples Correlations

		N	Correlation	Sig.
Pair 1	One Hour & One Day	40	.862	.000

Paired Samples Test

		Paired Differences					t	df	Sig. (2-tailed)
		Mean	Std. Deviation	Std. Error Mean	95% Confidence Interval of the Difference Lower	95% Confidence Interval of the Difference Upper			
Pair 1	One Hour – One Day	3.20000	2.53679	.40110	2.38869	4.01131	7.978	39	.000

Figure 4.5 Results of paired *t*-test.

> **BOX 4.4 What if paired *t*-test was applicable and one applies unpaired *t*-test?**
> In addition to being an inexcusable mistake, this would be a loss to the researcher. The unpaired *t*-test is less powerful, as the variance is higher in unpaired *t*-test. In SPSS, paired *t*-test is applied through selection of two different columns as opposed to unpaired *t*-test where only one column is test variable, the other being a grouping variable. Thus, the chances of making such a mistake inadvertently is unlikely.

6. Parametric tests comparison with >2 groups: analysis of variance

To compare the means of more than two independent groups, the analysis of variance (ANOVA) test is applied. The outcome variable is continuous, and the categorical variables (groups) are more than two. Thus, ANOVA is an extension of the independent *t*-test when more than two groups are to be compared. The ANOVA that we are discussing is actually a One-Way ANOVA, also called uncommonly as a One-Factor ANOVA or between–subjects ANOVA. Two-Way ANOVA is a statistical technique where two independent variables (instead of one) can be compared simultaneously to understand the interrelationship between factors and influencing variables. Whenever ANOVA is mentioned alone, it signifies One-Way ANOVA. ANOVA is used to test means in >2 different groups, interventions, or changes in measures/scores.

6.1 Applying one-way ANOVA

Before applying ANOVA, one must ensure its applicability and assumptions. The dependent variable is a scaled variable whose mean and standard deviation can be calculated and compared with the >2 categorical groups. As discussed earlier, the three assumptions for applying ANOVA are similar to other parametric tests:
1. Normally distributed data or nearly normally distributed,
2. Homogeneity of Variance/homoscedasticity in the sample,
3. Independence of the variable.

   Among these three assumptions, the one that needs to be checked is normal or near-normal data distribution. It is important to note that even approximately normal data satisfy this criterion as ANOVA, like *t*-test, is significantly "robust" to violations of normality, especially if the sample size is not too small. The normality check is explained in chapter 3. (*Analyze > Descriptive Statistics > Explore > Normality plots with tests*). If the data do not fulfill this criterion, then the nonparametric alternative, the Kruskal–Wallis test, can be applied. Homogeneity of variance, the second assumption, is automatically checked and resolved as in an unpaired *t*-test. Levene's test for equality of variances automatically tests this assumption. If the data fail this assumption (significant Levene's test), then Welch's ANOVA results should be used. SPSS does all this automatically.

Let us discuss the steps needed to perform ANOVA. The data we will use to understand the application of ANOVA is from a data set of a related paper (different data) on the association of breakfast frequency with obesity (Faizi et al., 2014) available as *3. Adolescents_BMI.sav*.

The following research question and hypothesis will be used:

Research question: Is irregular breakfast intake associated with a higher BMI?

H_0: There is no difference in the mean BMI for age Z score of adolescents who take breakfast rarely, irregularly, and regularly.

H_A: There is a difference in the mean BMI for age Z score of adolescents who take breakfast rarely, irregularly, and regularly.

The steps in the application of **ANOVA** are as follows:

1. Open data file—*3.Adolescents_BMI.sav* and go to *Analyze > Compare Means > One-Way ANOVA* (Fig. 4.6).
2. In the One-Way ANOVA box > transfer dependent variable (bmi_z) to *Dependent list* and *factor* variable (breakfast_freq) in their respective boxes.
3. Click *Options* to open us the Options box. Select *Descriptive, Homogeneity of variance test*, and *Welch* and click *Continue*.
4. Click *OK* to obtain the results of ANOVA in output window as four set of tables (Fig. 4.7).

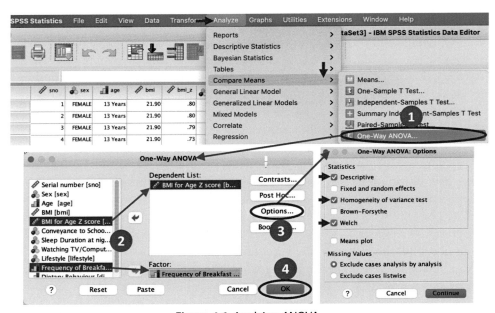

Figure 4.6 Applying ANOVA.

Descriptives

BMI for Age Z score

	N	Mean	Std. Deviation	Std. Error	95% Confidence Interval for Mean		Minimum	Maximum
					Lower Bound	Upper Bound		
Rarely (<2/Wk)	88	1.1081	.55488	.05915	.9905	1.2256	.25	2.56
Irregularly (3–5 times/wk)	390	.5725	.58643	.02970	.5142	.6309	−.84	2.56
Regularly (6–7 times/wk)	938	−.4215	.77212	.02521	−.4709	−.3720	−1.93	2.25
Total	1416	−.0526	.88878	.02362	−.0990	−.0063	−1.93	2.56

Test of Homogeneity of Variances

		Levene Statistic	df1	df2	Sig.
BMI for Age Z score	Based on Mean	13.678	2	1413	.000
	Based on Median	15.411	2	1413	.000
	Based on Median and with adjusted df	15.411	2	1356.854	.000
	Based on trimmed mean	14.672	2	1413	.000

ANOVA

BMI for Age Z score

	Sum of Squares	df	Mean Square	F	Sig.
Between Groups	398.583	2	199.292	391.557	.000
Within Groups	719.177	1413	.509		
Total	1117.760	1415			

Robust Tests of Equality of Means

BMI for Age Z score

	Statistic[a]	df1	df2	Sig.
Welch	484.462	2	250.724	.000

a. Asymptotically F distributed.

Figure 4.7 Results of ANOVA.

6.2 Interpretation of results of ANOVA

The results of ANOVA contain four tables of interest: (1) descriptives, (2) test of homogeneity of variances, (3) ANOVA, and (4) robust test of equality of means (Fig. 4.7). They and are explained below.

1. Descriptives: The mean BMI for age Z score was 1.11 ± 0.55, 0.57 ± 0.59, and -0.42 ± 0.77 in adolescents who took breakfast rarely, irregularly, and regularly, respectively.

2. Test of homogeneity of variances: This is a vital assumption tested through Levene's statistic. As the mean BMI for age Z score was significant (Levene Statistic: 13.68, $df = 2$, $P < .001$), this assumption is violated. Therefore, Welch's ANOVA should be used to report the results.

3. ANOVA: The difference between groups-adolescents who took breakfast rarely, irregularly, and regularly was significant with F (2, 199.29) = 391.56, $P < .001$. This ANOVA should be reported if the assumption of homogeneity of variances was not violated.

4. Robust tests of equality of means: As the assumption of homogeneity of variance is violated, Welch ANOVA values must be reported instead of simple ANOVA. The difference among adolescents who took breakfast rarely, irregularly, and regularly was significant with Welch's ANOVA test (2, 250.72) = 484.46, $P < .001$.

Thus, the null hypothesis is rejected, and the results can be written as follows.

The mean BMI for age Z score was found to reduce from 1.11 ± 0.55 to 0.57 ± 0.59 and −0.42 ± 0.77 in adolescents who took breakfast rarely, irregularly, and regularly, respectively. On applying Welch's ANOVA test, the mean difference in BMI for age Z scores was found to be statistically significant, Welch's ANOVA test (2, 250.72) = 484.46, P < .001.

Box 4.5 highlights the implications of wrong usage of ANOVA instead of Welch's ANOVA.

6.3 Post hoc ANOVA test

There is a difference between independent *t*-test and ANOVA test interpretation. As only two group means are compared in *t*-tests, a significant test indicates that the two means differ significantly from each other. However, in ANOVA, there are more than two groups, and a significant ANOVA indicates that the means differ but not whether the means of one group differ with the other. For example, we do not know whether the means significantly differ between groups a and group b, b and c, or even between groups a and c. For example, the mean BMI for age *Z* score was 1.11 ± 0.55, 0.57 ± 0.59, and −0.42 ± 0.77 in adolescents who took breakfast rarely, irregularly, and regularly, respectively. A significant ANOVA does not indicate whether there is a significant difference between adolescents who took breakfast rarely versus irregularly or irregularly versus regularly or even between rarely versus regularly etc. For this, we need to perform a post hoc ANOVA test. *A wrong but tempting error is to perform multiple t-tests, such as a t-test between adolescents who took breakfast rarely versus regularly, and get these results. However, such an approach increases the chances of type 1 or α error.*

Post hoc (Latin, meaning "after this") tests are *posteriority* tests and are only applicable if the results of ANOVA are significant. Therefore, if the *F* test or Welch's ANOVA test is significant, we employ a post hoc ANOVA test.

6.4 Selecting appropriate post hoc ANOVA test

There are several post hoc tests easily applicable through statistical software such as SPSS. We refrain from an advanced statistical discussion on post hoc test selection but explain a simple guide in Fig. 4.8. Essentially, there are two things to keep in mind. First, if the

---

BOX 4.5 What if one uses ANOVA results instead of Welch's ANOVA despite nonhomogeneity of variance?

This would be a mistake. The alpha error of the test results will increase. Infact, violating the homogeneity of variances leads to a bigger alpha error than violations of normality assumption in ANOVA.

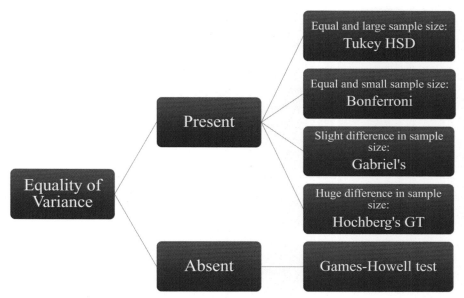

Figure 4.8 Selecting appropriate post hoc ANOVA test.

homogeneity of variance is not present, as checked via Levene's test earlier, then we use the Games—Howell test. If homogeneity of variance is present, then the second important thing is the sample size of the groups in question.

Four situations could be present:

1. Sample size—equal and large: use Tukey's Honest Significant Difference Testing (Tukey's HSD). This is mentioned as Tukey in SPSS, as we see later.
2. Sample size—equal and small: use Bonferroni.
3. Sample size—slight differences: use Gabriel's.
4. Sample size—huge differences: use Hochberg's GT2.

6.5 Applying post hoc ANOVA test

1. Open data file—*3.Adolescents_BMI.sav* and go to *Analyze > Compare Means > One-Way ANOVA* (Fig. 4.9).
2. In the One-Way ANOVA box > transfer dependent variable (bmi_z) and factor variable(breakfast_freq) in their respective boxes.
3. Click Post Hoc to open the Post Hoc box. Select the appropriate test according to Fig. 4.8 (in our case, Games—Howell, since our data failed equality of variance in the ANOVA test).
4. Click OK to obtain the results of post hoc test in output window (Fig. 4.10).

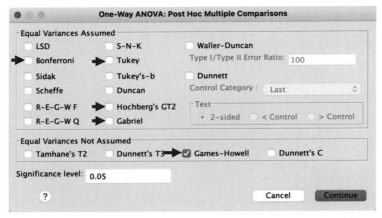

Figure 4.9 Applying post hoc ANOVA test.

Multiple Comparisons

Dependent Variable: BMI for Age Z score
Games–Howell

(I) Frequency of Breakfast	(J) Frequency of Breakfast	Mean Difference (I–J)	Std. Error	Sig.	95% Confidence Interval Lower Bound	95% Confidence Interval Upper Bound
Rarely (<2/Wk)	Irregularly (3–5 times/wk)	.53553*	.06619	.000	.3787	.6924
	Regularly (6–7 times/wk)	1.52953*	.06430	.000	1.3770	1.6821
Irregularly (3–5 times/wk)	Rarely (<2/Wk)	–.53553*	.06619	.000	–.6924	–.3787
	Regularly (6–7 times/wk)	.99400*	.03895	.000	.9026	1.0854
Regularly (6–7 times/wk)	Rarely (<2/Wk)	–1.52953*	.06430	.000	–1.6821	–1.3770
	Irregularly (3–5 times/wk)	–.99400*	.03895	.000	–1.0854	–.9026

*. The mean difference is significant at the 0.05 level.

Figure 4.10 Results of post hoc ANOVA test.

6.6 Interpretation of results of post hoc ANOVA test

1. The first thing to note is that post hoc ANOVA test results follow a significant ANOVA test.

2. Post hoc Games–Howell test was applied to find the significance of the difference between the different frequencies of breakfast. All three pair-wise analyses were significant. The mean difference in BMI for age Z score between those who had breakfast rarely versus those who had it irregularly was 0.54 (95% CI: 0.38–0.69) and was statistically significant on the post hoc Games–Howell test ($P < .001$). The mean difference in BMI for age Z score between those who had breakfast rarely versus those who had it regularly was 1.53 (95% CI: 1.38–1.68) and was statistically significant on the post hoc Games–Howell test ($P < .001$). Additionally, the mean difference in

BMI for age Z score between those who had breakfast irregularly versus those who had it regularly was 0.99 (95% CI: 0.90−1.08). It was statistically significant on the post hoc Games−Howell test ($P < .001$).

7. Repeated-measures ANOVA

Earlier, we saw how an independent t-test compares independent groups and paired t-test compares paired/related groups such as pre−post measures. For more than two groups, ANOVA is used instead of an independent t-test, and Repeated-Measures ANOVA or RMANOVA is used instead of paired t-test. Thus, RMANOVA is an extension of paired t-tests for more than two measures. We need to remember that, like paired t-tests, RM-ANOVA is not limited to the same groups' repeated measures but also related group measures. Thus, RMANOVA is used to test means at >2 different times, interventions, or changes in measures/scores within the same/related groups (such as twins).

7.1 Applying RMANOVA

Before applying RMANOVA, one must ensure its applicability.
- The dependent variable is a scaled variable whose mean and standard deviation can be calculated and has to be compared at more than two different times/stages/conditions.
- The assumptions of RMANOVA are the same as ANOVA except that instead of homogeneity of variance/homoscedasticity in the sample, the assumption of "sphericity" must be met. Sphericity is the homogeneity of variances in a between-subjects ANOVA and is violated when the variances of the *differences* between all the combinations of paired/related groups are not equal. Sphericity is measured as e (epsilon), and its violation causes an increase in Type 1 or an error. In most statistical software, the assumption of sphericity is tested, and in case it is violated, an adjusted test value is also calculated. In SPSS, sphericity is tested by Mauchly's sphericity test. If Mauchly's test is significant (<0.05), then the assumption of sphericity is violated.

There is a difference in the approach of variability measures in RMANOVA as compared to ANOVA (Fig. 4.11). In ANOVA, the total variability (sum of squares total—SS_T) is due to between-group variability and within-group variability. Between-group variability is the sum of squares between variables (SS_b), whereas within-group variability is the error (SS_w or SS_{error}). In RMANOVA, this large error-within-group variability (SS_w) is measured as variability in individual subjects' measure (subjects variability $= SS_{subjects}$) and error variability (SS_{error}) otherwise. The important thing to note is that RMANOVA gives us a more precise measure giving full value to individual differences and a reduced error. Individual difference is a significant variability when we measure blood pressure, height, BMI, pulse rate, or any values over time, as these values have a specific biological variability among people.

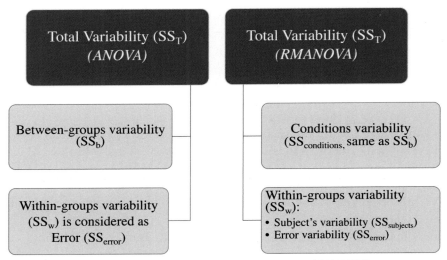

Figure 4.11 Variability measures in ANOVA and RMANOVA.

The data for the RMANOVA application is from the research where the release of fluorides after applying different fluoride agents on teeth was measured after 1 hour, 1 day, and 1 week (Data Name—*3.Fluorides_Dental.sav*). The researcher intends to measure whether the fluoride release has reduced significantly with time after application or not (within subjects). The hypothesis is as follows:

H_0: There is no difference in the mean fluoride release with time from 1 hour to 1 day and 1 week after applying different fluoriding agents.

H_A: There is a reduction in the mean fluoride release with time from 1 hour to 1 day and 1 week after applying different fluoriding agents.

However, in practical terms, we would also want to check whether there is a significant difference in the decrease in fluoride release between the different agents (i.e., between-subjects variation). Fortunately, we can do this together while applying RM-ANOVA in SPSS. For this, the hypothesis could be:

H_0: There is no difference in the mean fluoride release with time between different fluoriding agents—sodium fluoride (NaF), stannous fluoride (SnF2), and acidulated phosphate fluoride (APF).

H_A: There is a reduction in the mean fluoride release with time between different fluoriding agents—sodium fluoride (NaF), stannous fluoride (SnF2), and acidulated phosphate fluoride (APF).

The steps in the application of **RMANOVA** are as follows:

1. Open data file—*3.Fluorides_Dental.sav* and click *Analyze > General Linear Model > Repeated Measures* (Fig. 4.12).

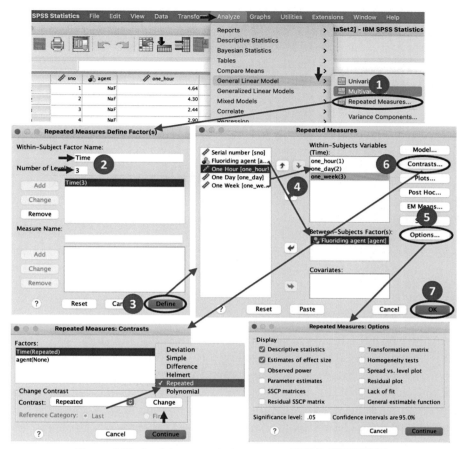

Figure 4.12 Applying repeated-measures ANOVA (RMANOVA).

2. In Repeated Measures dialog window, we have to first create Factor along with its variables and define their characteristic, which would be used in the next step. In *Within-Subject Factor*, enter *Factor Name* and the *Number of levels*. By default, in *Within-Subject Factor Name*: factor1 is written. The factor is the categorical variable across which one wants to compare the dependent variable (fluoride release). The factor in our example is the "time" and should be named as such. The number of levels is the number of subgroups in our factor. In our data there are three levels—1 h, 1 day, and 1 week. The number of levels, in this case, is three because measures to be compared have been taken at 1 h, 1 day, and 1 week.
3. Click *Define* and the main Repeated Measure dialog window opens up.
4. Here *Within-Subjects variables* and *Between-Subjects Factor(s)* are to be transported in the respective box. It is important to note that the three levels should be arranged in the

order of occurrence, that is, One hour is (1), One Day is (2), and One Week is (3). This is why we should drag the levels one by one, chronologically. In the between-subjects factors, the "agent" should be selected to know the difference between different agents, which is fluoriding agent.

5. In Repeated Measures dialog box, click *Options* and Select *Descriptive Statistics* and *Estimates of effect size*.

6. To command SPSS to use Repeated Measures for analysis, click *Contrast* to open new dialog box and Select time (Within-Subject Factor) and change contrast to "Repeated" instead of polynomial from drop-down menu. Remember to click "Change" after choosing repeated. Unless you click change, it stays as the default "polynomial." Once it changes to repeated, it will show in the Factors box after the factor name, such as Time (Repeated).

7. Now click *OK* to get the results in output window of SPSS.

8. Results: The results are clubbed and shown in Fig. 4.13. It shows the descriptive statistics, tests of sphericity, tests of within-subject effects, tests of within-subject contrasts, and tests of between-subjects effects. Fig. 4.14 helps in deciding which within-subjects test to use.

7.2 Post hoc RMANOVA

In RMANOVA, if the between-subject effects are significant, it does not tell us which subject is significant to each other. This is similar to ANOVA and post hoc ANOVA discussion mentioned earlier. Post hoc (Latin, meaning "after this") tests are *posteriority* tests and are only applicable if the results of between-subjects effects in RMANOVA are significant. In our example above, a statistically significant difference was seen between the different agents using RMANOVA, $F(3,12.34) = 342.95$, $P < .001$. However, we want to know whether the mean fluoride release between fluoriding agents is significant. For this, we need to apply post hoc tests.

7.3 Applying post hoc RMANOVA

The steps in applying post hoc RMANOVA is similar to the RMANOVA application (Fig. 4.12). Just two additional steps are needed (Fig. 4.15).

The steps in the application of **post hoc RMANOVA** is as follows:

1. In the main Repeated Measures Box, click *Options* and Select *Descriptive Statistics*, *estimates of effect size*, and *homogeneity tests* and click *Continue*.

2. Again, from Repeated Measures Box, click *Post Hoc Box* and Select Post hoc tests for (agents) > Select appropriate test. Since the sample size is equal and small, choose *Bonferroni* (Fig. 4.8) and *Games—Howell* if the equal variances assumption is violated.

3. Results: Two results are relevant: (1) Levene's test of equality of error variance and (2) Post hoc tests for multiple comparisons (Fig. 4.16)

Descriptive Statistics

	Fluoriding agent	Mean	Std. Deviation	N
One Hour	NaF	3.7140	.68571	10
	SnF2	7.8300	.59994	10
	APF	3.3000	.46638	10
	Control	.5000	.04110	10
	Total	3.8360	2.69508	40
One Day	NaF	.5020	.06680	10
	SnF2	.8860	.04300	10
	APF	.7160	.05816	10
	Control	.4400	.02309	10
	Total	.6360	.18569	40
One Week	NaF	.4430	.02584	10
	SnF2	.7120	.06339	10
	APF	.5010	.06226	10
	Control	.4030	.02111	10
	Total	.5148	.12894	40

Mauchly's Test of Sphericity[a]

Within Subjects Effect	Mauchly's W	Approx. Chi-Square	df	Sig.	Greenhouse-Geisser	Huynh–Feldt	Lower-bound
					Epsilon[b]		
Time	.030	122.861	2	.000	.508	.552	.500

Tests of Within–Subjects Effects

Source		Type III Sum of Squares	df	Mean Square	F	Sig.	Partial Eta Squared
Time	Sphericity Assumed	283.805	2	141.903	1783.155	.000	.980
	Greenhouse–Geisser	283.805	1.015	279.564	1783.155	.000	.980
	Huynh–Feldt	283.805	1.104	257.180	1783.155	.000	.980
	Lower–bound	283.805	1.000	283.805	1783.155	.000	.980
Time * agent	Sphericity Assumed	164.552	6	27.425	344.628	.000	.966
	Greenhouse–Geisser	164.552	3.046	54.031	344.628	.000	.966
	Huynh–Feldt	164.552	3.311	49.705	344.628	.000	.966
	Lower–bound	164.552	3.000	54.851	344.628	.000	.966
Error(Time)	Sphericity Assumed	5.730	72	.080			
	Greenhouse–Geisser	5.730	36.546	.157			
	Huynh–Feldt	5.730	39.727	.144			
	Lower–bound	5.730	36.000	.159			

Tests of Within–Subjects Contrasts   Multivariate Tests[a]

Source	Time	Type III Sum of Squares	df	Mean Square	F	Sig.	Partial Eta Squared
Time	Level 1 vs. Level 2	409.600	1	409.600	1753.291	.000	.980
	Level 2 vs. Level 3	.588	1	.588	238.969	.000	.869
Time * agent	Level 1 vs. Level 2	242.567	3	80.856	346.103	.000	.966
	Level 2 vs. Level 3	.225	3	.075	30.538	.000	.718
Error(Time)	Level 1 vs. Level 2	8.410	36	.234			
	Level 2 vs. Level 3	.089	36	.002			

Tests of Between–Subjects Effects

Source	Type III Sum of Squares	df	Mean Square	F	Sig.	Partial Eta Squared
Intercept	110.523	1	110.523	3070.539	.000	.988
agent	37.033	3	12.344	342.949	.000	.966
Error	1.296	36	.036			

Figure 4.13 Choosing the right within-subjects effect test.

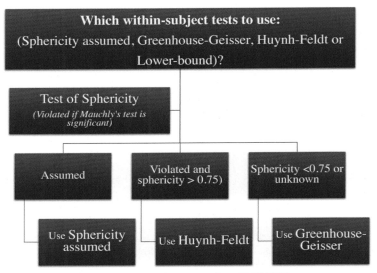

Figure 4.14 Applying post hoc RMANOVA.

7.4 Interpretation of results of post hoc RMANOVA test

1. The first thing to note is that post hoc RMANOVA test results follow a significant between-subjects RMANOVA test.
2. Levene's test of equality of error variances was found to be significant for means at 1 h and 1 week (Fig. 4.16). Therefore, the assumption of equal variances is violated, and Games—Howell Test must be reported.
3. The test interpretation can be written as follows after the results of RMANOVA: *Post hoc Games—Howell test was applied to find the significance of the difference between the different fluoriding agents. The mean difference in fluoride release between Stannous Fluoride (SnF2) and APF was the highest, with a mean difference of 1.64 (95% CI: 1.38—1.89). This was followed by the mean difference in fluoride release between stannous fluoride (SnF2) and sodium fluoride (NaF) at 1.59 (95% CI: 1.29—1.89). Both these differences were statistically significant, with P < .001. The mean difference in mean fluoride release between sodium fluoride and acidulated phosphate fluoride was 0.0473 (95% CI: 0.23—0.32), which was statistically nonsignificant.*

8. ANOVA, ANCOVA, MANOVA, and MANCOVA

ANOVA stands for analysis of variance, ANCOVA for analysis of covariance, M-ANOVA for multivariate analysis of variance, and MANCOVA for multivariate analysis of covariance. All these tests are variants of analysis of variance and have a dependent variable that is continuous. There is only one dependent variable in ANOVA and ANCOVA, whereas, in MANOVA and MANCOVA (M for multivariate), we have two/or more dependent variables. Among independent variables, Factor is a term used

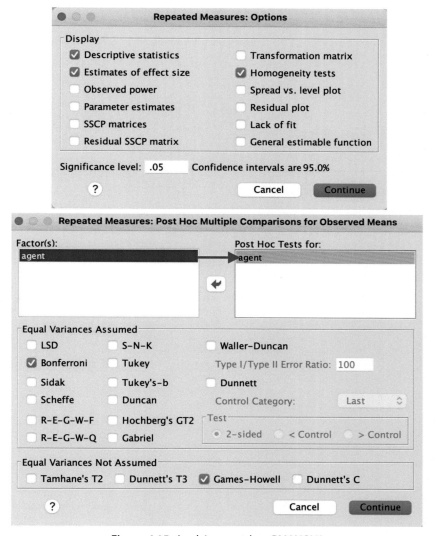

Figure 4.15 Applying post hoc RMANOVA.

for categorical variables and Covariate for continuous variables. In both ANOVA and M-ANOVA, the independent variables are one/more categorical variables (factors). On the other hand, the addition of *C* is for covariance, and it means the addition of one/more continuous variables (covariates). A detailed explanation with examples is given in Table 4.1.

When we apply RMANOVA, there is a test result showing multivariate tests just after descriptives (Fig. 4.13). This multivariate test is valid regardless of assumptions of

Levene's Test of Equality of Error Variances[a]

		Levene Statistic	df1	df2	Sig.
One Hour	Based on Mean	8.152	3	36	.000
	Based on Median	7.126	3	36	.001
	Based on Median and with adjusted df	7.126	3	19.656	.002
	Based on trimmed mean	8.065	3	36	.000
One Day	Based on Mean	2.356	3	36	.088
	Based on Median	1.368	3	36	.268
	Based on Median and with adjusted df	1.368	3	22.811	.278
	Based on trimmed mean	2.437	3	36	.080
One Week	Based on Mean	6.867	3	36	.001
	Based on Median	2.898	3	36	.048
	Based on Median and with adjusted df	2.898	3	19.852	.061
	Based on trimmed mean	6.345	3	36	.001

Multiple Comparisons

	(I) Fluoriding agent	(J) Fluoriding agent	Mean Difference (I–J)	Std. Error	Sig.	95% Confidence Interval Lower Bound	95% Confidence Interval Upper Bound
Bonferroni	NaF	SnF2	−1.5897*	.08485	.000	−1.8266	−1.3528
		APF	.0473	.08485	1.000	−.1896	.2842
		Control	1.1053*	.08485	.000	.8684	1.3422
	SnF2	NaF	1.5897*	.08485	.000	1.3528	1.8266
		APF	1.6370*	.08485	.000	1.4001	1.8739
		Control	2.6950*	.08485	.000	2.4581	2.9319
	APF	NaF	−.0473	.08485	1.000	−.2842	.1896
		SnF2	−1.6370*	.08485	.000	−1.8739	−1.4001
		Control	1.0580*	.08485	.000	.8211	1.2949
	Control	NaF	−1.1053*	.08485	.000	−1.3422	−.8684
		SnF2	−2.6950*	.08485	.000	−2.9319	−2.4581
		APF	−1.0580*	.08485	.000	−1.2949	−.8211
Games–Howell	NaF	SnF2	−1.5897*	.10504	.000	−1.8869	−1.2924
		APF	.0473	.09723	.961	−.2298	.3245
		Control	1.1053*	.07853	.000	.8608	1.3499
	SnF2	NaF	1.5897*	.10504	.000	1.2924	1.8869
		APF	1.6370*	.09073	.000	1.3797	1.8943
		Control	2.6950*	.07032	.000	2.4762	2.9138
	APF	NaF	−.0473	.09723	.961	−.3245	.2298
		SnF2	−1.6370*	.09073	.000	−1.8943	−1.3797
		Control	1.0580*	.05800	.000	.8778	1.2382
	Control	NaF	−1.1053*	.07853	.000	−1.3499	−.8608
		SnF2	−2.6950*	.07032	.000	−2.9138	−2.4762
		APF	−1.0580*	.05800	.000	−1.2382	−.8778

Figure 4.16 Post hoc RMANOVA results: multiple comparisons.

sphericity. This multivariate analysis of variance is called MANOVA and is preferred when there are two dependent variables (continuous) instead of one. To clear the confusion between ANOVA, MANOVA, ANCOVA, and MANCOVA, see Table 4.1.

Table 4.1 Difference between ANOVA, ANCOVA, MANOVA, and MANCOVA.

Test	Meaning	Comparison groups	
		Data type	Example
Dependent variable: Test score (continuous measure)			
One-way ANOVA	Compares the score in one factor	One factor: categorical variable	Level of education (Primary, High School, Graduation)
Two-way ANOVA	Compares the score in two factors	Both factors are categorical variables	Level of education (Primary, High School, Graduate) & Residence (Rural/ Urban)
ANCOVA	Compares the score with a factor and a continuous independent variable	One factor: categorical and one covariate: continuous	Level of education (Primary, High School, Graduate) & Number of Hours Sleeping
Dependent variables: 1. Test score 2. Monthly salary (both continuous measures, can be more than two)			
MANOVA	MANOVA is "multivariate" ANOVA which means it has two continuous response variables		
One-way MANOVA	Compares the score in one factor	One factor: categorical variable	Level of education (Primary, High School, Graduation)
Two-way MANOVA	Compares the score in two factors	Both (or more) factors are categorical variables	Level of education (Primary, High School, Graduate) & Residence (Rural/ Urban)
MANCOVA	Compares the score with a factor and one continuous independent variable	One factor: categorical and one covariate: continuous	Level of education (Primary, High School, Graduate) & Number of Hours Sleeping

Note. Factors are used for categorical variables and covariates for continuous.

References

Faizi, N., Khan, Z., Amir, A., & Azmi, S. A. (2015). Sleep duration and its effect on nutritional status in adolescents of Aligarh, India. *South African Journal of Child Health, 9*(1), 18. https://doi.org/10.7196/sajch.777

Faizi, N., Khan, I. M., Amir, A., Azmi, S. A., Ahmad, A., & Khalique, N. (2014). Breakfast skipping and proposed effects of breakfast on obesity: A school based study in adolescents in Aligarh, India. *Annals of Tropical Medicine and Public Health, 7*(1), 43—47. https://doi.org/10.4103/1755-6783.145011

Knief, U., & Forstmeier, W. (2021). Violating the normality assumption may be the lesser of two evils. *Behavior Research Methods, 53*(6), 2576–2590. https://doi.org/10.3758/s13428-021-01587-5

Pagano, M., & Gauvreau, K. (2000). *Principles of biostatistics*. Brooks/Cole.

Student. (1908). The probable error of a mean. *Biometrika*, 1–25.

Welch, B. L. (1947). The generalisation of student's problems when several different population variances are involved. *Biometrika, 34*(1–2), 28–35. https://doi.org/10.1093/biomet/34.1-2.28

Wikipedia contributors. Student's t-test [Internet]. (2022 Nov 24). *Wikipedia, The Free Encyclopedia*, 11:22 UTC [cited 2022 Dec 1]. Available from: https://en.wikipedia.org/w/index.php?title=Student%27s_t-test&oldid=1123560646.

CHAPTER 5

Nonparametric tests*

Whenever I read statistical reports, I try to imagine my unfortunate contemporary, the average Person, who, according to these reports, has 0.66 children, 0.032 cars, and 0.046 TVs.

Kato Lomb

1. Nonparametric methods

Measurements such as mean, variance, and standard deviation of the population are called parameters, and to predict these parameters with accuracy, the data should meet the assumption of normal distribution. Therefore, parametric tests can only be applied after the research data pass the normalcy assumption. If the data violate normal or even near-normal distribution, they can be subjected to data transformations, randomization procedures, generalized linear models that assume Gaussian errors, or simply apply nonparametric tests (Knief & Forstmeier, 2021). Nonparametric tests allow statistical inference without assuming that the sample drawn from a population has a normal or near-normal distribution. The characteristics and advantages of nonparametric test are highlighted in Box 5.1.

Consider a situation where the outcome is on ordinal or Likert scale, e.g., *1—Totally Satisfied to 5—Totally Dissatisfied*, or where the outcome is a rank, e.g., *APGAR score*, or where there are outliers; in all of these conditions, a nonparametric test is a viable option for their analysis. Because the nonparametric tests do not have a distribution assumption, they are often called as distribution-free tests. They provide statistical inference by ranking the individual data rather than the data itself as the parametric test does.

> **BOX 5.1 Characteristics and advantages of nonparametric test**
> It does not make an assumption about population parameters, so it does not require normal or near-normal distribution.
> > It can be used to analyze nominal, ordinal, ranked data, and outliers.
> > The tests are based on the median, which can be better in some situations (skewed data).
> > These tests are valid even with a small sample size.

---

*For datasets, please refer to companion site: https://www.elsevier.com/books-and-journals/book-companion/9780443185502

Biostatistics Manual for Health Research
ISBN 978-0-443-18550-2, https://doi.org/10.1016/B978-0-443-18550-2.00003-7

Because some information is lost in the process, it makes them less powerful. It is always recommended to keep the parametric test as the first choice for significance testing, unless the dataset does not meet the assumptions for parametric tests.

Thus, despite all these advantages, efforts should be made to apply parametric statistics whenever applicable. This is because nonparametric tests are less powerful, that is, if there is an actual effect, nonparametric tests are comparatively less likely to detect it. So, before applying any nonparametric test in SPSS, it is often advisable to assess the dataset for normalcy. This is described in detail in Chapter 3 Statistical tests of significance. If it violates the assumption, and if data transformations, randomization procedures, and generalized linear models cannot make it near normal, choose the test of significance from Fig. 5.1, based on your dataset. In Fig. 5.1, the choices for the application of nonparametric tests for continuous data based on the exposure variables is shown. Other tests for categorical outcomes are described in Chapter 7. Categorical variables.

2. Mann—Whitney *U* test

Mann—Whitney *U* test is the distribution-free alternative to the independent/unpaired *t*-test. Rarely, it is also called as Mann—Whitney—Wilcoxon (MWW/MWU), Wilcoxon rank-sum test, or Wilcoxon—Mann—Whitney test. The alternative to paired *t*-test or dependent *t*-test is called sign test or Wilcoxon signed-rank test. Paired alternative test will always have the term *"sign"* in it. To clear the confusion, we will use the most commonly used term—Mann—Whitney *U* test. Whenever the outcome/dependent variable is either a continuous variable which is not normally distributed or is an ordinal variable, we apply this test. The independent variable or comparison of the outcome is between two groups.

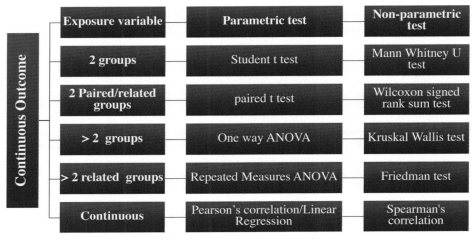

Figure 5.1 Nonparametric statistical tests.

2.1 The assumptions for Mann–Whitney *U* test

- There should be one dependent variable *having* continuous (e.g., IQ score) or ordinal value (e.g., Likert items).
- There should be one independent variable *having* two categories (i.e., a dichotomous variable).
- *Independence of observations*—the variable should not be paired or related (e.g., pre and post or before and after).

There are three methods to find statistical significance in nonparametric tests—asymptotic, Monte Carlo, and Exact method. Box 5.2 below gives a guide for use.

2.2 Applying Mann–Whitney *U* test

To understand the application of the *Mann–Whitney U test*, we use a dataset based on a research question we have used before.

Research Question: Is inadequate sleep duration at night (IASDN) associated with a higher BMI for age? The dataset that we use is named as *3. Adolescents_BMI.sav*. The following hypothesis will be used for our data set, from a related paper (different data) on the association of sleep duration with obesity (Faizi et al., 2015):

H_0: There is no difference in the mean BMI for age Z score of adolescents with IASDN as compared to those with adequate sleep duration at night (ASDN)

H_A: There is a difference in the mean BMI for age Z score of adolescents with IASDN as compared to those with ASDN.

Steps in application of Mann–Whitney *U* test are as follows:

1. Open data file (*3. Adolescents_BMI.sav*). Go to *Analyze > Nonparametric Tests > Legacy Dialogs > Two-Independent Samples* (Fig. 5.2). A Two-Independent-Samples Tests dialog box will open up.
2. In the *Two-Independent-Samples Tests* Box, enter "BMI for Age *Z* score" as a *Test variable* (a scale variable) and "Sleep duration at night" as a *Grouping variable* (Fig. 5.3).

BOX 5.2 Asymptotic versus Monte Carlo versus Exact: which method should we use in nonparametric significance calculation?

By default, SPSS uses the asymptotic method. For a more precise estimate, a Monte Carlo estimation should be done. However, if the sample size is small, we should prefer the Exact tests. Computing the Exact tests take some time, so please be patient if the output gives results after a while. Sometimes, when the data have more than three categories or when the sample size is large, SPSS is unable to calculate the Exact test. In such cases, Monte Carlo remains the best option to calculate a precise estimate.

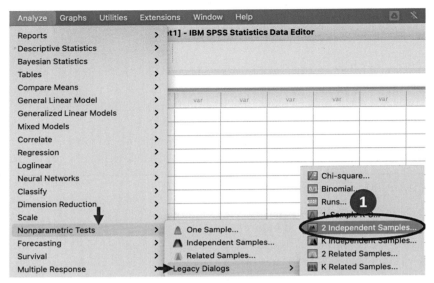

Figure 5.2 Selecting Mann–Whitney *U* test.

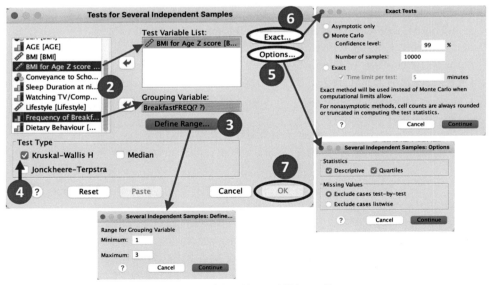

Figure 5.3 Applying Mann–Whitney *U* test.

3. Note the question mark in the *grouping variable* "Sleepatnight" Below, there is an option to define the groups. Here, the groups coded were 1 and 2 (for IASDN and ASDN, respectively); this should be entered in *Define groups*. The critical point is that in case there are multiple categories in the subgroup, one can choose to apply Mann—Whitney test between any two groups whose codes are defined here (Fig. 5.3).

4. Under the Test Type section, choose the *Mann—Whitney U test.*
5. To select the method to perform analysis, click on *Exact* on the top right corner, opening up a new dialog box in Fig. 5.3. The Exact Tests box has three options, and by default, SPSS performs *Asymptotic* only. For more precision, we will choose "*Monte Carlo*" methods and click continue to return to the Two-Independent-Sample dialog box. See Box 5.1.
6. We then click *Options*, and in the new dialog box, we choose *Descriptive* and *Quartiles* to get an idea of the parameters of the sample.
7. Finally, after all the steps, the *OK* button will highlight in blue, and should be clicked.

2.3 Interpretation of results of Mann—Whitney *U* test

There will be three tables in results output of Mann—Whitney *U* test (Fig. 5.4): (1) descriptive statistics, (2) Mann—Whitney ranks, and (3) test statistics.

The Mann—Whitney *U* test compares the two groups for statistical significance. There are three essential things to note from the results (Fig. 5.4):

Descriptive Statistics

	N	Mean	Std. Deviation	Minimum	Maximum	25th	Percentiles 50th (Median)	75th
BMI for Age Z score	1416	-.0526	.88878	-1.93	2.56	-.7000	-.1400	.5300
Sleep Duration at night	1416	1.76	.425	1	2	2.00	2.00	2.00

Ranks

	Sleep Duration at night	N	Mean Rank	Sum of Ranks
BMI for Age Z score	IASDN	334	1113.82	372017.00
	ASDN	1082	583.38	631219.00
	Total	1416		

Test Statistics[a]

			BMI for Age Z score
Mann–Whitney U			45316.000
Wilcoxon W			631219.000
Z			-20.724
Asymp. Sig. (2–tailed)			.000
Monte Carlo Sig. (2–tailed)	Sig.		.000[b]
	99% Confidence Interval	Lower Bound	.000
		Upper Bound	.000
Monte Carlo Sig. (1–tailed)	Sig.		.000[b]
	99% Confidence Interval	Lower Bound	.000
		Upper Bound	.000

a. Grouping Variable: Sleep Duration at night

b. Based on 10000 sampled tables with starting seed 2000000.

Figure 5.4 Results of Mann—Whitney *U* test.

1. The first table shows descriptive variables: This has limited use in interpreting results as opposed to its parametric counterpart (t-test), where it is beneficial. The table calculated descriptive of the variables in the analysis including mean and median, but during interpretation, we required outcome (bmi_z) descriptive split across two categories of exposure variable (sleep_night). We shall calculate this in the next step.

2. The second table shows the ranks of the two groups for the Mann−Whitney U test. The average or mean rank of BMI for age Z score in those with IASDN at 1113.82 was higher than those with ASDN at 583.38. Let us see whether this is statistically significant or not.

3. The third table shows the test statistics. The Mann−Whitney U test statistic is U. According to our chosen method; the value U is 45,316.00. The P-value that we have decided to use is through the Monte Carlo Sig. (two-tailed), the value of which is 0.000 (that is <0.001).

Thus, the null hypothesis is rejected, but we need a measure of central tendency of outcome variable across exposure variable to express the result. Hence, the median of bmi_z split across sleep_night has to be measured separately to express the results.

Steps to measure the median of one continuous variable across groups

1. We need to measure the median "BMI for Age Z score" divided across the two categories of "Sleepatnight" variable. This can be done by splitting the whole dataset into two groups using the split function using the "Sleepatnight" variable. So, go to *Data > Split file*, and a new dialog box will open, as shown in Fig. 5.5.

2. In the new dialog box of Split File, click the radio button of *Compare groups* to activate it.

3. Transfer the variable, you want to use for splitting the datasheet. In this case, shift "Sleepatnight" to the right side under *Group Based*.

4. Click *OK* to activate the split function. The output window will open by conforming that the Split function is activated across the selected variable.

5. We will now measure the central tendency as discussed in the third chapter. Go to *Analyze > Descriptive Statistics > Frequency*, and a new dialog box of Frequencies will open up, as shown in Fig. 5.6.

6. Transfer the continuous variable of interest, that is, "BMI for Age Z score," under the *Variable* box.

7. To inform SPSS what to measure, click *Statistics*, which will open a new dialog box.

8. In the Frequency: Statistics dialog box, check *Median* and *Quartiles* and click *Continue* to return to the frequency box.

9. In the Frequency dialog box, Display frequency tables at the left bottom are constantly checked by default. It is suggested to uncheck the *Display frequency tables*. This is not essential, but if it remains checked, the output window will display unnecessary tables that are of no use and could be annoying. Click *OK* to get the desired result of the median and quantile in the output window (Fig. 5.7).

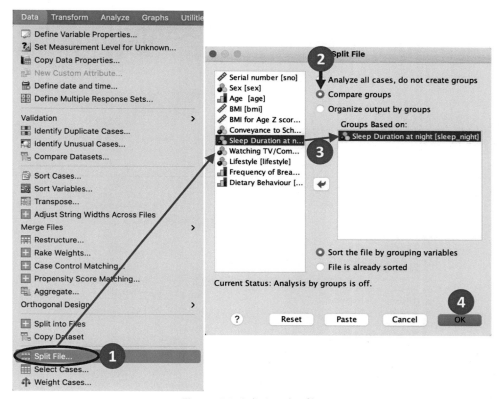

Figure 5.5 Splitting the file.

So, the median BMI for Age Z score for IASDN group is 0.61 ($n = 334$, IQR 0.42–0.97), and for ASDN is -0.38 ($n = 1082$, IQR -0.86–0.06). Thus the null hypothesis is rejected and the results should be reported as follows:

The BMI for age Z score in adolescents with inadequate Sleep Duration at Night (Mdn = 0.61) was higher than the ones with adequate Sleep Duration at Night (Mdn = −0.38). The difference was statistically significant on applying Mann–Whitney U test, U (N_{IASDN} = 334, N_{ASDN} = 1082) = 45,316.00, P < .001.

3. Wilcoxon signed-rank test

Wilcoxon signed-rank test (aka Wilcoxon signed rank-sum test) is the distribution-free alternative to paired t-test. The dependent variable or outcome should either be a continuous variable that is not normally distributed or is an ordinal variable. It should not be confused with the Wilcoxon sum rank test, the sparingly used synonym of the Mann–Whitney U test. Wilcoxon signed-rank test is analyzed based on the *signs* and magnitude

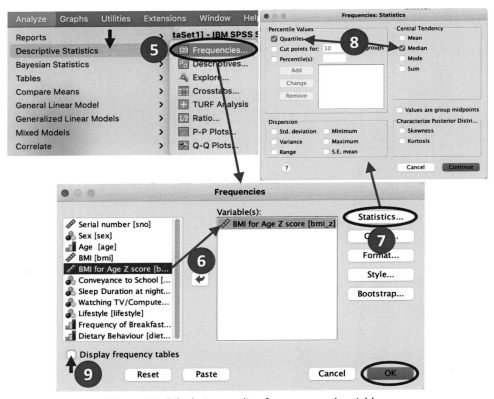

Figure 5.6 Calculating median for nonnormal variables.

of the observed differences between two paired continuous variables. As discussed in the paired *t*-test section, the data compares two sets of continuous or ordinal scores measured on the same/related participants. Thus, change in score between two related or matched pairs or the same subjects at two different times, is assessed by Wilcoxon signed rank-sum test.

3.1 Assumptions of Wilcoxon signed-rank test

- The dependent variable should be measured as continuous (such as IQ score) or ordinal value (such as Likert items).
- The independent variable should consist of two categorical, related, or matched pairs (Before and after).
- *Independence of observations*—the observations should be independent.

Statistics

Figure 5.7 Median across two groups of "Sleepatnight" variable.

BMI for Age Z score

IASDN	N	Valid	334
		Missing	0
	Median		.6100
	Percentiles	25	.4200
		50	.6100
		75	.9725
ASDN	N	Valid	1082
		Missing	0
	Median		−.3800
	Percentiles	25	−.8625
		50	−.3800
		75	.0600

3.2 Applying Wilcoxon signed rank-sum test

The data that we will use to understand the application of the Wilcoxon signed-rank sum test is the one that we have used before. A dietary intervention (ketogenic diet) was given for a month to a sample, and their pre and postintervention weights were measured. The researcher intends to determine whether a 1-month Keto diet reduces weight significantly. The hypothesis is as follows:

H_0: There is no difference in the subjects' weight after 1 month of the ketogenic diet.

H_A: There is a difference in the subjects' weight after 1 month of the ketogenic diet.

The steps in the application of the Wilcoxon signed-rank sum test are as follows:

1. Open data file (*5. Keto_diet.sav*). Go to *Analyze > Nonparametric Tests > Legacy Dialogs > Two-Related Samples* (Fig. 5.8).
2. In Two-Related-Samples Tests Box, transfer our variables "Preintervention Wt" under *Variable1* and "Postintervention Wt" as *Variable2* in the *Test Pairs* box (Fig. 5.9).
3. By default, the Wilcoxon is checked under the Test Type box; if not, select Wilcoxon.

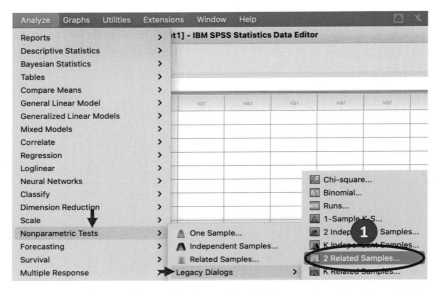

Figure 5.8 Selection of two related samples for Wilcoxon signed-rank sum test.

4. On clicking Options, a dialog box opens, where we click *descriptive* to get an idea of the sample (Fig. 5.9).
5. As soon as we click the *Exact* button, its dialog box opens. This box has three options, and by default, SPSS performs *Asymptotic* only. We will choose methods for more precision as the sample size is small. See details in Box 5.2.
6. After clicking *Continue* in the Exact Box, followed by *OK* in the main box, we get the results in the output window. There are three tables in results: [1] Descriptive statistics, [2] for Wilcoxon Signed Ranked Tests, and [3] Test Statistics.

3.3 Interpretation of results of Wilcoxon signed rank-sum test

The Wilcoxon signed-rank sum test compares the two groups (pre and postweight) for statistical significance. There are three essential things to note from the results (Fig. 5.10):

1. The first table shows descriptive variables: It provides an overview of central tendency weight of pre and postintervention. So we can conclude that the median weight of the person reduced from 71.15 kg (IQR: 64.80—77.60) to 68.70 kg (IQR: 62.00—77.20) after ketogenic diet intervention.
2. The second table shows the ranks of the two groups for the Wilcoxon signed rank-sum test. In 38 cases, the postintervention wt-preintervention weight is negative; it has decreased. In 11 cases, the postintervention wt. is higher, and it has not changed in one case. Since, in most cases, the postintervention wt is lower, we conclude that

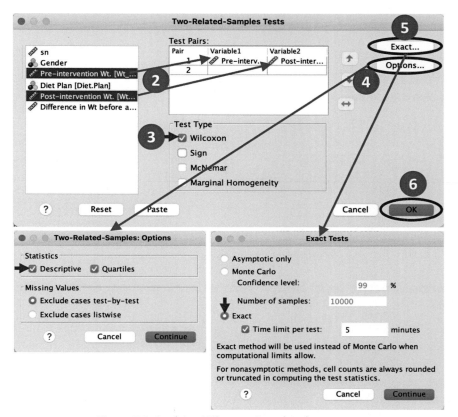

Figure 5.9 Applying Wilcoxon signed rank-sum test.

the postintervention wt is lower than preintervention wt- but is it statistically significant?

3. The third table shows the test statistics. The Wilcoxon signed-rank sum test statistics show that the z value is -5.17, and the P-value is <0.001. Note that the P-value of our chosen method is given in the third line [Exact Sig. (two-tailed)] of the table, the second line is for the default—Asymptotic method.

Thus, the null hypothesis is rejected; the weight decreases after 1 month of the ketogenic diet. The results should be reported as follows:

After 1 month of the ketogenic diet, the postintervention wt (Mdn = 68.70) reduced from the Pre-intervention wt (Mdn = 71.15). The difference was statistically significant on applying the Wilcoxon signed-rank sum test (z = −5.17, P < .001).

Note: The test options for two related test types: Wilcoxon, Sign, McNemar, and Marginal Homogeneity are discussed in Box 5.3.

Descriptive Statistics

	N	Mean	Std. Deviation	Minimum	Maximum	25th	Percentiles 50th (Median)	75th
Pre-intervention Wt.	50	71.872	9.5974	58.3	103.1	64.800	71.150	77.600
Post-intervention Wt.	50	69.590	9.3194	54.2	98.5	62.000	68.700	77.200

Wilcoxon Signed Ranks Test

Ranks

		N	Mean Rank	Sum of Ranks
Post-intervention Wt. – Pre-intervention Wt.	Negative Ranks	38[a]	29.80	1132.50
	Positive Ranks	11[b]	8.41	92.50
	Ties	1[c]		
	Total	50		

a. Post-intervention Wt. < Pre-intervention Wt.

b. Post-intervention Wt. > Pre-intervention Wt.

c. Post-intervention Wt. = Pre-intervention Wt.

Test Statistics[a]

	Post-intervention Wt. – Pre-intervention Wt.
Z	–5.174[b]
Asymp. Sig. (2–tailed)	.000
Exact Sig. (2–tailed)	.000
Exact Sig. (1–tailed)	.000
Point Probability	.000

a. Wilcoxon Signed Ranks Test

b. Based on positive ranks.

Figure 5.10 Results of Wilcoxon signed-rank sum test.

4. Nonparametric tests comparison with >2 groups: Kruskal–Wallis test

We have discussed the nonparametric tests used to compare two groups—the Mann–Whitney U test and the Wilcoxon signed-rank sum test—the nonparametric alternative of the independent t-test and paired t-test. Similarly, when the number of groups is more than two, the nonparametric choices for ANOVA and RMANOVA are the Kruskal–Wallis test and the Friedman test, respectively. Apart from these two, a few other specific tests are also available in SPSS, reserved for particular instances (Table 5.1). For more than two non-normal independent variables, either Kruskal–Wallis test or Jonckheere–Terpstra test (aka Jonckheere Trend test) are available. The Kruskal–Wallis test is used when the grouping variable is independent, such as treatment-A versus treatment-B versus treatment-C. On the other hand, Jonckheere–Terpstra test is applied when the independent grouping variables are ordered or ranked, such as treatment-A low versus normal versus high dose.

On the other hand, if the grouping variables are related, the Friedman test, Kendall's W test, and Cochran's Q test are the options. Friedman is the nonparametric alternative to RMANOVA, and is used to compare more than two related/paired continuous variables. Kendall's W test (aka Coefficient of concordance) measures agreement between raters by normalization of Friedman's statistic between 0 and 1, where 0 stands for no agreement and 1 for complete agreement. Cochran's Q test is reserved for comparing binary/dichotomous data between more than two groups, like categorical variables with binary responses (e.g., painful versus painless, improved versus not improved, etc., compared with >2 groups). We will discuss Cochran's Q test in the chapter on categorical variables.

BOX 5.3 Two related test types: Wilcoxon, Sign, McNemar, and marginal homogeneity

Wilcoxon test is a nonparametric alternative to paired t-test and is applied on related/paired observations.

The sign test is used in paired variables like Wilcoxon signed-rank test but is weaker than the same. Instead of measuring the *signs* and magnitude of the observed differences between two paired continuous variables like the Wilcoxon test, it converts the variable into plus and minus as per its status below or above the median. It does not value the magnitude of the paired differences and is thus seldom used.

McNemar test or McNemar chi-square test is a test for paired/related categorical variables, where there is a dichotomous or binary change. For example, the pass/fail proportions among 20 students in Maths and Science or the proportion of anemic and nonanemic patients before and after an intervention. This is discussed further in the chapter on Categorical variables. Marginal Homogeneity test is an extension of McNemar test if the category is more than two. For example, mild, moderate, and severe anemia before and after an intervention in 20 patients.

Table 5.1 Nonparametric tests with more than two comparison groups.

Test	Grouping variable	Comparison groups (groups >2)	Remark
Kruskal–Wallis test	Independent	Independent groups	Nonparametric alternative to ANOVA
Jonckheere–Terpstra test		Independent but ordered groups	Ordinal data
Friedman test	Related	Related or matched groups	Nonparametric alternative to RMANOVA
Kendall's W test		Measure of agreement among raters	Coefficient of concordance
Cochran's Q test		Related/matched groups with only binary/dichotomous response	Categorical variables test

4.1 The assumptions for Kruskal–Wallis test

- There should be one dependent variable *having* continuous (e.g., IQ score) or ordinal value (e.g., Likert items)
- There should be one independent variable *having more than* two categories
- *Independence of observations*—the variable should not be paired or related (before and after)

However, we must note that if the grouping/independent variable has an ordinal nature, we should choose Jonckheere–Terpstra test in the Tests for Several Independent Samples Box (Table 5.1).

4.2 Applying Kruskal–Wallis test

The data that we will use to understand the application of the Kruskal–Wallis test is based on the research question we have discussed earlier: Is irregularity of breakfast intake or skipping breakfast associated with a higher prevalence of BMI for age? The dataset that we use is named as *3. Adolescents_BMI.sav*. The following hypothesis will be used for our data set, from a related paper (different data) on the association of breakfast skipping with obesity (Faizi et al., 2014):

H_0: There is no difference in the mean BMI for age Z score of adolescents who take breakfast rarely, irregularly, and regularly.

H_A: There is a difference in the mean BMI for age Z score of adolescents who take breakfast rarely, irregularly, and regularly.

Steps in application of the Kruskal–Wallis test are as follows:

1. Open data file (*3. Adolescents_BMI.sav*). Go to *Analyze > Nonparametric Tests > Legacy Dialogs > K Independent Samples* (Fig. 5.11).
2. A new dialog box of Tests for Several Independent Samples will open up, as shown in Fig. 5.12. Among the variables on the left side, scroll down to select and enter "BMI for Age Z score" as the *Test Variable* and "Frequency of Breakfast" as the *grouping variable*.
3. As soon as the grouping variable is entered, one can see a question mark in brackets. This means that we need to *Define range* of the grouping variable we are interested in testing. The BreakfastFREQ has three values, 1 for rarely, 2 for irregularly and 3 for

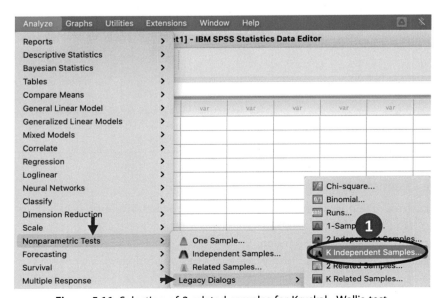

Figure 5.11 Selection of 2 related samples for Kruskal–Wallis test.

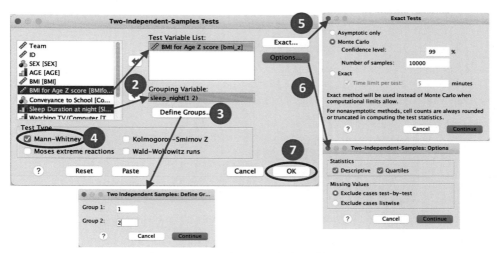

Figure 5.12 Applying Kruskal—Wallis test.

regularly. We are interested in measuring all three; hence we define our range as 1 for minimum and 3 for maximum.

4. At the left bottom end, we command SPSS for test type. Since we are interested in the *Kruskal—Wallis H* test here, we chose the same. If the data has ordinal or ranked grouping variables, the *Jonckheere—Terpstra test* should be selected.

5. Click the option to open a new dialog box. Here we choose *Descriptive* and *Quartiles* to get an idea of our summary measures in the result.

6. We will inform SPSS to choose the method for calculating significance by clicking the *Exact* button. The Exact Tests box has three options; by default, SPSS performs analysis using the *Asymptotic* method. For more precision, we will choose the "Monte Carlo" method as discussed in Box 5.2.

7. We get the results after clicking *Continue* in the Exact Box and *OK* in the main box. There would be three tables in results: [1] Descriptive statistics, [2] for Kruskal—Wallis Test Ranks, and [3] Test Statistics.

4.3 Interpretation of results of Kruskal—Wallis test

The Kruskal—Wallis test compares >2 groups for statistical significance in cases where the outcome/dependent variable is ordinal or continuous but not normally distributed. The essential things to note from the results are as follows (Fig. 5.13):

1. The descriptive values in the result of the Kruskal—Wallis test have limited use in the interpretation of results. As discussed in Mann—Whitney *U* test, we shall calculate median of BMIZ across breakfast group. This is done by splitting (Data > Split file), followed by finding their median and SD (Analyze > Descriptive

Descriptive Statistics

	N	Mean	Std. Deviation	Minimum	Maximum	25th	Percentiles 50th (Median)	75th
BMI for Age Z score	1416	−.0526	.88878	−1.93	2.56	−.7000	−.1400	.5300
Frequency of Breakfast	1416	2.60	.604	1	3	2.00	3.00	3.00

Kruskal–Wallis Test

Ranks

		N	Mean Rank
BMI for Age Z score	Rarely (<2/Wk)	88	1225.26
	Irregularly (3–5 times/wk)	390	1031.24
	Regularly (6–7 times/wk)	938	525.83
	Total	1416	

Test Statistics^{a,b}

			BMI for Age Z score
Kruskal–Wallis H			570.713
df			2
Asymp. Sig.			.000
Monte Carlo Sig.	Sig.		.000^c
	99% Confidence Interval	Lower Bound	.000
		Upper Bound	.000

a. Kruskal Wallis Test
b. Grouping Variable: Frequency of Breakfast
c. Based on 10000 sampled tables with starting seed 299883525.

Figure 5.13 Results of Kruskal–Wallis test.

Variables > Frequencies) as shown in Fig. 5.5 and Fig. 5.6. The results of medians are shown in Fig. 5.14.

2. The second table shows the ranks of the two groups for the Kruskal–Wallis H test. In 1416 subjects, those who took breakfast rarely had a mean rank of 1225.26, as compared to 1031.24 in those who took breakfast irregularly and 525.83 in those who took breakfast regularly. So, skipping breakfast seems to increase the BMI for age Z score. But is this statistically significant?

3. The third table shows the test statistics. The test statistic, that is, Kruskal–Wallis $H = 570.71$ with a df of 2. As we have chosen the Monte Carlo method for estimation, the P-value is <0.001.

4. Thus, the null hypothesis is rejected; there is a difference in the mean BMI for age among those taking breakfast rarely, irregularly, and regularly. To express this result clearly, we need a measure of central tendency, calculated by splitting the outcome variable (bmi_z) across exposure variable (breakfast_freq) given in Fig. 5.14.

5. The median BMI for age Z score in those who took breakfast rarely, irregularly, and regularly was 0.96, 0.47, and −0.48, respectively.

The null hypothesis is rejected and the final results should be reported as follows:

The BMI for age Z score decreases in adolescents with an increase in breakfast skipping (rarely, irregularly, regularly). The median BMI for age Z score of those taking breakfast rarely, irregularly, and regularly was 0.96, 0.47, and −0.48, respectively. A Kruskal–Wallis H test shows a significant difference in BMI for age Z scores with an increase in breakfast skipping, $H(2) = 570.71, P < .001$.

5. Nonparametric tests comparison with >2 related or repeated measures: Friedman test

Friedman test is applied for related or repeated measure variables when they are three or more. While we will discuss the application of the Friedman test in detail, we reiterate

Frequencies

Statistics

BMI for Age Z score

Rarely (<2/Wk)	N	Valid	88
		Missing	0
	Median		.9600
	Percentiles	25	.6600
		50	.9600
		75	1.5625
Irregularly (3–5 times/wk)	N	Valid	390
		Missing	0
	Median		.4700
	Percentiles	25	.1800
		50	.4700
		75	.8500
Regularly (6–7 times/wk)	N	Valid	938
		Missing	0
	Median		−.4800
	Percentiles	25	−.9700
		50	−.4800
		75	−.0700

Figure 5.14 Median across three groups of outcome variable.

that three nonparametric tests are applicable in >2 related samples—Friedman Test, Kendell's W and Cochran's Q.

As discussed earlier (Table 5.1), Kendall's W is specifically applied to measure agreement or concordance among different raters or same raters in different times/situations. Cochran's Q is a categorical variable test that measures the statistical significance of >2 related/matched groups with only binary/dichotomous response (nominal variables) and is discussed in detail along with other categorical variables. Thus, Cochran's Q is identical to the Friedman test but is applicable when all responses are binary. It is an extension of the McNemar test to the k-sample situation.

5.1 Assumptions of Friedman test

Friedman Test is an extension of the Wilcoxon signed-rank test, with more than two groups. It is also the nonparametric alternative of RMANOVA and is applied because of its distribution-free nature, that is, its applicability in nonnormal distributions.

- The dependent variable should be measured as continuous variable that is not normally distributed (such as IQ score) or ordinal value (such as Likert items).
- The independent variable should consist of more than two categorical, related, or matched pairs (Before and after).

5.2 Applying Friedman test

To apply the Friedman test, we will use a study that measured Fluoride release after applying two professionally applied fluoride agents—(1) sodium fluoride (from hereon, NaF) and (2) stannous flouride (from hereon, SnF2). Usually, fluoride release decreases after application. We compare the difference in fluoride release after 1 h to that after 1 day and 1 week regardless of the fluoride agent used. Friedman test is ideally meant to compare only whether the fluoride release decreases significantly with time after applying fluoride agents or not. The hypothesis is as follows:

H_0: There is no difference in the mean fluoride release with time from 1 h to 1 day and 1 week after application of different fluoriding agents.

H_A: There is a reduction in the mean fluoride release with time from 1 h to 1 day and 1 week after application of different fluoriding agents.

Steps in application of Friedman test are as follows:

1. Open data file (*3. Fluorides_Dental.sav*). Go to *Analyze > Nonparametric Tests > Legacy Dialogs > K Related Samples* (Fig. 5.15).

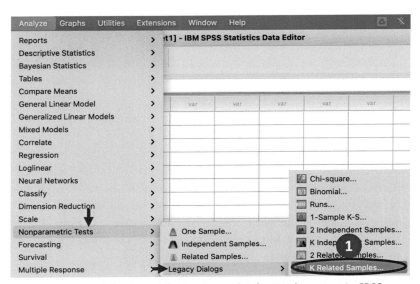

Figure 5.15 Selection of *K*-related samples for Friedman test in SPSS.

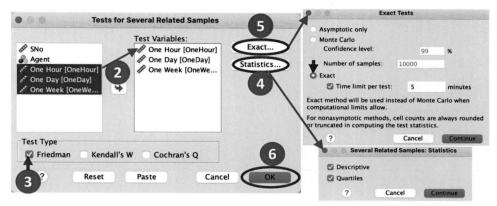

Figure 5.16 Applying Friedman test.

2. In the "Tests for Several Related Samples" box, enter *Test variables*—1 h, 1 day, and 1 week. (Fig. 5.16).

3. Under the Test Type Box, the *Friedman test* is chosen by default in the bottom left corner. If not, check the radio button against Friedman's test.

4. Click Statistics, and a new dialog box named Several Related Samples: Statistics opens up. We choose both *Descriptives* and *Quartiles* in the Statistics box.

5. Click *Exact* to open the exact tests box. The Exact Tests box has three options; by default, SPSS performs *Asymptotic* only. For more precision, and since we have a smaller sample size, we will choose "Exact" methods as discussed in Box 5.2 earlier in this chapter.

6. We get the results after clicking *Continue* in the Exact Tests box and Several Related Samples: Statistics box and *OK* in Tests for Several Related Samples Box.

5.3 Interpretation of results of Friedman test

1. The first thing to note in the result output of Friedman test (Fig. 5.17) is that there are three tables—(1) descriptive statistics, (2) ranks, and (3) test statistics.

2. Descriptive statistics: This is the first box and is very important for expressing the result. As the distribution is nonnormally distributed, we use median instead of mean to express our results. The median Fluoride release is 3.66 (IQR: 1.03−6.23) at 1 h, 0.60 (IQR: 0.47−0.80) at 1 day, and 0.42 (IQR: 0.46−0.61).

3. The second table shows the ranks of the three groups for Friedman's test. The mean rank at 1 h is 2.98, at one day—1.96 and at one week—1.06. So, Fluoride release seems to decrease with time (1 h, 1 day, and 1 week). But is this statistically significant?

4. The third table shows the test statistics. The test statistic, that is, Friedman $\chi^2 = 75.60$ with a df of 2. Since we have chosen the Exact method for estimation, the *P*-value

Descriptive Statistics

	N	Mean	Std. Deviation	Minimum	Maximum	25th	Percentiles 50th (Median)	75th
One Hour	40	3.8360	2.69508	.44	8.58	1.0300	3.6600	6.2300
One Day	40	.6360	.18569	.37	.93	.4700	.6000	.8050
One Week	40	.5148	.12894	.37	.84	.4200	.4600	.6100

Friedman Test

Ranks

	Mean Rank
One Hour	2.98
One Day	1.96
One Week	1.06

Test Statistics[a]

N	40
Chi–Square	75.600
df	2
Asymp. Sig.	.000
Exact Sig.	.000
Point Probability	.000

a. Friedman Test

Figure 5.17 Results of Friedman test.

is <0.001. Thus, the null hypothesis is rejected; there is a decrease in the Fluoride release over time. Additionally, suppose we are further interested in knowing whether there is a significant difference between 1 h and 1 day or 1 day and 1 week or 1 h and 1 week. In that case, we can apply Wilcoxon signed rank-sum test for the post hoc assessment. The procedure for the Wilcoxon test is given earlier. In this case, the pairs chosen would be 1 h—1 day, 1 day—1 week, and 1 h—1 week. While this serves our purpose, the ideal tests applicable for such post-hoc test after Friedman's test are Conover and/or Nemenyi tests (not available in SPSS). Another important point to note is that Friedman's test are more like sign tests which doesn't give value to magnitude like the Wilcoxon tests. However, post-hoc tests are automatically performed through legacy dialogs (See Box 5.4).

The result is expressed as follows:

The Median (IQR) fluoride release reduced over time. The fluoride release decreased from 3.66 (1.03—6.23) after 1 h to 0.60 (0.47—0.80) after 1 day, and further to 0.42 (0.46—0.61) after 1 week. On applying Friedman test, this was found to be statistically significant, $\chi^2(2) = 75.60$, P < .001. Post hoc analysis with Wilcoxon signed-rank tests was conducted with exact

BOX 5.4 Legacy dialog versus run: two ways of commanding nonparametric tests in SPSS

In SPSS, there are two ways of commanding nonparametric tests. One way is to choose legacy dialogs and choose the exact test options as we have used in this chapter. The other way is to directly run the command (Analyze > Nonparametric tests > Independent samples/Related Samples). This opens up another window where the fields are filled for the variables and *Run* command is given. Both the methods produce the same results. We perform the legacy dialog method as it gives more control over the test type we are interested in. However, the run command is beneficial as it provides the post hoc results along with the test results.

method. There was a significant reduction in fluoride release between 1 h and 1 day (Z = −5.37, P < .001), 1 day and 1 week (Z = −5.20, P < .001) and between 1 h and 1 week (Z = −5.51, P < .001).

Note: There are two ways of commanding nonparametric tests in SPSS. The difference is explained in Box 5.4.

References

Faizi, N., Khan, Z., Amir, A., & Azmi, S. A. (2015). Sleep duration and its effect on nutritional status in adolescents of Aligarh, India. *South African Journal of Child Health, 9*(1), 18. https://doi.org/10.7196/sajch.777

Faizi, N., Khan, I. M., Amir, A., Azmi, S. A., Ahmad, A., & Khalique, N. (2014). Breakfast skipping and proposed effects of breakfast on obesity: A school based study in adolescents in Aligarh, India. *Annals of Tropical Medicine and Public Health, 7*(1), 43−47. https://doi.org/10.4103/1755-6783.145011

Knief, U., & Forstmeier, W. (2021). Violating the normality assumption may be the lesser of two evils. *Behavior Research Methods, 53*(6), 2576−2590. https://doi.org/10.3758/s13428-021-01587-5

CHAPTER 6

Correlation*

The classification of facts, the recognition of their sequence and relative significance is the function of science, and the habit of forming a judgment upon these facts unbiased by personal feeling is characteristic of what may be termed the scientific frame of mind.

—**Karl Pearson**

1. Continuous outcome and exposure

Correlations are the statistical test of significance that show relations between two continuous variables—outcome/dependent variable and exposure/independent variable (Fig. 6.1). As both the variables are measurable and continuous, correlation provides more information than other parametric tests.

Correlation gives three important results:

1. **Significance:** Whether there is a significant correlation between the two variables. If it is significant (with a P-value of $<.05$), it indicates that the probability of this being

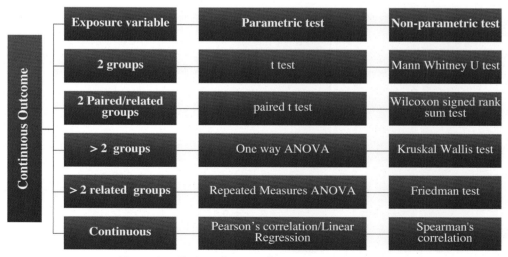

Figure 6.1 Choice of tests with continuous outcomes.

*For datasets, please refer to companion site: https://www.elsevier.com/books-and-journals/book-companion/9780443185502

Biostatistics Manual for Health Research
ISBN 978-0-443-18550-2, https://doi.org/10.1016/B978-0-443-18550-2.00002-5

due to chance alone is very limited. This is similar to the deduction of any association test such as *t*-test and ANOVA.

2. **Strength:** Correlation is distinct from other tests of significance because it also measures the strength of correlation. This is indicated by the correlation coefficient (r). If $r = 1$, it indicates that the two variables are perfectly correlated, implying that a change by one unit in one variable would lead to a change in the other variable by one unit as well. On the other hand, if $r = 0$, it implies no correlation between the two variables, and one cannot predict the change in the second variable through changes in the first variable (Fig. 6.2).

3. **Direction:** This adds furthermore value to strength. Whether one variable increases/ decreases by an increase in the second variable can be predicted through the direction. For example, if there is a one-unit increase in one variable and $r = +0.5$, it signifes that the other variable increases by 0.5 units. Similarly, for one unit increase in one variable and $r = -0.5$, there is a decrease in 0.5 units of the other.

Both exposure and outcome need to be continuous for Pearson's correlation, which is a parametric test. Whenever correlation is used alone, it implies Pearson's correlation. Spearman's correlation is an alternative to Pearson's correlation for nonparametric continuous data. Spearman's correlation can also be applied to ordinal data. We discuss other forms of correlation and similar tests used for agreement and concordance later in this chapter. It is important to note that many of these agreement tests are not synonymous with correlation.

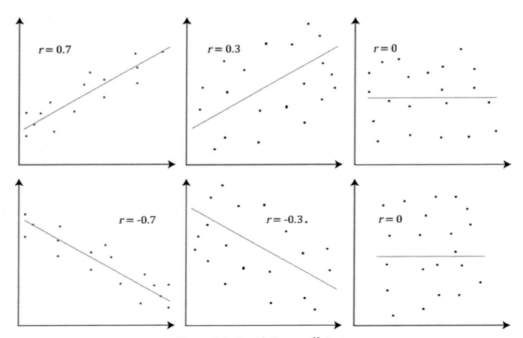

Figure 6.2 Correlation coefficient.

2. Correlation versus association

Some researchers confuse correlation with association. Although both are measures of relationship between two variables, correlation provides additional measures such as strength between variables and direction. The difference between association and correlation is as follows:

1. While the term association may be used broadly, correlation is a more specific technical term.

2. Association maybe used as a general term for any relationship between two variables, whereas correlation is a strict technical term for a linear relationship between two variables. For example, poor dietary behavior and obesity may be associated with each other. However, correlation, also indicates an increasing/decreasing trend between them. For instance, daily calorie consumption (kcalories) could be correlated with body mass index (BMI, measured in kg/m^2).

3. Association can be measured by tests such as t-test or ANOVA, whereas correlation is measured through Pearson's or Spearman's correlation. While association measures only significance, correlation also measures "strength" and "direction." Hence, tests of associations usually have a test statistic (t or F value), a degree of freedom (df), and a P-value for significance. In correlation, there is a correlation coefficient (r), its direction, and P-value for significance.

4. Association is synonymous with dependence as it measures significance between a dependent outcome/variable and an independent variable/exposure/explanatory variable (Altman & Krzywinski, 2015). Correlation is a measure of strength between two continuous variables in the strict sense and is a bivariate relation.

5. There could be a U-shaped association; for example, obesity may be common at both extremes of per capita income. However, correlation is a linear relationship between variables. Spearman's correlation can measure curvilinear relations as well, but it has to be monotonic, that is, in one direction, U or W-shaped associations cannot be correlated.

3. Pearson's correlation test

Pearson's correlation is the parametric test for correlation between two continuous (scaled-interval/ratio) variables. The assumptions to apply the test are as follows: (1) normal distribution, (2) independence of observations, and (3) linear relationship. If the first assumption, that is, normalcy, is not met or if one variable is ordinal in nature, a nonparametric alternative known as Spearman's correlation or Spearman's rho can be applied. Spearman's correlation can be applied to curvilinear relationships (in ranked or ordinal data). However, the relationship in any correlation must be monotonic, that is, as the value of one variable increases or decreases, so does the value of the other variable either increase/decrease.

Measuring normality tests must be done for both the variables through the Shapiro—Wilk test, as detailed in Chapter 3. After measuring the assumption of normality, the two continuous variables should be selected for Pearson's correlation test. Spearman's correlation, the Pearson's correlation nonparametric or distribution-free alternative, should be applied if the normality assumption fails.

3.1 Applying Pearson's correlation

Let us discuss the steps needed to perform Pearson's Correlation. The data we will use to understand the application of Pearson's Correlation is from a data set from a related paper (different data) on the association of vitamin D level and Parathormone (PTH) levels available as *6. Vit D_PTH*.sav.

The research question and hypothesis are:

Research question—Is vitamin D level correlated with PTH levels? The hypothesis is as follows.

H_o: There is no correlation between vitamin D and PTH levels.

H_A: There is a correlation between vitamin D and PTH levels.

The steps in the application of Pearson's correlation test are as follows:

1. Open data file (*6. Vit D_PTH.sav*) and go to *Analyze > Correlate > Bivariate* (Fig. 6.3).
2. This will open up Bivariate Correlations dialog box, where we need to select the variables to correlate. In our case, vit_d and pth_level are to be transferred to *Variables box* in center.
3. Under the Correlation Coefficients selection box, Tick *Pearson* correlation (Do note Kendall's tab-b and Spearman are the other options to choose). Keep *Two-tailed* significance and *Flag significant* correlations selected.
4. Click OK to perform correlation analysis which will be present in output window (Fig. 6.4).
5. Results: Since correlation is best appreciated through a scatter diagram graph, we must make a graph on the word file, as shown in Fig. 6.5. By convention, the Y-axis shows the outcome variable. We use a linear trendline to appreciate the trend in Pearson's correlation better. We also specify the Pearson's correlation coefficient in the graph.

3.2 Results of Pearson's correlation

The results of Pearson's correlation are best presented through a scatter diagram. Scatter diagrams can be easily drawn through Microsoft Word/Excel. The SPSS can also be used for making figures, but they won't be editable on the manuscript's word file. In SPSS it

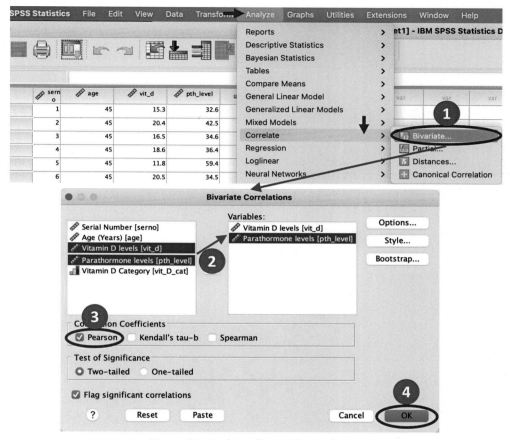

Figure 6.3 Applying Pearson's correlation.

can be drawn by going to *Graphs > Legacy Dialogs > Scatter/Dot*. Then select *Simple Scatter > Define* and shift vit_d to *X Axis* and pth_level to *Y Axis*. Click OK to draw the scatter graph.

The result and scatter diagram are shown in Figs. 6.4 and 6.5.

The important things to note from the results are as follows:

1. Correlations: The SPSS result output shows only one table of correlations (Fig. 6.4). All three things essential in a correlation—(1) strength, (2) significance, and (3) direction—are mentioned. As we see in Fig. 6.4, Pearson's correlation coefficient (r) is −0.765. This means the direction is negative (−) and the strength is −0.765. This indicates that for one unit increase in one variable, the other decreases by 0.765 units. The correlation is significant with a P-value <.001 (Software usually writes 0.000 for values below 0.001).

Correlations

		Vitamin D levels	Parathormone levels
Vitamin D levels	Pearson Correlation	1	−.765[**]
	Sig. (2–tailed)		.000
	N	102	102
Parathormone levels	Pearson Correlation	−.765[**]	1
	Sig. (2–tailed)	.000	
	N	102	102

**. Correlation is significant at the 0.01 level (2–tailed).

Figure 6.4 Results of Pearson's correlation.

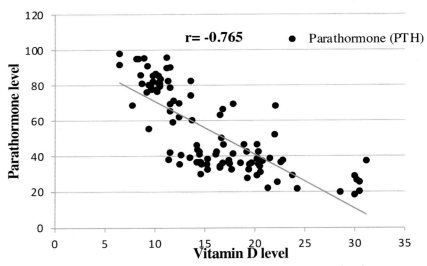

Figure 6.5 Correlation of parathormone and vitamin D levels.

2. Strength interpretation. How do we comment on the quality of strength? There are many guidelines/standards available to do so (Chan, 2003; Mukaka, 2012; Schober & Schwarte, 2018). It is entirely up to the researcher to choose one from these and remain consistent. We follow the standard guidelines in Table 6.1 (Chan, 2003). As we can see, 0.765 falls in "moderately strong" strength according to the values in Table 6.1. One must note that one is a perfect relationship and is extremely rare in health research.

Thus, the null hypothesis is rejected as PTH and vitamin D levels are significantly correlated. The results can be expressed as follows: *The Parathormone level and vitamin D*

Table 6.1 Interpreting the strength of the correlation coefficient.

Correlation coefficient	Strength
≥ 0.8	Very strong
0.6–0.79	Moderately strong
0.3–0.59	Fair
<0.3	Poor
0	No correlation

levels were significantly correlated on Pearson's correlation test with a moderately strong strength at $r(102) = -0.76$, $P < .001$. *The correlation can be seen in* Fig. 6.5.

4. Spearman's correlation test

As discussed earlier, Pearson's is a parametric test and is applicable only if the distribution of the variables is normal. If this assumption is violated, Spearman's correlation test, a nonparametric/distribution-free alternative, can be used. In case one of the variables is ordinal, then also Spearman's correlation can be applied. As we discussed earlier, Spearman's correlation appreciates curvilinear relationship and is valid if the relationship is monotonic, that is, as the value of one variable increases, the other variable either increases or decreases. For applying Spearman's correlation, we will take two examples—(1) for continuous data and (2) for ordinal data.

4.1 Applying Spearman's correlation to continuous data

We use the same data and hypothesis as we did in Pearson's correlation for this application. The research question—Is vitamin D level correlated with PTH levels? The hypothesis is as follows.

H_o: There is no correlation between vitamin D and PTH levels.

H_A: There is a correlation between vitamin D and PTH levels.

The steps in the application of Spearman's correlation test are as follows:

1. Open data file (6. *Vit D_PTH.sav*) and go to *Analyze > Correlate > Bivariate* (Fig. 6.3).
2. In the Bivariate Correlations box > select the *Variables* to correlate (vit_d and pth_level)
3. Tick Spearman's correlation coefficient. Keep *Two-tailed significance* and *Flag significant correlations* selected.
4. Results: After clicking *OK*, we get a single table of correlations (Fig. 6.6).
5. Results: Since correlation is best appreciated through a scatter diagram graph, we must make a graph on the word file, as shown in Fig. 6.7. By convention, the Y-axis shows the outcome variable. We can use a logarithmic trendline to appreciate

Correlations

			Vitamin D levels	Parathormone levels
Spearman's rho	Vitamin D levels	Correlation Coefficient	1.000	−.802[**]
		Sig. (2–tailed)	.	.000
		N	102	102
	Parathormone levels	Correlation Coefficient	−.802[**]	1.000
		Sig. (2–tailed)	.000	.
		N	102	102

**. Correlation is significant at the 0.01 level (2–tailed).

Figure 6.6 Results of Spearman's correlation.

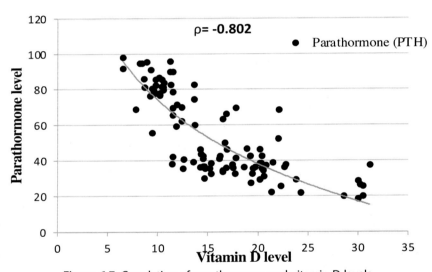

Figure 6.7 Correlation of parathormone and vitamin D levels.

the curvilinear trend in Spearman's correlation better, as we have done in this case. We also specify Spearman's correlation coefficient (ρ) in the graph.

4.2 Results of Spearman's correlation

The results of Spearman's correlation are best presented through a scatter diagram. Scatter diagram can be easily drawn through Microsoft Word/Excel. The SPSS can also be used for making figures, but they will not be editable on the manuscript's word file. The scatter diagram for the result is shown in Fig. 6.7.

The important things to note from the results are as follows:

1. Correlations: The SPSS result output shows only one table of correlations (Fig. 6.6). All the three things are important in a correlation—(1) strength, (2) significance, and (3) direction are mentioned in it. As we see in Fig. 6.6, Spearman's correlation coefficient (r) is −0.802. This means that the direction is negative (−), and the strength is −0.802. This indicates that for one unit increases in one variable and the other decreases by 0.802 units. The correlation is significant with a P-value $<.001$ (Software usually writes 0.000 for values below 0.001).

2. Strength interpretation. As per the standard guidelines of in Table 6.1 (Chan, 2003), 0.802 falls in "very strong" strength according to the values.

3. Thus, the null hypothesis is rejected as PTH and vitamin D levels are significantly correlated. The results can be expressed as follows: *The Parathormone level and vitamin D levels were significantly correlated on Spearman's correlation test with a very strong strength at r(102) = −0.80, P < .001. The correlation can be seen in* Fig. 6.7.

4. Important point: If you look at the graph in Fig. 6.5 and compare it to Fig. 6.7, the difference in trend is better appreciated. The data is more suitable for curvilinear (nonparametric) trend than linear (parametric) trend. Note that the correlation via Spearman's is stronger ($\rho = -0.80$ as compared to $r = 0.76$), so it is a better correlation test for this data. In fact, in the data used for Pearson's correlation, both the vitamin D level and PTH level violate the assumption of normality and have a significant normality test result. Hence, Pearson's correlation should not be applied at all.

4.3 Applying Spearman's correlation on ordinal data

We use the same data (*6. Vit D_PTH.sav*) for this application, but instead of vitamin D levels, we use the three ordinal categories based on the vitamin D levels—deficient, insufficient, and normal (labeled as vit_d_cat). The research question is—Is vitamin D level categories correlated with PTH levels? The hypothesis is as follows.

H_o: There is no correlation between vitamin D level categories (deficient, insufficient and normal) and PTH levels.

H_A: There is a correlation between vitamin D level categories (deficient, insufficient and normal) and PTH levels.

The steps in the application of Pearson's correlation test are as follows:

1. Open data file (*6. Vit D_PTH.sav*) and go to *Analyze > Correlate > Bivariate*.
2. In the Bivariate Correlations box > select the *Variables* to correlate (vit_d_cat and pth_level)>Tick *Spearman's* correlation coefficient (Fig. 6.8).
3. After clicking *OK*, we get a single table of correlations (Fig. 6.9).
4. Results: Since correlation is best appreciated through a scatter diagram graph, we must make a graph on the word file, as shown in Fig. 6.10. By convention, the Y-axis shows the outcome variable. We can use a logarithmic trendline to appreciate

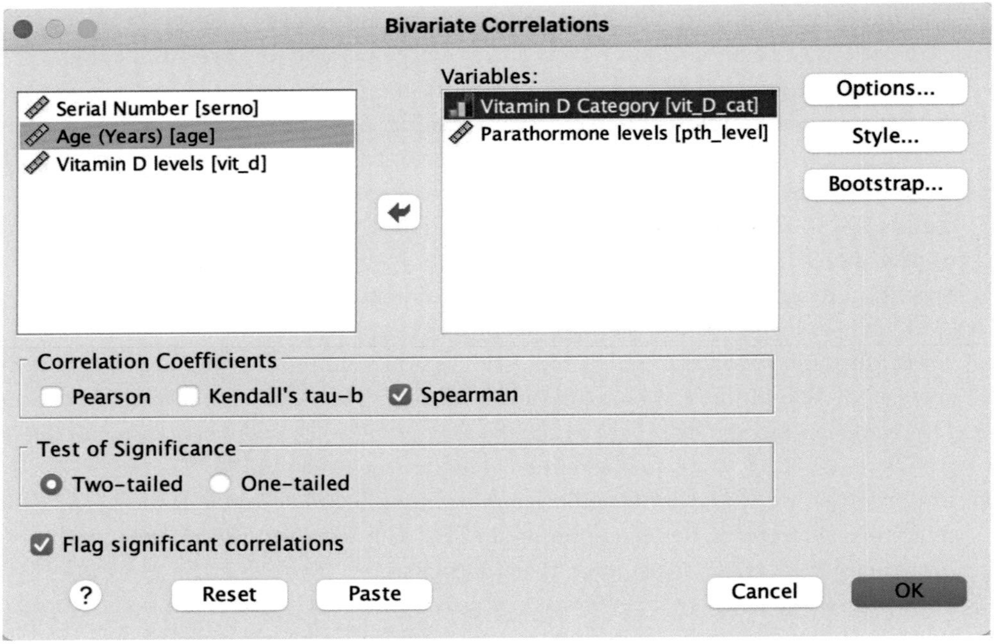

Figure 6.8 Applying Spearman's correlation: selecting variables (ordinal).

Correlations

			Vitamin D Category	Parathormone levels
Spearman's rho	Vitamin D Category	Correlation Coefficient	1.000	−.594[**]
		Sig. (2-tailed)	.	.000
		N	102	102
	Parathormone levels	Correlation Coefficient	−.594[**]	1.000
		Sig. (2-tailed)	.000	.
		N	102	102

**. Correlation is significant at the 0.01 level (2-tailed).

Figure 6.9 Results of Spearman's correlation (ordinal).

the trend in Spearman's correlation better as we have done in this case. We also specify Spearman's correlation coefficient (ρ) in the graph.

4.4 Results of Spearman's correlation on ordinal data

The important things to note from the results are as follows:

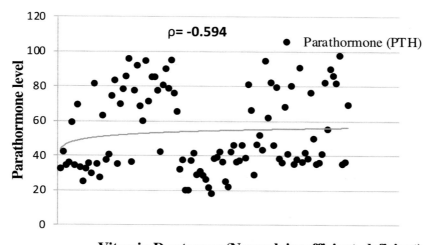

Figure 6.10 Results of Spearman's correlation (ordinal).

1. Correlations: The SPSS result output shows only one table of correlations (Fig. 6.9). All the three things are important in a correlation—(1) Strength, (2) Significance and Direction are mentioned in it. As we see in Fig. 6.9, Spearman's correlation coefficient (r) is −0.594. This means that the direction is negative (−), and the strength is −0.594. This indicates that for one unit increases in one variable, the other decreases by 0.594 units. The correlation is significant with a P-value <.001 (Software usually writes 0.000 for values below 0.001).

2. Strength interpretation. As per the standard guidelines in Table 6.1 (Chan, 2003), 0.594 falls in "fair" strength according to the values.

3. Thus, the null hypothesis is rejected as PTH and vitamin D levels are significantly correlated. The results can be expressed as follows: *The Parathormone level and vitamin D categories of deficient, insufficient, and normal were significantly correlated on Spearman's correlation test with a fair strength at r(102) = −0.59, P < .001. The correlation can be seen in* Fig. 6.10 .

4. Important point: Comparing the graphs in Figs. 6.5, 6.7, and 6.10, one realizes that the trends in ordinal variables are least appreciable. That is because an ordinal variable is seldom worth a correlation. In ordinal variables, tests of associations can serve an equally, if not more critical value. For example, if ANOVA (Chapter 4) was applied in this data, the results would be: *The mean Parathormone levels were found to decrease from 83.74 ± 11.15 to 49.65 ± 19.94 and 26.13 ± 6.80 in vitamin D deficient, insufficient, and normal categories, respectively. On applying Welch's ANOVA test, the mean difference in Parathormone levels was statistically significant, Welch's ANOVA test (2, 18.83) = 104.95.46, P < .001. Post hoc Games-Howell test was applied to find the significance of*

the difference in means between vitamin D deficient, insufficient, and normal categories. The mean difference in parathormone levels between vitamin D deficient with insufficient was 34.09 (95% CI: 25.38−42.80), between deficient and normal was 57.60 (95% CI: 47.39−67.82), while the mean difference between insufficient and normal was 23.52 (95% CI: 14.13−32.90). These mean differences were significant on the post hoc Games-Howell test (P < .001).

5. Therefore, whenever we have ordinal data, it is better to use a test of associations. An important recommendation is to *never categorize data unless absolutely necessary*. Here, Spearman's correlation of exact values of vitamin D gives a clearly better result than categorized vitamin D values.

5. Correlation versus concordance

Correlation and concordance are two different terms in research, and substituting one for the other is erroneous. Correlation means co-relation as in "relatedness," which signifies whether two different variables on the same case/patient are related or not. If one increases/decreases, does the other increase/decrease, and how strongly does it do so? On the other hand, "agreement" between two measures means whether two different tests on a single case/patient agree with each other. This agreement is called Concordance (Lowenstein & Badgett, 1993).

If the question is whether analysis of pulse or mental status score is related to blood alcohol concentration, then correlation can be used. However, the case differs if the question is whether pulse or mental status score provides an accurate estimation of blood alcohol concentration and could be used as a replacement or proxy measure. In the latter case, correlation cannot be used, but a concordance based test must be used. The blunder of using correlation as a measure of agreement/concordance is highlighted through example in Box 6.1.

6. Agreement: Kendall's τ, Kendall's W, and kappa

The three tests that often cause confusion are Kendall's tau, Kendall's W, and kappa test. Kendall's $τ$ (tau) is a rank correlation test and is an option when applying correlation along with Pearson and Spearman (Fig. 6.3). Kendall's W is a measure of concordance, and more about it is given in the chapter on the nonparametric test. Kappa test ($κ$) is a method to measure agreement in nominal/ordinal variables.

6.1 Kendall's tau (τ)

While applying correlation tests, there are three options for correlation coefficient test types—Pearson's, Kendall's tau-b, and Spearman's. Generally, whenever we say Kendall's tau, it stands for Kendall's tau-b and not a or c. We would not be discussing the

BOX 6.1 The blunder of using correlation as a measure of agreement/concordance

There is a significant difference between correlation and concordance, and there are instances of inappropriate use of correlation in scientific papers. The three critical points of concern are:

1. Correlation is a measure of relatednesses, such as the correlation between iron levels and hemoglobin levels in the body. Concordance is a measure of agreement, such as the agreement between hemoglobin measured through Wintrobe's method versus Westergreen's method.

2. If two measures are correlated, it does not indicate replaceability/interchangeability. Even a very strong correlation does not imply agreement/replaceability. For example, a very strong correlation of 0.85 was found using two different methods of assessing gestational age-Robinson, and Dubowitz (Serfontein & Jaroszewicz, 1978), leading to a false assumption of agreement/replaceability. This was pointed out later by Altman and Bland (1983). It was evident from their data that a baby with a gestational age of 35 weeks by the Robinson method could have been anything between 34 and 39.5 weeks by the Dubowitz method, clearly irreplaceable. Even in the example above, vitamin D levels and parathormone levels are very strongly correlated but clearly not replaceable.

3. Suppose one uses a new screening/diagnostic tool/test and uses correlation as a test measure. It could be misleading because (a) systematic bias in measures cannot be overruled and (b) it would lead to an unreliable diagnostic cut-off value (Lowenstein et al., 1993). For example, if the newer measure (test measure device) is consistently 10 units more than the actual measure (gold measure device), it could have a high correlation. But if they are replaced with each other, it would be a diagnostic blunder in terms of diagnostic cut-off values.

latter two because we seldom use them in health research. Pearson's is a parametric test, unlike Kendall's tau-b and Spearman's, which are nonparametric and are applicable to ordinal variables (rank correlation). However, Kendall's tau is more accurate when sample sizes are small and uses a concordant-discordant pairing while ranking between the two variables. In the continuous data correlation where we applied Spearman's, the Kendall's tau (τ) result is also significant with τ (102) $= -0.61$, $P < .001$. Essentially the features of Kendall's tau (τ) are as under:

1. Applies only to pairs (bivariate/two only) of ranked lists and measures the correlation;
2. Values are in the range $[-1, 1]$.
3. Similar to Spearman's rank correlation, but better when sample sizes are small.
4. In SPSS, it is a choice while applying Correlation (one can choose one of Pearson, Spearman, and Kendall's tau). [*Analyze > Correlate > Independent-Bivariate > Choose Kendall's tau*].

6.2 Kendall's coefficient of concordance *W*

Kendall's coefficient of concordance *W* is a measure of concordance between raters rating through several (>2) ranked lists. Essentially the features of Kendall's coefficient of concordance *W* are as under:

1. Summarizes the concordance between several (>2) ranked lists, specifically applied to measure agreement or concordance among different raters or same raters in different times/situations.
2. It ranges from 0 to 1.
3. In SPSS, it is applied by choosing *Analyze > Nonparametric Tests > Legacy Dialogs > K Related Samples > Choose Kendall's W.*
4. Kendall's coefficient of concordance is discussed in detail in the chapter on Testing for reliability and agreements.

6.3 Kappa test (κ)

Kappa test (κ) is a measure of agreement of nominal/ordinal assessments by different raters on the same sample. Essentially the features of the kappa test (κ) are as under:

1. Measures the degree of agreement of the nominal/ordinal assessments made by multiple appraisers when assessing the same samples.
2. It ranges from 0 to 1, with 1 having a perfect agreement and 0 meaning no agreement.
3. There are two types of kappa test—Cohen's kappa and Fleiss kappa. While *Cohen's kappa* is applicable between two such appraisers/raters, Fleiss's kappa is applicable for more than two.
4. For Cohen's kappa application: *Analyze > Descriptive Statistics > Crosstabs > Statistics > Choose kappa.*
5. For Fleiss' kappa application: *Analyze > Scale > Reliability Analysis > Select Appropriate variables for* "Items" *and* "Ratings." Since Fleiss kappa is an interrater test applicable for more than two raters, remember that all the raters, such as rater A, rater B, and rater C variable should be entered in the rater box. After variable selection, choose Fleiss kappa options in "Statistics." Please note that Fleiss kappa can be found only in SPSS 26 or later versions.
6. Discussed in detail in the chapter on Testing for reliability and agreements.

7. Measuring concordance/agreement

This section will explore the understanding on how to measure concordance/agreement correctly. Let us discuss this in different scenarios to understand the application clearly (Table 6.2).

7.1 Scenario 1: Nominal data

1. Two teachers have rated the same group of students separately in two categories: Pass/Fail.

Table 6.2 Data and applicable test of concordance.

Type of data	Test to apply for agreement/concordance
Scenario 1: Nominal data	Kappa test (if between two raters–Cohen's, 3 or more–Fleiss's kappa)
Scenario 2: Ordinal data with two raters	Cohen's kappa + Kendall's tau (correlation)
Scenario 3: Ordinal data with >2 raters	Fleiss' kappa + Kendall's W (coefficient of concordance)

2. Three or more teachers have rated the same group of students separately in two categories: Pass/Fail.
3. Two different tests analyze the same blood samples to find whether the sample is anemic/not anemic.
4. Two observers rated postdenture cosmetic correction as improved/not improved.

7.2 Scenario 2: Ordinal data with two raters

1. Two teachers have rated the performance of the same group of students separately as: Good/Better/Best.
2. Two different tests analyze the same anemic blood samples to characterize the sample as mild/moderate/severe anemia.
3. Two observers rated postdenture cosmetic correction as poor/fair/good improvement.
4. Comparison of rating of the performance of the same group of students as—Good/Better/Best between a teacher and a standard computerized algorithm.
5. A new test's analysis of anemic blood samples graded as mild/moderate/severe anemia compared with the grading by an established method.

7.3 Scenario 3: Ordinal data with more than two raters

1. Three teachers have rated the performance of the same group of students separately as: Good/Better/Best.
2. Three different tests analyze the same anemic blood samples to characterize the sample as mild/moderate/severe anemia.
3. Three observers rated postdenture cosmetic correction as poor/fair/good improvement compared with measurement-based computer algorithms.

7.4 The real difference between the three tests

In the case of two raters on ordinal data, we can apply both the Kappa and Kendall's tau tests. What is the real difference? This is answered in Box 6.2. We also elaborate on this through an example.

Let us look at an example of academic grades (range: 1—10) given to 10 students by different raters—Amar, Akbar, and Anthony. This will help us understand the relative significance of the three tests for ordinal variables. The datasheet is given in the data file named *6. Raters.sav*. Note: Kappa for comparisons between two is Cohen's kappa and for >2 is Fleiss kappa. While the example uses Kappa for elaboration, kindly note that only weighted Cohen's kappa should be applied on ordinal variables. Fleiss kappa is applicable on both nominal and ordinal variables, but has other conditionalities. To know further details about the kappa test, please refer to the chapter on reliability agreement (Chapter 9).

7.4.1 Case 1: Amar and Akbar (Table 6.3)

The only difference between Amar and Akbar is in the first five students. Akbar grades 1, 2, 3, 4, 5 as 2, 3, 4, 5 and 6. However, the differential gradation is slight and uniform. That is why Kendall's tau is higher than kappa. For kappa, the first five students were misclassified (regardless of their uniformity/pattern), and therefore its value drops to near/below 50%. On the contrary, despite the misclassification, Kendall's appreciates that the relative difference in magnitude.

BOX 6.2 What is the real difference between using kappa and Kendall's for the same dataset?

The real difference is when we use ordinal variables. Kappa treats all misclassifications equally, whereas Kendall's gives value to the magnitude of difference. For example, if 5 is rated as 1 or 4 is rated as 1. For kappa, they are both equally misqualified, whereas Kendall's treats the former (5 rated as 1) worse than the latter (4 rated as 1). This is specifically important for ordinal variables. In nominal variables, this is not a problem at all since there is no gradation/order/ranking between categories (e.g., anemia or no anemia)—regardless of the number allotted to them unlike ordinal variables (e.g., mild < moderate < severe). Weighted Kappa test improves the applicability of Kappa for ordinal variables.

Table 6.3 Amar and Akbar gradings.

Rater	Grades										Test results
Amar	1	2	3	4	5	6	7	8	9	10	Kappa (A and B): 0.444
Akbar	2	3	4	5	6	6	7	8	9	10	Kendall's tau: 0.989

7.4.2 Case 2: Amar and Anthony (Table 6.4)

This is a similar case, with Anthony marking wrong grades with the first five students. However, the first student is graded better than Akbar. Therefore, the difference is greater in the first student's marks than in the previous example, and Kendall's tau appreciates this difference. Kendall's tau is reduced to 0.978. For kappa, it is still a misclassification of five students and the values are same.

7.4.3 Case 3: Akbar and Anthony (Table 6.5)

There is only one difference between Akbar and Anthony. The difference is in the grading of the first student. Look at the jump in kappa value or agreement, because there is only one misclassification.

7.4.4 Case 4: Amar is a standard program

Important point: *If Amar was a standard rater or a computer-based algorithm, then who is a better replacement?* The first thing to note is that a kappa of 0.444 means both of them have a similar (and not so good) agreement with the standard. However, Kendall's tau helps us answer this. Akbar is a better replacement than Anthony, with Kendall's tau at 0.989 compared to 0.978, respectively. This is true even though Akbar and Anthony are both replaceable to each other (Case 3).

7.4.5 Case 5. All three are nonstandard raters (Table 6.6)

If all the three are nonstandard raters, Fleiss' kappa and Kendall's coefficient of concordance are good enough measures. Fleiss kappa is 0.575, indicating a better agreement

Table 6.4 Amar and Anthony gradings.

Rater	Grades										Test results
Amar	1	2	3	4	5	6	7	8	9	10	Kappa (A and C): 0.444
Anthony	3	3	4	5	6	6	7	8	9	10	Kendall's tau: 0.978

Table 6.5 Akbar and Anthony gradings.

Rater	Grades										Test results
Akbar	2	3	4	5	6	6	7	8	9	10	Kappa (A and C): 0.886
Anthony	3	3	4	5	6	6	7	8	9	10	Kendall's tau: 0.989

Table 6.6 Amar, Akbar, and Anthony gradings.

Rater	Marks										Test results
Amar	1	2	3	4	5	6	7	8	9	10	Fleiss kappa: 0.575
Akbar	2	3	4	5	6	6	7	8	9	10	Kendall's coefficient of
Anthony	3	3	4	5	6	6	7	8	9	10	concordance: 0.475

when the three are taken together. However, Kendall's coefficient of concordance is 0.475. Please remember that this is only for illustration, otherwise Fleiss kappa is only applicable for nonunique raters (Chapter 9).

References

Altman, D. G., & Bland, J. M. (1983). Measurement in medicine: The analysis of method comparison studies. *The Statistician, 32*(3), 307. https://doi.org/10.2307/2987937

Altman, N., & Krzywinski, M. (2015). Points of significance: Association, correlation and causation. *Nature Methods, 12*(10), 899–900. https://doi.org/10.1038/nmeth.3587

Chan, Y. H. (2003). Biostatistics104: Correlational analysis. *Singapore Medical Journal, 44*(12), 614–619.

Lowenstein, S. R., Koziol-McLain, J., & Badgett, R. G. (1993). Concordance versus correlation. *Annals of Emergency Medicine, 22*(2), 269. https://doi.org/10.1016/S0196-0644(05)80225-2

Mukaka, M. M. (2012). Statistics corner: A guide to appropriate use of correlation coefficient in medical research. *Malawi Medical Journal, 24*(3), 69–71. http://www.ajol.info/index.php/mmj/article/download/81576/71739.

Schober, P., & Schwarte, L. A. (2018). Correlation coefficients: Appropriate use and interpretation. *Anesthesia and Analgesia, 126*(5), 1763–1768. https://doi.org/10.1213/ANE.0000000000002864

Serfontein, G. L., & Jaroszewicz, A. M. (1978). Estimation of gestational age at birth. Comparison of two methods. *Archives of Disease in Childhood, 53*(6), 509–511. https://doi.org/10.1136/adc.53.6.509

CHAPTER 7

Categorical variables*

Statistics is the grammar of science

Karl Pearson.

1. Categorical variables

Not everything in life is measurable quantitatively, such as the different states of morbidity. The headache you had yesterday after watching the cacophony on a TV news debate is not really twice as bad as the headache you had last week or the one before. But you know for sure that the severity was greater. Regardless of their measurement potential, their counts yeilds useful statistics such as the prevalence of hypertension increasing with age, the prevalence of anemia increasing in pregnancy, higher prevalence of severe hypertension in obese individuals, etc. When both, the outcome/dependent variable and exposure/independent variable are categorical in nature, the following tests are applicable (Fig. 7.1). It is worth remembering that categorical variables could be nominal or ordinal. If the exposure variables are independent and not paired/related with each other, regardless of the number of groups, the chi-square test or exact tests are applicable. If the exposure variables are paired or related, then McNemar's test and Cochran's Q test are applicable, if there are two groups and >2 groups, respectively.

2. Independent exposure variables: chi-square test

Chi-square tests are applicable when both outcome and exposure variables are categorical, regardless of the number of groups being compared. The chi-square test, also χ^2 test is not a square but a summary statistic. The square does not mean that it is a mathematical square of any kind, it is a traditional name.

The famous statistician, Karl Pearson, explained χ^2 test in his seminal paper published in 1900 CE (Pearson, 1900). Chi-square tests are a wide range of tests that are nonparametric and robust. A few types of chi-square tests are Pearson's χ^2 test, McNemar's χ^2 test, Mantel—Haenszel χ^2 test, etc. However, by convention χ^2 test is a Pearson's χ^2 test, unless the name is specified. The chi-square test statistic is based on approximation;

---

*For datasets, please refer to companion site: https://www.elsevier.com/books–and–journals/book–companion/9780443185502

Biostatistics Manual for Health Research
ISBN 978-0-443-18550-2, https://doi.org/10.1016/B978-0-443-18550-2.00001-3

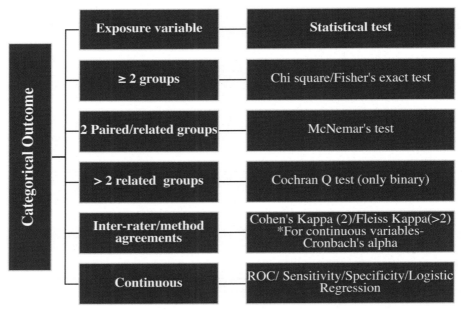

Figure 7.1 Choice of tests with categorical outcomes.

> ## BOX 7.1 Measuring the strength of a chi-square test
> Chi-square tests are robust to data distributions and assumptions regarding equality of variance, etc. This makes chi-square test an easily computable and widely applicable test (McHugh, 2012). However, chi-square tests are "significant tests" that comment on whether the rows and columns have a significant trend of difference. It does not comment on the effect size or strength of such associations. There are three different measures of effect size for nominal variables—Phi (φ), Cramer's V (V), and odds ratio (OR), and one for ordinal variable—Somer's *d* (Somer's delta). The φ and OR can only be used in 2 × 2 contingency tables. For ordinal variables, we prefer Somer's *d* as it gives us values considering the variables as independent and dependent.

calculating the expected count in each cell and the deviation from the expected count and observed count (Box 7.1).

2.1 The assumptions for chi-square test

- Both the variables (exposure and outcome) should be categorical.
- Independence of observations—variable should not be paired or related.
- Mutually exclusive groups—an individual cannot belong to more than one cell in the contingency table.
- No cell should have an *expected value* less than 1, and an *expected value* of less than 5 in no more than 20% of the cells in the contingency table. For example, in a 2 × 2 table

(4 cells in total and each cell is 25% of the total number of cells), no cell should have an expected value of <5.

While the first three assumptions are self-explanatory, the last assumption needs be checked before interpretation. The SPSS results, the expected counts are given and you can decide whether to use the chi-square statistics or choose its alternative. To apply this test in SPSS, the data should be in form of frequency counts (exact values) and not in percentages or proportions.

2.2 Applying the chi-square (χ^2) test

The data that we will use to apply chi-square test are based on the following hypothesis from a paper on the association of depression and clinical symptoms of infection in HIV/ AIDS patients (Alvi et al., 2018). In this dataset, you will find exposure variables of clinical symptoms at three time intervals (initial stage, 1 year ago, and currently) and outcome variable of depression. Please note that the dataset is modified from the actual result for this exercise.

H_0: There is no association of current clinical stage of infection with being depressed.
H_A: There is an association of current clinical stage of infection with being depressed.
Steps in application of χ^2 *test* are as follows:
1. Open the data set *7.HIV_Depression.sav*. Go to Analyze > Descriptive Statistics > - Crosstabs (Fig. 7.2).
2. Remember to put outcome/dependent variable (in our case *Depression status*) in Column and independent variable (*Clinical.Symptoms.Current*) in Rows.
3. Click *Statistics* to open new dialog box, select *chi-square*, and *Phi and Cramer's V* under Nominal *and Risk* for measuring effect size. Click *Continue* to return to Crosstabs box.
4. Click *Cell* to open new dialog box, select *Observed* under Counts and *Rows* under Percentages. Click *Continue* to return to Crosstabs box.
5. Click *OK* to get results in the output window.

2.3 Interpretation of results of the chi-square (χ^2) test

There will be four tables in the result output of chi-square test: (1) crosstab, (2) chi-square test, (3) symmetric measures, and (4) risk estimate (Fig. 7.3). The chi-square test compares the two groups for statistical significance. There are three essential things to note from the results (Fig. 7.3):
1. Crosstab [1]: This is useful in interpreting results and observing the trend. The chi-square analyzes the association of columns with rows by preparing cross-tabulation. Here we see that depression was observed in 12.0% (30/249) of patients who were asymptomatic, compared to 20.6% (40/185) who had symptoms. As expected, a reverse trend is seen in patients without depression: 88.0% versus 78.4%. Let us check if this is statistically significant or not in the next table. As the chi-square test is based on approximation, we can obtain the expected count in each cell by selecting it in the Cells dialog box for a better appreciation of the fourth assumption.

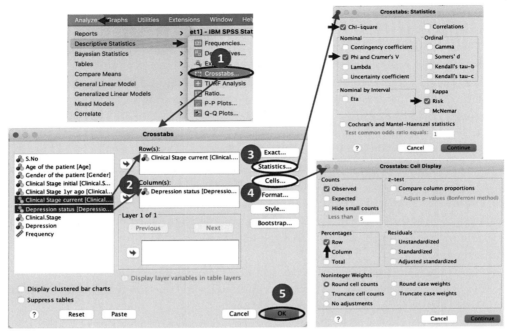

Figure 7.2 Applying chi-square (χ^2) test.

Clinical Stage – Symptomatic or not * Depression status Crosstabulation Depression status

			Yes	No	Total
Clinical Stage current	Asymptomatic	Count	30	219	249
		% within Clinical Stage current	12.0%	88.0%	100.0%
	Symptomatic	Count	40	145	185
		% within Clinical Stage current	21.6%	78.4%	100.0%
Total		Count	70	364	434
		% within Clinical Stage current	16.1%	83.9%	100.0%

Symmetric Measures

		Value	Approximate Significance
Nominal by Nominal	Phi	-.129	.007
	Cramer's V	.129	.007
N of Valid Cases		434	

Chi-Square Tests

	Value	df	Asymptotic Significance (2–sided)	Exact Sig. (2–sided)	Exact Sig. (1–sided)
Pearson Chi-Square	7.191ᵃ	1	.007		
Continuity Correctionᵇ	6.501	1	.011		
Likelihood Ratio	7.111	1	.008		
Fisher's Exact Test				.008	.006
Linear–by–Linear Association	7.175	1	.007		
N of Valid Cases	434				

a. 0 cells (0.0%) have expected count less than 5. The minimum expected count is 29.84.
b. Computed only for a 2x2 table

Risk Estimate

		95% Confidence Interval	
	Value	Lower	Upper
Odds Ratio for Clinical Stage current (Asymptomatic / Symptomatic)	.497	.296	.833
For cohort Depression status = Yes	.557	.361	.860
For cohort Depression status = No	1.122	1.027	1.226
N of Valid Cases	434		

Figure 7.3 Results of chi-square test.

2. Test Statistics [2]: The second table shows the chi–square statistics along with their variations. It includes test statistics for Pearson chi–square, continuity correction, likelihood ratio, Fisher's exact test, and linear–by–linear association. The first thing to

note in this table is the table footnote for "*a*," which tests the fourth assumption of the chi-square test. If the expected count of less than 5 is present in less than 20.0% of cells, then the assumption is met, and Pearson chi-square statistics can be used. The Pearson chi-square statistics is 7.191 with a degree of freedom of 1 and the *P* value of 0.007 (asymptotic 2-tailed, explained later).

3. Effect size [3 and 4]: The third table and fourth table show effect sizes and are only available if we select *Phi and Cramer's V* under Nominal and *Risk* in *Statistics* dialog box. Since in our example we are dealing with the nominal variables—depressed/ not depressed and asymptomatic/symptomatic, we chose Phi and Cramer's V. For ordinal variables, Somer's *d* (Somer's delta) should be used. Phi is only applicable for 2×2 tables, while Cramer's V is more widely applicable. When Phi was used, the strength of association was reported to be -0.129. As per the standard guidelines given in Table 7.1, 0.129 falls into the "moderate" strength. Sometimes, the Odds ratio (OR) is a preferred way of expressing the strength of association in the chi-square test. As shown in Fig. 7.3, the Odds ratio for asymptomatic HIV/AIDS patients developing depression as compared to symptomatic is 0.497, while OR for symptomatic as compared to asymptomatic will be 2.014 (inverse of previous OR, 1/0.497). Similarly, the 95% confidence interval is also reported (0.296—0.833), and inversing them provides 95% confidence interval for symptomatic to asymptomatic (1.200—3.378).

4. Thus, the null hypothesis is rejected as Depression and Clinical staging are significantly associated. The results can be expressed as follows:
   Depression was more common in patients with symptomatic HIV/AIDS clinical stage (21.6%) as compared to asymptomatics (12.0%). Depression and symptomatology of HIV/AIDS were significantly associated on the chi-square test with test statistics χ^2 (1, n = 434) = 7.191, P = .007 and a moderate strength with Phi, $\varphi = -0.129$. The odds of developing depression for clinically symptomatic patients were 2.01 (95% CI: 1.20—3.38) times higher than asymptomatic HIV/AIDS patients.

2.3.1 Guide to interpret effect sizes in chi-square test

This is interpreted as Pearson's correlation, where a value of 0 indicates no association. There are subtle differences to this, as a value of >0.25 is considered a very strong

Table 7.1 A guide to interpret strength of association of categorical values.

Phi and Cramer's V value	Interpretation
>0.25	Very strong
0.16—0.25	Strong
0.11—0.15	Moderate
0.06—0.10	Weak
0—0.05	No or very weak

association (Akoglu, 2018). A guide to grading the strength of association is given based on recommendations (Akoglu, 2018), and our value of −0.129 indicates a moderate strength of association (Table 7.1). The strength of interpretation gives us an idea of clinical significance or outcome as opposed to statistical significance. This is also important while dealing with another significant categorical variable, as the relative strengths of the association will help in clinical significance between the two statistically significant exposures/variables/risk factors.

2.4 Post hoc comparison of the chi-square test

The chi-square test analyses the association of columns with rows by preparing crosstab and indicates whether there is an association between the categories of the two variables. It is a good measure of trend. Irrespective of number of categories, if there is a significant association between any two pairs, the chi-square test will give significant results. For 2 × 2 contingency tables, this is not an issue as there are only two pairs and thus results can be easily appreciated. In the example above, this can be easily visualized as clinically symptomatic patients had a higher proportion of being depressed. However, in case of three or more categories in exposure and/or outcome variables, a post hoc pairwise comparison is needed to understand which two pairs are significant. If we were to compare Depression (*Depression.status* in our dataset) across four WHO clinical stages (*WHO.Stage.Current*), we would get 4 × 2 contingency table, and if the chi-square test gives us a significant association, we may need to break down the table into multiple 2 × 2 pairs and analyze the chi-square test with Bonferroni corrections. Although the current version of SPSS does not perform this, we may estimate it using adjusted residuals, procedures of which are out of the scope of this book. Odds ratios are also only calculated in SPSS for 2 × 2 tables, although they can be calculated using logistic regression in such cases. Please read the chapter on regression for the same.

Note: There is a distinct test named as chi-square for the goodness of fit which is explained in Box 7.2.

3. Alternatives to chi-square test

3.1 Fisher exact test

Sir Ronald A. Fisher laid the foundation for modern statistical science and gave us many statistical concepts, including analysis of variance (ANOVA), Student's *t*-test, and Fisher exact test. Unlike chi-square test which is based on approximations, Fisher exact test computes exact *P*-values from all possible combinations of the data. Thus, it can be used in situations where chi-square tests are not applicable. Fisher exact test assumes a directional hypothesis and is based on a one-tailed presumption. The interesting lady tasting tea experiment related to the origins of the Fisher test is shown in Box 7.3.

BOX 7.2 Chi-square tests for goodness of fit

Pearson's chi-square goodness-of-fit test or one-sample goodness-of-fit test is a different test than the chi-square test for independence. It is a single-sample nonparametric test, used to predict whether the distribution of cases in a categorical variable follows an already known distribution. In other words, it assesses the "goodness of fit," summarizing the discrepancy between observed and expected values. This can be performed by following command: *Analyze > Nonparametric Tests > Legacy Dialogs > Chi-square.*

BOX 7.3 Lady tasting tea experiment

"Some people will tell you there is a great deal of poetry and fine sentiment in a chest of tea" said Ralph Waldo Emerson. Tea taster Muriel Bristol claimed that she could distinguish whether tea or milk was added first by tasting the tea. Ronald Fisher conducted a randomized experiment with eight cups—four of each variety—to test whether or not her claim could reject the null hypothesis. The experiment is described in Fisher's book *The Design of Experiments* (Fisher, 1971). Fisher's description of this experiment in less than 10 pages is considered as an example of his extraordinary descriptive, calculative and experimental clarity. Given the small sample size, the statistical test used was Fisher's exact test.

3.1.1 The assumptions for Fisher exact test

The assumptions of Fisher's exact test are similar to the chi-square test except for the cell's expected values:

- Both the variables (exposure and outcome) should be categorical.
- Independence of observations—variable should not be paired or related.
- Mutually exclusive groups—an individual cannot belong to more than one cell in the contingency table.

The assumption that no cell should have an expected value less than 1, and less than 5 is more than 20% of total cell are not required for Fisher exact test. Thus, Fisher exact test can be used if the dataset fails this assumption for chi-square test.

3.1.2 Applying the Fisher exact test

The steps in the application of the Fisher exact test are the same as the χ^2 test given above Fig. 7.2. By default, SPSS calculates Fisher whenever we apply chi-square in a 2 × 2 contingency tables. For tables other than 2 × 2, you need to click *Exact* box in Crosstab dialog box and then select *Exact* (Fig. 7.4). The statistics will be calculated in the second chi-square tests table and the interpretation is the same as the chi-square test.

Figure 7.4 Exact dialog box in crosstab.

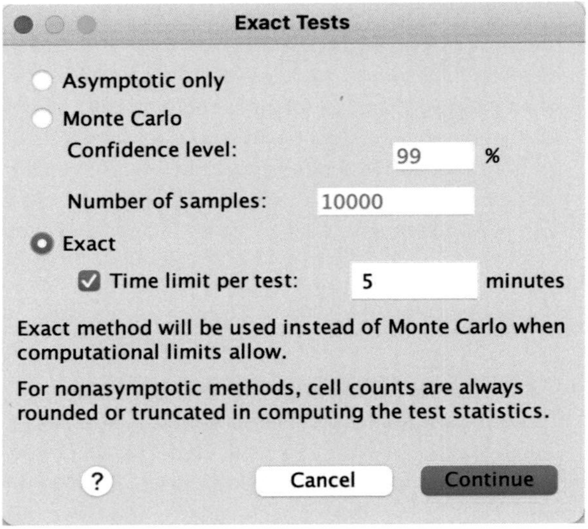

3.2 Chi-square with continuity correction

Frank Yates, an English statistician, demonstrated that in 2×2 contingency table, especially when the sample size is toward the lower side, chi-square approximations are suboptimal and tend to give significant values even when they are not (Type I error) (Yates, 1934). While chi-square calculations are based on the sum of [(observed − expected)^2/expected], Yates' correction of 0.5 transforms the calculation to the sum of [(|observed − expected| − 0.5)^2/expected] (Riffenburgh, 2012). This reduces the chi-square value and increases its P-value, reducing the significance and Type 1 error. The advantage of the chi-square with continuity correction is that it is applicable to small sample-size situations and unlike Fisher's exact test, it can be calculated by hand. This was the reason for its wide popularity and preference over Fisher's exact test in the past. Fisher's exact test, which can now can be performed in a few clicks, is rightly the preferred test.

3.3 Likelihood ratio test

Also known as log-likelihood ratio test or G-test, is another alternative to Pearson's chi-square. Unlike Fisher's exact test, it is useful when the sample size is large (>1000). When computing statistics, it measures how far the observed data are from the null expectation and derives their ratios. The computation involves complicated statistical modeling. The likelihood ratio test gives approximately the same results as the chi-square test; the decision to use is based on personal preference. In the biomedical field, researchers are familiar with the chi-square test, so it is always a good idea to use it over likelihood ratio test. However, if the data are log-linear in nature, the likelihood ratio test is preferable.

3.4 Linear by linear association

Linear by linear association (also known as the Mantel—Haenszel test) is useful when the dataset contains ordinal variables, that is, Likert scale, small/medium/large. An important principle to remember is that dichotomous ordinal variables should be treated as nominal variables for statistical purposes. The SPSS computes linear-by-linear association in the chi-square test table for all the data. Remember to select Somer's d for measuring effect size when using linear by linear association. Spearman's rank correlation and Kendall's tau discussed in the chapter on correlation are also useful in such situations.

3.5 Cochran—Mantel—Haenszel chi-square test

The Cochran and Mantel—Haenszel statistic is used in the analysis of stratified/matched categorical data. This test detects whether there are significantly differences between data across multiple/repeated tables. Apart from the measure of association, Mantel—Haenszel test has many applications in statistics, such as estimating common odds ratio and assessing confounding. Fortunately, most statistical software including SPSS, can compute the Cochran—Mantel—Haenszel test as a test of independence of $2 \times 2 \times n$, involving dichotomous exposure and outcome variables stratified by a third categorical variable.

3.5.1 Applying the Cochran—Mantel—Haenszel chi-square test

The data we will use to understand the application of the Cochran—Mantel—Haenszel test are the same as we used in the chi-square test based on the following hypothesis from a paper on the association of depression and clinical stage of infection in HIV/ AIDS patients (Alvi et al., 2018).

H_0: Depression does not vary with clinical symptoms of HIV/AIDS after controlling for the gender.

H_A: Depression varies with clinical symptoms of HIV/AIDS after controlling for the gender.

Apart from all the assumptions for the chi-square test, Cochran—Mantel—Haenszel test also has the assumption that all observations are identically distributed across the different repeats, which is tested by the homogeneity of odds ratios across the third variable. The homogeneity of the odds ratio assumption is checked in the results through the Breslow-Day test (should not be significant).

The steps to apply Cochran—Mantel—Haenszel test in SPSS are as follows:

1. Open the data set 7.*HIV_Depression*.sav. Go to Analyze > Descriptive Statistics > - Crosstabs (Fig. 7.5).

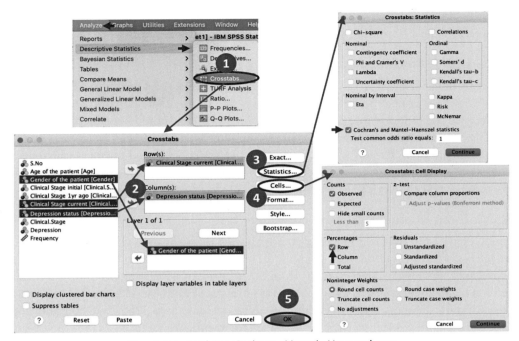

Figure 7.5 Applying Cochran—Mantel—Haenszel test.

2. Remember to put the outcome/dependent variable (in our case *Depression status*) in Column and independent variable (*Clinical Stage current*) in Rows. The third variable (*Gender*) is transferred under Layer box.

3. Click *Statistics* to open a new dialog box, select *Cochran's and Mantel—Haenszel Statistics* and click *Continue* to return to Crosstabs box.

4. Click *Cell* to open a new dialog box, select *Observed* under count and *Rows* under Percentage. Click *Continue* to return to Crosstabs box.

5. Click *OK* to get results in output window.

3.5.2 Interpreting the results of the Cochran—Mantel—Haenszel chi-square test

There will be four tables in the results output of Cochran's and Mantel—Haenszel test: (1) crosstabulation, (2) tests of homogeneity of odds ratio, (3) Cochran's and Mantel—Haenszel test, and (4) common odds ratio (Fig. 7.6).

1. Crosstabulation [1]: You will observe three crosstabs, two across categories of a third variable (male and female) and one with the total cases. Here we see that depression was observed in 9.0% of males who were asymptomatic as opposed to 23.3% of males who were having symptoms, while the reverse trend is seen in males without depression. Similarly, 15.5% of asymptomatic females and 17.9% of symptomatic females

Clinical Stage current * Depression status * Gender of the patient Crosstabulation

Gender of the patient				Depression status Yes	No	Total
Male	Clinical Stage current	Aymtomatic	Count	12	121	133
			% within Clinical Stage current	9.0%	91.0%	100.0%
		Symtomatic	Count	30	99	129
			% within Clinical Stage current	23.3%	76.7%	100.0%
	Total		Count	42	220	262
			% within Clinical Stage current	16.0%	84.0%	100.0%
Female	Clinical Stage current	Aymtomatic	Count	18	98	116
			% within Clinical Stage current	15.5%	84.5%	100.0%
		Symtomatic	Count	10	46	56
			% within Clinical Stage current	17.9%	82.1%	100.0%
	Total		Count	28	144	172
			% within Clinical Stage current	16.3%	83.7%	100.0%
Total	Clinical Stage current	Aymtomatic	Count	30	219	249
			% within Clinical Stage current	12.0%	88.0%	100.0%
		Symtomatic	Count	40	145	185
			% within Clinical Stage current	21.6%	78.4%	100.0%
	Total		Count	70	364	434
			% within Clinical Stage current	16.1%	83.9%	100.0%

Tests of Homogeneity of the Odds Ratio

	Chi-Squared	df	Asymptotic Significance (2-sided)
Breslow-Day	2.829	1	.093
Tarone's	2.826	1	.093

Tests of Conditional Independence

	Chi-Squared	df	Asymptotic Significance (2-sided)
Cochran's	7.458	1	.006
Mantel-Haenszel	6.714	1	.010

Under the conditional independence assumption, Cochran's statistic is asymptotically distributed as a 1 df chi-squared distribution, only if the number of strata is fixed, while the Mantel-Haenszel statistic is always asymptotically distributed as a 1 df chi-squared distribution. Note that the continuity correction is removed from the Mantel-Haenszel statistic when the sum of the differences between the observed and the expected is 0.

Mantel-Haenszel Common Odds Ratio Estimate

Estimate				.478
ln(Estimate)				-.738
Standard Error of ln(Estimate)				.271
Asymptotic Significance (2-sided)				.007
Asymptotic 95% Confidence Interval	Common Odds Ratio	Lower Bound		.281
		Upper Bound		.814
	ln(Common Odds Ratio)	Lower Bound		-1.270
		Upper Bound		-.206

The Mantel-Haenszel common odds ratio estimate is asymptotically normally distributed under the common odds ratio of 1.000 assumption. So is the natural log of the estimate.

Figure 7.6 Results of Cochran's and Mantel—Haenszel test.

were depressed. Same as the chi-square crosstab, this is useful in interpreting results and observing the trend.

2. Tests of Homogeneity of Odds Ratio [2]: The second table tests the assumption of the Mantel—Haenszel test, and measures odds ratio of Outcome (Depression) across exposure (Clinical symptoms), which should be the same in the different categories of a third variable (gender). Both Breslow-Day and Tarone's test results are nonsignificant, so we meet the assumption of homogeneity and we can safely use the Mantel—Haenszel test.

3. Tests of Conditional Independence and their effect size [3 and 4]: The third table gives Cochran's and Mantel—Haenszel test statistics, which are tests of conditional independence. We can make out from the table that both Cochran's and Mantel—Haenszel tests are significant and thus we can reject H_0 and accept H_A. Thus, depression and clinical symptoms are associated even after controlling for gender. The effect sizes can be taken from the table of odds ratio. Thus common odds ratio for asymptomatic HIV/AIDS patients developing depression as compared to symptomatic is 0.478 (95% CI: 0.281—0.814), while OR for symptomatic as compared to asymptomatic will be 2.09 (1/0.478) with 95% CI: 1.23—3.56 (1/0.814 and 1/0.281).

4. Thus, the null hypothesis is rejected as Depression and Clinical staging are significantly associated across gender. The results can be expressed as follows:
Depression was higher in symptomatic HIV/AIDS patients (21.6%) than in asymptomatic patients (12.0%). Depression and Clinical staging of HIV/AIDS were significantly associated on Mantel—Haenszel chi-square test with test statistics χ^2MH (1, N = 434) = 6.714, P = .01

and the common odds of developing depression was 2.09 (95% CI: 1.23–3.56) times higher for clinical symptomatic patients than for asymptomatic after adjusting gender.

Important Note: The three methods of chi-square test calculations are asymptotic, exact, and Monte Carlo methods. They are discussed in Box 7.4.

4. Two related exposure variables: McNemar's test

The McNemar's test is also known as McNemar's chi-square tests. Whenever the chi-square is mentioned alone, it is considered as Pearson's chi-square test; all the alternative chi-square tests must be mentioned by their names. The McNemar's test is applicable to pretest–posttest data of same (paired), or matched/related individuals. This test finds whether two related groups with dichotomous dependent variable differ statistically or not. In this sense, it can be considered as paired *t*-test equivalent for a non-parametric dichotomous dependent variable.

BOX 7.4 Asymptotic versus exact method versus Monte Carlo

In SPSS, while interpreting the results from the chi-square tests table as well as applications of exact tests, three different terms can be seen—Asymptotic and Exact significance as well as Monte Carlo Method. Their use and interpretation are as follows:

Asymptomatic Sig: It is based on assumption that the data has a sufficient sample size and follows a particular distribution (chi-square distribution). It should be preferred when the assumption of tests is met and the sample size is large enough.

Exact Method: When the data do not follow the assumption of the test, the asymptotic significance may be unreliable (Mehta & Patel, 2011). Thus, when you have a small, disbalanced, or poorly distributed sample, the exact method should be selected to calculate significance. In this, the *P*-value from all possible combinations of the data is computed. Therefore, this method is computationally intensive and time consuming, especially if the sample size is more than 30. Be patient when using this test because it will take a while. If the sample size is extremely large, you should not apply this test unless you want to be tortured in this fashion.

Monte Carlo Method: Sometimes the data violates the test assumptions despite a large sample size. Computing exact tests can be time consuming and exceed the memory limits of the computers. In such situations, the Monte Carlo method is the best alternative. The Monte Carlo method of computing significance is based on the repeated sampling method, which is computationally less intensive and produces results quickly. So, it can be used when your computer fails to compute the exact test.

By default, SPSS calculates asymptotic significance but you can command it to calculate Exact or Monte Carlo in all Crosstabs and Nonparametric analysis by clicking an exact button (Fig. 7.4).

4.1 The assumptions for McNemar's test

- Participants should be paired or matched/related.
- Both variable should be nominal and dichotomous (2 × 2).
- Participants should be independent of each other.
- Mutually exclusive groups.

The McNemar's test has one more condition, namely a sufficient samples of discordant pairs (>30). Remember, it is not the sample size but the number of discordant pairs. However, if this fails, we can safely use exact significance that is automatically reported by SPSS when applying the McNemar's test.

4.2 Applying McNemar's test

The data that we will use to understand the application of Mc Nemar's test is the same that we used in the chi-square test. The research question is on the patients under treatment. Do they become asymptomatic with treatment over time? The hypothesis is as follows:

H_0: During treatment, the proportion of symptomatic HIV patients at the initial stage of the disease does not change over time.

H_A: During treatment, the proportion of symptomatic HIV patients at the initial stage of the disease changes over time.

The steps in application of *McNemar's test* are as follows (Fig. 7.7): In SPSS, we can run McNemar's test in two different ways, in Crosstab along with chi-square test, and under nonparametric test. We will demonstrate both the methods. In nonparametric test, McNemar's test is chosen automatically on adding two paired categorical data and in this approach, the test statistics is also calculated. However, for descriptive data, crosstab methods is more appropriate.

1. Open the dataset *7.HIV_Depression*.sav. Go to *Analyze > Nonparametric tests > Related Samples* (Fig. 7.7).
2. This will open *Two or More Related Sample* dialog box. Click on the *Fields* tab in the top center.
3. Transfer both paired variables (*Clinical stage initial and Clinical stage current*) to Test Fields.
4. Click *Run* to get the results in output window.
5. We recommend that you also run McNemar's test from the crosstab option to get the descriptives for interpreting the results. This is easy and is similar to applying chi-square tests, keep *Clinical stage current* in the Column and *Clinical stage initial* in the Row. Instead of chi-square, select *McNemar* and *Risk* in Crosstabs:Statistics dialog box (Fig. 7.8).

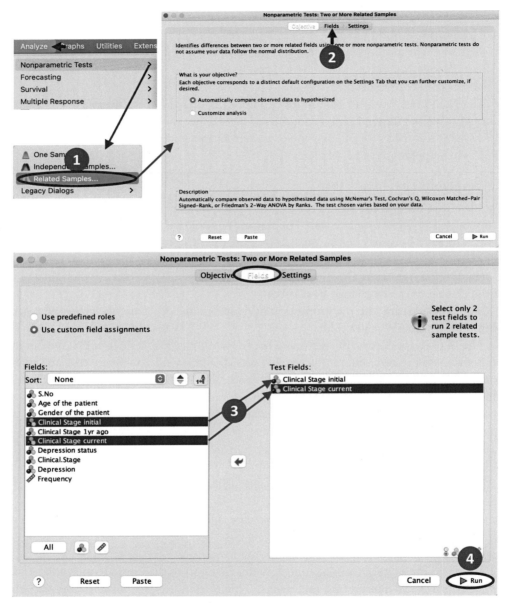

Figure 7.7 Applying McNemar's test.

4.3 Interpretation of results of McNemar's test

In the results output of the crosstab analysis for the *McNemar* test, two tables will be displayed: (1) Crosstab and (2) chi-square test (Fig. 7.9). In the results from nonparametric

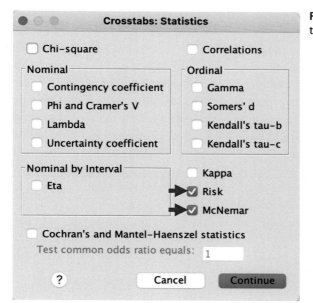

Figure 7.8 Statistics dialog box in cross-tab for running *McNemar* test.

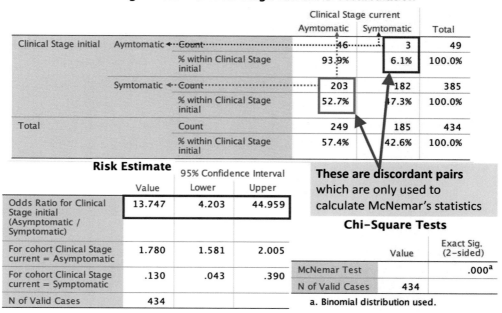

Figure 7.9 Results from crosstab analysis for *McNemar* test.

test analysis for *McNemar* test, the two tables are (3) hypothesis test summary and (4) McNemar test (Fig. 7.10).

McNemar's test compares the two discordant pairs for statistical significance. Three essential things can be seen from the results (Figs. 7.9 and 7.10):

1. Crosstab [1]: This is useful in interpreting results and observing the trend. The McNemar test considers only the discordant pairs i.e., the paired observations with discord or difference. We can see that 6.1% of those who were asymptomatic at the initial stage were currently symptomatic and 52.7% of those who were symptomatic at the initial stage were currently asymptomatic (these are discordant pairs). These are the two different proportions that McNemar's test analyzes. It is should also be noted that the total number of discordant pairs is $3 + 203 = 206$, which is more than 30, so McNemar's asymptotic significance is reliable.

2. Chi-square tests and Hypothesis test summary [2 and 3]: Table 2 shows the exact significance of the McNemar's test (Fig. 7.9). The first table in the nonparametric test analysis—Hypothesis test summary gives better results and calculates the asymptotic significance (Fig. 7.10). The *P*-value is <0.001 in both.

3. McNemar's test [4]: The second table from the nonparametric test analysis calculates the test significance of McNemar's test, which is not calculated in crosstab analysis. McNemar's test statistics is 192.2. One important thing to note is that this is a test of associations and does not provide information about the strength of the association. Unfortunately, current versions of SPSS do not calculate the effect size of McNemar's

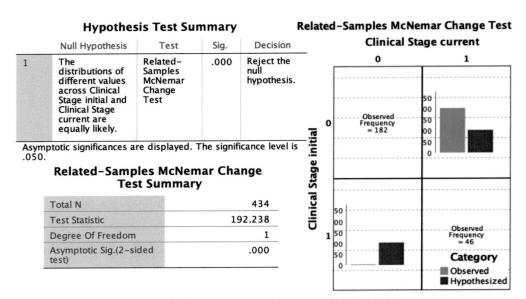

Figure 7.10 Results from nonparametric test analysis for *McNemar* test.

test, that is, Cohen's *g*. However, one can use the odds ratio function to express the strength in absence of Cohen's *g* value to some extent (Muller & Cohen, 1989). The Odds of being currently asymptomatic was 13.747 [95% CI (4.203—44.959)] compared with the initial stage.

4. Thus, the null hypothesis is rejected as the clinical stage at the initial and clinical stage at current are significantly different. The results can be expressed as follows:

During treatment, the proportion of symptomatic HIV patients at the initial stage of the disease changed over time to the current stage. About 52.7% of patients became asymptomatic in contrast to their initial stage, while 6.1% of asymptomatic patients became symptomatic. Thus, the proportion of symptomatic HIV patients at the initial stage of the disease reduced over time. This was significant on applying McNemar's test with McNemar's χ^2 (1, N = 434) = 192.2, P < .001. The Odds of being currently asymptomatic was 13.747 [95% CI (4.203—44.959)] as compared to the initial stage.

Note: The case of erroneous application of the chi-square test instead of McNemar's chi-square test on paired data is explained in Box 7.5.

5. More than two related exposure variables: Cochran's *Q* test

The Cochran's *Q* test is an extension of McNemar's test with three or more (*k*) related samples, each with nominal dichotomized responses. It can be considered a special case of the nonparametric Friedman's rank test, where responses are dichotomous instead of continuous. An example of paired exposure variables can be the data of individuals measured at baseline, at 1 month, and at 6 months, while example of matched data may be matched individuals with similar characteristics exposed to three or more interventions (two individuals acting as proxies measured once on the same thing).

5.1 The assumptions for Cochran's *Q* test

- One dichotomous outcome variable and one independent variable with three or more levels or repetition.

BOX 7.5 What if we apply the Pearson's chi-square test instead of the McNemar's test on paired data?

The chi-square test analyses the association of all columns with rows by cross-tabulation. In a 2 × 2 contingency table, the information from four cells is used to calculating significance. The McNemar's test only observes the difference in discordant pairs, that is, two cells, to calculate the significance. To test the hypothesis of proportional difference between paired data, the information from two cells is sufficient. Thus, McNemar's test is more powerful to assess the difference between proportions on paired data as only two cells are tested.

- Participants should be independent from each other.
- Mutually exclusive.

The Cochran's Q test has one additional condition of adequate samples. Although, if this fails, we can safely use exact significance, which is also reported by SPSS.

5.2 Applying Cochran's Q test

The data we will use to understand the application of the Cochran's Q test are the same as we used in the chi-square test and McNemar's test. The research question is do HIV patients under treatment become asymptomatic over time (measured at baseline, 1 year ago, and current stage)? The hypothesis is as follows:

H_0: During treatment, the proportion of symptomatic HIV patients does not change from baseline to one year ago and current stage.

H_A: During treatment, the proportion of symptomatic HIV patients changes from initial to one year ago and current stage.

Steps in application of Cochran's Q test in SPSS are follows:

In SPSS, we can run the Cochran's Q test in two different ways: (1) automatically running from *Related Samples* under nonparametric test or (2) from *Legacy dialogs*. We will demonstrate both the methods. In *Related Samples*, Cochran's Q test is chosen automatically on adding more than two paired categorical data. This approach performs post hoc tests as well and is therefore preferable (Fig. 7.11).

1. Open the data set *7.HIV_Depression.sav*. Go to *Analyze > Nonparametric tests > Related Samples*.
2. This will open Two or More Related Sample dialog box. Click *Fields* tab in top center.
3. Transfer three paired variables (*Clinical stage initial, Clinical stage 1 year ago* and *Clinical stage current*) to Test Fields.
4. Click *Run* to get results in output.

5.3 Interpretation of results of the Cochran Q test

There will be three tables in the results output in addition to some graphs: (1) Hypothesis test summary, (2) Related-samples Cochran's Q test, (3) Graph of related-samples Cochran's Q test, and, (4) Pairwise comparisons (Fig. 7.12).

There are three essential things to note from the results (Fig. 7.12):

1. Hypothesis test summary [1]: This table provides the asymptotic significance, which is below the assumed significance level ($P < .001$), thus null hypothesis is rejected.
2. Cochran's Q test [2]: The second table calculates Cochran's Q test statistic as 283.48, with a significance P-value $<.001$. One important thing to note is that this is a test of statistical significance and does not provide information about the strength of the

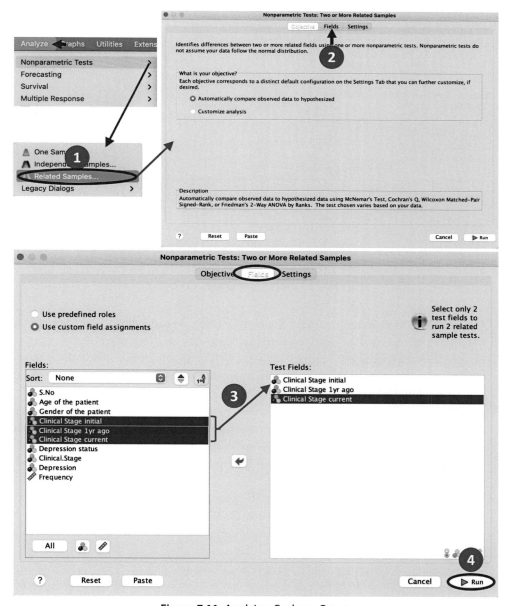

Figure 7.11 Applying Cochran Q test.

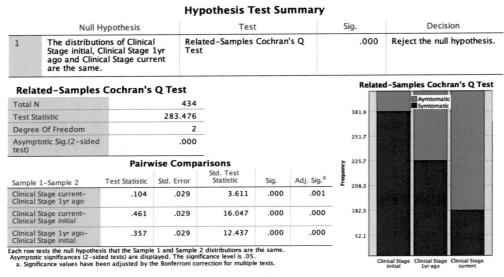

Figure 7.12 Results of Cochran Q test.

association. Unfortunately, current versions of SPSS do not calculate the effect size of Cochran's Q test, that is, chance-corrected measures of effect size—R.

3. Graph of related-samples Cochran's Q test [3]: The graph clearly shows that the proportion of asymptomatic increased after treatment and should be reported in the results. To know the exact proportion of symptomatic and asymptomatic individuals in the three time intervals, you need to check *Frequencies* from: Analyze > Descriptive Statistics > Frequencies and enter Clinical stage initial, 1 year ago, and current as variables. After starting treatment, the proportion of symptomatic decreased from 88.7% (385/434) at the baseline to 53% (230/434) one year ago and to 42.6% (185/434) currently.

4. Pairwise comparisons [4]: This provides the post hoc results and indicates which stages differ significantly from each other. In this table, we can observe all three pairs are significantly different from each other after adjusting through Bonferroni correction.

5. The results can be expressed as follows:

During treatment, the proportion of symptomatic patients decreased from 88.7% (385/434) at the baseline to 53% (230/434) one year ago and to 42.6% (185/434) currently (Refer to graph). The HIV patients had significantly different proportions of asymptomatic at the baseline, at one year ago, and currently on Cochran's Q test with test statistics $\chi^2 C$ (2, N = 434) = 283.5, P < .001. In post hoc analysis, all three pairs were found to be statistically different (P < .01).

6. Analyzing the summary data

Sometimes entered data in SPSS or any other electronic software is not available and only a summary table is available. This situation may also arise when we need to perform analysis on frequency data, either from secondary data from hospital records or from published research. In both situations, we can perform analysis on the summary data in the form of frequencies. To do this, we need to create new variables along with the frequency variable with weighting of cases. Suppose the summary data in the form of 2 × 2 table, we can create a *Frequency* variable as depicted in the SPSS data view (Fig. 7.13).

As shown in Fig. 7.13, when you have data on grouped frequencies (crosstab) you need to perform few steps. First create three new variables: independent (*Clinical Stage*) and dependent (*Depression status*) variables corresponding to the row and column of the 2x2 table, and a third variable *Frequency*. Next, assign a numeric value to the categories for the row and column variables and enter them into the SPSS data view. Finally, add the frequency corresponding to the categories into the *Frequency* variable in the SPSS data view.

Now you need to command SPSS to consider the newly created *frequency* variable to Weight cases.

1. Create the variable as shown in Fig. 7.13. Hover the mouse pointer over *Data* and click *Weight cases*.
2. A new dialog box will open as shown in Fig. 7.14. Check *Weight cases by* to activate the *Frequency Variable* box.
3. Locate the newly created variable *Frequency* and drop it under *Frequency Variable*.
4. Click *OK* to execute the Weight cases function.

		Depression status		Total
		Yes	No	
Clinical Stage	Asymptomatic	30	219	249
	Symptomatic	40	145	185
Total		70	364	434

	Clinical.Stage	Depression	Frequency
1	1	1	30
2	1	2	219
3	2	1	40
4	2	2	145
5	.	.	.

Figure 7.13 Crosstab of clinical stage across depression along with new variable created as frequencies in SPSS.

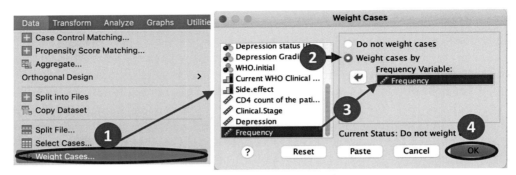

Figure 7.14 Steps for weight cases function in SPSS.

Now, try performing the chi-square analysis on the variable of *Clinical Stage* and *Depression* you just created and compare the results with the results in Fig. 7.3. They will be exactly the same!

Note: Do not forget to reset the Weight cases function after you have done the analysis.

References

Akoglu, H. (2018). User's guide to correlation coefficients. *Turkish Journal of Emergency Medicine, 18*(3), 91—93. https://doi.org/10.1016/j.tjem.2018.08.001

Alvi, Y., Khalique, N., Ahmad, A., Khan, H. S., & Faizi, N. (2018). Prevalence of depression among HIV-positive patients treated with antiretrovirals at different stage of infection. *HIV and AIDS Review, 17*(4), 243—248. https://doi.org/10.5114/hivar.2018.80255

Fisher, R. A. (1971). *The design of experiments*. Hafner Press.

McHugh, M. L. (2012). The chi-square test of independence. *Biochemia Medica, 23*(2), 143—149. https://doi.org/10.11613/BM.2013.018

Mehta, C. R., & Patel, N. R. (2011). *IBM SPSS exact tests* (pp. 23—24). IBM Corporation.

Muller, K., & Cohen, J. (1989). Statistical power analysis for the behavioral sciences. *Technometrics, 31*(4), 499. https://doi.org/10.2307/1270020

Pearson, K. (1900). On the criterion that a given system of deviations from the probable in the case of a correlated system of variables is such that it can be reasonably supposed to have arisen from random sampling. The London, Edinburgh, and Dublin Philosophical Magazine. *Journal of Science, 50*(302), 157—175.

Riffenburgh, R. (2012). Statistics in medicine. In *Statistics in medicine*. Elsevier Inc. https://doi.org/10.1016/C2010-0-64822-X

Yates, F. (1934). Contingency tables involving small numbers and the χ^2 test. *Supplement to the Journal of the Royal Statistical Society, 1*(2), 217. https://doi.org/10.2307/2983604

CHAPTER 8

Validity*

The classification of facts and the formation of absolute judgments upon the basis of this classification—judgments independent of the idiosyncrasies of the individual mind—essentially sum up the aim and method of modern science.

—**Karl Pearson.**

1. Validity

The term validity refers to the extent of a test to accurately measure what it intends to measure. In this sense, validity is akin to accuracy. In contrast, reliability is a term that refers to the stability or consistency of information and is similar to reproducibility/repeatability (Abramson & Abramson, 2011). In this sense, reliability is akin to precision. Fig. 8.1 explains the concepts for understanding. However, in reality, an unreliable measure cannot have high validity.

1.1 Types of validity

Validity can be classified in different ways. One way of classifying validity is in terms of internal and external validity. Internal validity is the validity of inferences for the study population, whereas the validity outside that population is external validity (Abramson & Abramson, 2011). A sound study design, data collection, and analysis ensure good internal validity. External validity or generalizability is only possible if the internal validity is good. However, external validity can be poor even if internal validity is high, especially when the study has a controlled or restricted population group (exclusions). Epidemiological and research method books delve further into these two types of validity.

In terms of appraisal, validity is divided into four types—construct, criterion, content, and face validity (Fig. 8.2).

The different types of validity are further defined on the basis of Dictionary of Epidemiology as follows (Porta, 2014):
1. **Construct validity**: "*The extent to which the measurement corresponds to theoretical concepts (constructs) concerning the phenomenon under study. For example, if on theoretical grounds the phenomenon should change with age, a measurement with construct validity would reflect such a change.*" Construct validity is the overarching concern of validity and ensures that the construct of the measure is well aligned. It is further divided into convergent

---

*For datasets, please refer to companion site: https://www.elsevier.com/books-and-journals/book-companion/9780443185502

Biostatistics Manual for Health Research
ISBN 978-0-443-18550-2, https://doi.org/10.1016/B978-0-443-18550-2.00012-8

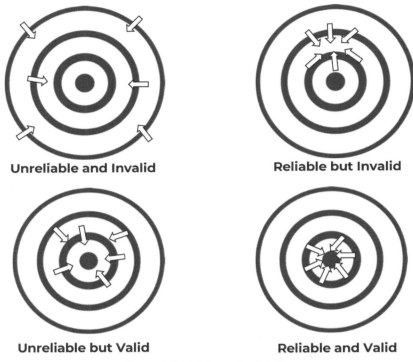

Unreliable and Invalid   **Reliable but Invalid**

Unreliable but Valid   **Reliable and Valid**

Figure 8.1 Validity and reliability.

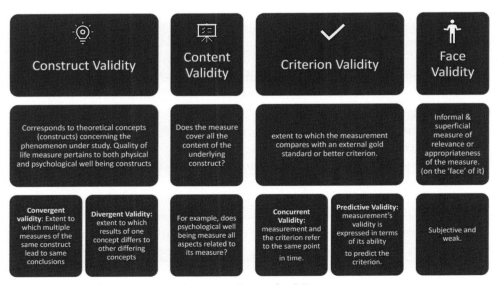

Figure 8.2 Types of validity.

and discriminant/divergent validity. Convergent validity is the extent to which the related constructs lead to same conclusions. Divergent validity is the extent to which results of differing constructs lead to different conclusions.

2. **Content validity:** "*The extent to which the measurement incorporates the domain of the phenomenon under study. For example, a measurement of functional health status should embrace activities of daily living (occupational, family, and social functioning, etc.)*"

3. **Criterion validity:** "*The extent to which the measurement correlates with an external criterion of the phenomenon under study; ideally, a gold standard.*" Criterion validity is further divided into the following: (a) **Concurrent validity:** "*The measurement and the criterion refer to the same point in time.*" An example-clinical examination and comparison with microbiological examination at the same time or ELISA and Western Blot for HIV/AIDS at the same time. (b) **Predictive validity:** "*The measurement's validity is expressed in terms of its ability to predict the criterion. An example is an academic aptitude test that is validated against subsequent academic performance.*"

4. **Face validity:** "*The extent to which a measurement or a measurement instrument appears reasonable on superficial inspection.*" Based purely on lay judgment, this is based on whether the measure appears appropriate on the face of it.

In this manual, we will restrict our discussion to appraising validity in terms of data. The measure of certain diagnostic accuracy tests such as Sensitivity and Specificity are measures of concurrent validity.

2. Diagnostic test evaluation

Diagnostic test evaluation is an essential element in health research. We will first discuss the binary or dichotomous diagnostic tests that result in a test positive or a test negative outcome. Based on criterion validity, any set of tests can be measured for its concurrence with another criterion (ideally, a gold standard). Usually, any new testing method or composite index should be compared to the gold standard confirmatory test available for the test. For example, if Western Blot is a gold standard test for HIV/AIDS, the newly developed ELISA kit should be appraised against it for concurrent validity. Two such measures of concurrent validity are sensitivity and specificity. Another example could be a composite score for a disease developed on the basis of X-rays and clinical examination. This composite score could be compared to the gold standard MRI examination for its sensitivity and specificity. Any new diagnostic method that is cheaper or more efficient is of immense value in resource-limited settings. Thus, test evaluation is a very useful modality in health research. Screening tests are immensely useful in public health and are also evaluated through diagnostic test evaluations.

2.1 Tests for diagnostic test evaluation

While sensitivity and specificity are two commonest measures of diagnostic test evaluation, there are other tests that measure other important aspects in diagnostic test evaluation. About seven such tests are calculated for diagnostic test evaluation

Conceptual Dimension	Test	Calculation	Disease prevalence
Validity of Test (Concurrent Validity)	Sensitivity	(True Positive/True Positive + False Negative)*100	Not affected by prevalence
	Specificity	(True Negative/True Negative + False Positive)*100	Not affected by prevalence
Probability of Disease event (Bayes theorem)	Positive Predictive Value	(True Positive/True Positive + False Positive)*100	Affected by Disease Prevalence
	Negative Predictive Value	(True Negative/True Negative + False Negative)*100	Affected by Disease Prevalence
Likelihood ratio (Odds)	Positive Likelihood Ratio	Sensitivity/(1-Specificity)	Not affected by prevalence
	Negative Likelihood Ratio	(1-Sensitivity/Specificity)	Not affected by prevalence
Others	Diagnostic Accuracy	(True Positive + True Negative)/ (True Positive + False Positive + True Negative + False Negative)*100	Affected by Disease Prevalence

Figure 8.3 Diagnostic evaluation tests.

(Fig. 8.3)—sensitivity and specificity, positive and negative predictive value, positive and negative likelihood ratio, and diagnostic accuracy.

2.2 Sensitivity and specificity

Sensitivity and specificity are measures of concurrent validity in which the test is compared against a gold standard or a designated confirmatory test. If both sensitivity and specificity of a test is good, it is considered to have a high validity. Diagnostic test evaluation can be best understood through a 2*2 table as shown in Table 8.1.

2.2.1 Sensitivity

Sensitivity is defined as the probability that a diseased person is tested positive. It is also defined as the ability to detect true positives and is expressed as percentage (true positive rate).

$$\text{Sensitivity} = (\text{True Positive/Diseased})*100, \text{ or}$$

$$\text{Sensitivity} = (\text{True Positive/True Positive} + \text{False Negative})*100, \text{ or}$$

$$S_n = (a/a + c)*100 \text{ (based on Table 8.1)}$$

A test with 100% sensitivity will identify all the diseased people as positives, no one with negative test will have disease ($c = 0$). However, it could also include many

Table 8.1 Diagnostic test evaluation.

Test for evaluation	On the basis of gold standard/confirmatory test		Total
Result	Disease present	Disease absent	
Test positive	a	b	a + b
Test negative	c	d	c + d
Total	a + c	b + d	a + b + c + d

a = true positive, b = false positive, c = false negative, d = true negative.

nondiseased people as positives, because false positive (b) is not accounted for in this measure. Therefore, 100% sensitivity does not mean that all the positives are diseased, it only means that all the diseased people are positive. A good screening test must have a very high sensitivity so that it can detect all the potentially diseased individuals (even if it is at the cost of a few nondiseased people rated as positive).

2.2.2 Specificity

Specificity is defined as the probability that a nondiseased person is tested negative. It is also defined as the ability to detect true negative and is expressed as percentage (true negative rate).

$$\text{Specificity} = (\text{True Negative}/\text{Non} - \text{Diseased})*100, \text{ or}$$

$$\text{Specificity} = (\text{True Negative}/\text{True Negative} + \text{False Positive})*100, \text{ or}$$

$$S_p = (d/b+d)*100 \text{ (based on Table 8.1)}$$

A test with 100% specificity will identify all the nondiseased people as negatives, no one with a negative test will have the disease ($b = 0$). However, it could also include many diseased people as negatives, since false negatives (c) are not accounted for in this measure. Therefore, 100% specificity does not mean that all the negatives are nondiseased, it only means that all the nondiseased people are negative. A good diagnostic test must have a very high specificity so that it can confirm that the person does not have the disease.

2.2.3 Relative importance of sensitivity and specificity

Screening tests are often used in healthy populations and should have a high sensitivity; whereas, diagnostic tests are used in potential patients and should have a high specificity. Sometimes, diagnostic or confirmatory tests are very expensive and researchers often test a composite index or scale which is cheaper as a screening test. If the sensitivity is very high, then it is safe to say that the negatives do not have the disease and the positives are then considered for further evaluation and confirmation of the disease. For example, a composite score based on X-ray and Clinical examination is cheaper than MRI and could be compared for sensitivity and specificity against MRI. For this, all the patients in the study must undergo both the tests (composite score based on X-ray and clinical examination as well as MRI).

Although both sensitivity and specificity should be high for a good validity, there is often a tradeoff between sensitivity and specificity. As one increases, the other decreases. Therefore, their use is dependant on the context of use (screening or confirmation).

2.3 Positive and negative predictive values

Sensitivity and specificity are intrinsic values of a test and do not change from population to population. However, the probability of disease and clinical suspicion depends on prevalence of the disease in the population. For example, one of our friend was ELISA positive for Rubella during her first trimester screening. Expectedly, this caused a significant distress in family and they started looking at the sensitivity and specificity of the test.

As expected, it is wide ranging but generally high in most of the approved ELISA tests for Rubella (Hiebert et al., 2021). Let us suppose that the sensitivity was 70% and specificity 95%. Does that give us any insight into clinical suspicion of disease, based only on test results? Hardly, as the predictive values depend on local prevalence of the disease in question as well.

Positive predictive value (PPV) is the probability of positive test being truly positive or diseased. In probabilistic terms, this is written as probability of disease given test positive. In probabilistic terms, this can be further written as probability of disease given (symbolized by "|") a positive test, that is, **Disease | Test + ve**.

A 100% PPV, although quite impossible, means that all the positive test patients have the disease, that is there would be no false positive ($b = 0$).

Negative Predictive Value (NPV) is the probability of negative test being truly negative or nondiseased. In probabilistic terms, this is written as probability of absence of disease given a negative test. In probabilistic terms, this can be further written as probability of disease given a positive test (given is symbolized by "|"), that is, **No Disease | Test –ve**. A 100% NPV, although quite unlikely, means that all the negative test patients do not have the disease, that is there are no false negatives ($c = 0$).

Positive Predictive Value (PPV) = True Positive/(True Positive + False Positive)*100

PPV $= (a/a+b)$*100 (based on Table 8.1)

Negative Predictive Value (PPV) = True Negative/(True Negative + False Negative)*100

NPV $= (d/c + d)$*100 (based on Table 8.1).

2.3.1 Concept of conditional probability

As you would note from Fig. 8.3, PPV and NPV are concerned with disease predictivity and are not about the validity of a test. In other words, sensitivity and specificity are about the test, not the patient (Webb & Sidebotham, 2020). In contrast, PPV and NPV are about the patient (disease/no disease) and not about the test. Unlike a straightforward positive or negative test, we are dealing with uncertainty here. This uncertainty depends on a prior probability-prevalence of the disease.

Bayes' theorem in probability and statistics is used to describe the probability of one event based on prior condition. This conditional probability is helpful in understanding the PPV and NPV better. We delve into the calculation and dependence on disease prevalence through the Bayesian formula. Interested readers may read further about this in the paper by Webb & Sidebotham (2020).

In the following formula, P stands for probability, * for multiply, | for given. Also, P (Disease | Test + ve) = PPV and P(Test + ve | Disease) = Sensitivity (S_n)

$$P(Test + ve)*P(Disease|Test + ve) = P(Disease)*P(Test + ve|Disease)$$

$$\Rightarrow P(Disease|Test + ve) = [P(Disease)*P(Test + ve|Disease)]/P(Test + ve)$$

In other words, PPV = P (Disease)* S_n/P (Test + ve).

Thus, PPV is dependent on P(Disease) or prevalence.

2.3.2 Probability of the disease and validity of the test

How is the probability of disease (PPV) related with validity of a test (Sensitivity and Specificity)? To help the friend with positive ELISA about her concern, this concept is important. While we know that her test's sensitivity is 70% and specificity is 95%, what is her PPV? This can be calculated on the basis of formula given below:

$$PPV = (S_n * \text{Prevalence})/(S_n * \text{Prevalence}) + (1 - S_p)*(1 - \text{prevalence})$$

$$NPV = S_p*(1 - \text{Prevalence})/(1 - S_n)*\text{Prevalence} + S_p*(1 - \text{Prevalence})$$

$$PPV = \text{Positive Predictive Value, } NPV = \text{Negative Predictive Value, } S_n$$
$$= \text{Sensitivity, } S_p = \text{Specificity}$$

Based on the formula discussed earlier, the positive predictive value with different prevalences is shown in Table 8.2. With increase in the prevalence of a disease from 0.1% to 75%, the PPV jumps from 1.38% to 97.67%. In the Rubella example discussed earlier, the friend must be consoled using PPV. Suppose the prevalence is only 1% in her local area, then this means that the PPV is only 12.3%. Once she is consoled, she should revisit her Doctor and would be fully confirmed through a confirmatory test and other symptoms/manifestations of the disease. Therefore, clinician's suspicion and probability depend on the context and are dynamic. On the basis of one ELISA test for HIV/AIDS in India versus Swaziland, the same clinician will behave differently as the PPV changes (Swaziland has a significantly higher prevalence than India, but has seen spectacular progress in HIV/AIDS care in the last decade).

2.4 Positive and negative likelihood ratio

Sensitivity and specificity are about the validity of a test and predictive values are about the probability of diseases. Likelihood ratios are based on the odds of an event (disease in this case). Odds are distinct from probabilities as they are ratios of probabilities of an event

Table 8.2 Prevalence, validity and positive predictive value.

Prevalence of disease	Validity of test		Positive predictive value (PPV)
	Sensitivity	Specificity	
0.1%	70%	95%	1.38%
1.0%	70%	95%	12.39%
5.0%	70%	95%	42.42%
10%	70%	95%	60.87%
50%	70%	95%	93.33%
75%	70%	95%	97.67%

occurrence versus nonoccurrence. In the era of evidence-based medicine, likelihood ratio has become immensely important for patient consultations.

A positive likelihood ratio is applied when the test is positive. It measures the odds of the presence of a disease as opposed to the absence of a disease. In other words, the probability of a positive test given disease is present to the probability of positive test given it is absent (MedCalc Software, 2022).

A negative likelihood ratio is applied when the test is negative. It measures the odds of the presence of a disease as opposed to the absence of disease. In other words, the probability of a negative test given disease is present to the probability of a negative test given it is absent (MedCalc Software, 2022).

$$\text{Positive Likelihood ratio}(LR\ +) = \text{True positive rate}/\text{False positive rate, or}$$

$$LR+ = \text{Sensitivity}/(1 - \text{Specificity}) = S_n/(1 - S_p)$$

$$LR+ = (a/a+c)/(b/b+d) \text{ (based on Table 8.1)}$$

$$\text{Negative Likelihood ratio}(LR\ -) = \text{False negative rate}/\text{True negative rate, or}$$

$$LR- = (1 - \text{Sensitivity})/\text{Specificity} = (1 - S_n)/S_p$$

$$LR- = (c/a+c)/(d/b+d) \text{ (based on Table 8.1)}$$

In the previous example with a sensitivity of 70% and a specificity of 95%, the LR+ $[S_n/(1 - S_p)]$ is 14, and LR− is 0.32. An LR+ of 14 means that a person with a disease is 14 times more likely to be positive than a person without the disease. It is worth reiterating that unlike predictive values, likelihood ratios do not change with prevalence. If the local prevalence is not known and the clinician wants to get a sense of likelihood, LR

BOX 8.1 Probability, odds, and chance

The three terms probability, odds, and chance are often confusingly mentioned in dictionaries and were called a confusion pandemic when dictionary definitions were compared (Fulton et al., 2012). Probability is the expectation of an event occurrence and is expressed as a fraction. For example, in a 6-sided dice, the probability of getting 3 is 1/6 (only one side has 3/total sides). Odds is a ratio of probabilities of occurrence of a certain event to its nonoccurrence. For example in a 6-sided dice, the probability of odds of getting 3 is 1/5. This is calculated as the probability of getting 3 divided by the probability of not getting 3 (1/6 divided by 5/6 = 1/5). Another term is chance, which is synonymous to probability but usually expressed in percentages. The chance of getting 3 is 16.67%. Thus, the probability is a fraction ranging from 0 to 1, odds is a ratio, and chance is a percentage ranging from 0% to 100%.

becomes very useful. Before we go ahead, it is useful to clarify the difference between probability, odds, and chance (Box 8.1).

2.5 Diagnostic accuracy

Diagnostic accuracy is the potential of a test to correctly detect the presence or absence of disease. It also depends on the prevalence of the disease. Diagnostic accuracy is not as commonly used to describe a test evaluation as the other tests, especially in binary/dichotomous results.

$$\text{Diagnostic Accuracy} = (\text{True Positive} + \text{True Negative}/\text{All})*100$$

$$(\text{All} = \text{True Positive} + \text{True Negative} + \text{False Positive} + \text{False Negative})$$

$$\text{Diagnostic Accuracy} = (a+d/a+b+c+d)*100 \text{ (based on Table 8.1), or}$$

$$\text{Diagnostic Accuracy} = (\text{Sensitivity}*\text{Prevalence}) + \{\text{Specificity}*(1-\text{Prevalence})\}$$

$$= S_n*P + S_p*(1-P)$$

The diagnostic accuracy changes with a change in prevalence, as Table 8.3 shows. With a rise in prevalence ($S_n = 70\%$ and $S_p = 95\%$), the diagnostic accuracy drops if the test's sensitivity is lower than its specificity ($S_n < S_p$). However, if the test's sensitivity is higher than its specificity ($S_n > S_p$), the diagnostic accuracy rises with a rise in prevalence. This is distinct from PPV and NPV, as PPV always rises with a rise in prevalence of disease (and NPV always drops with a rise in prevalence), regardless of whether sensitivity or specificity is higher (Table 8.3).

Table 8.3 Prevalence and diagnostic test values.

Prevalence of disease (P)	Validity of test		Positive predictive value (PPV)	Negative predictive value (PPV)	Positive likelihood ratio (LR +)	Negative likelihood ratio (LR -)	Diagnostic accuracy
	Sensitivity (S_n)	Specificity (S_p)					
0.1%	70%	95%	1.38%	99.97%	14	0.32	94.97%
1.0%	70%	95%	12.39%	99.68%	14	0.32	94.75%
5.0%	70%	95%	42.42%	98.37%	14	0.32	93.75%
10%	70%	95%	60.87%	96.61%	14	0.32	92.50%
50%	70%	95%	93.33%	76.00%	14	0.32	82.50%
75%	70%	95%	97.67%	51.35%	14	0.32	76.25%

3. Diagnostic test evaluation: calculations

The calculation of the diagnostic test is easily done through different free online software. We use MedCalc-based screenshots in this manual (MedCalc Software, 2022). MedCalc calculates all the diagnostic tests through the 2*2 table such as Table 8.1. However, if someone is interested in calculating test values such as PPV and LR + through sensitivity and specificity, the free Diagnostic test calculator by Alan Schwartz can be used (Schwartz, 2022).

3.1 Applying diagnostic test evaluation

For the diagnostic test evaluation, the test for evaluation must ideally be compared with a gold standard test or at least an established confirmatory test. We take an example from a different setting for this application. The setting is a tertiary care hospital where the confirmatory diagnosis of this disease X is done through MRI. The MRI is both expensive and time-taking because of the patient load at the hospital. The predilection to the disease is also done through X-rays and clinical examination but ultimately the patients have to undergo an MRI. The surgery department devised a new score based on clinical examination and X-ray markers and called it Screen X scores. They want to use this score to reduce the patient load on MRI as well as expenses. For this, their screening test must have certain properties. So, the research objective is to analyze the diagnostic test evaluation of Screen X scores, as compared to MRI. Since sensitivity and specificity is a measure of concurrent validity, all the patients have to undergo both Screen X scoring as well as MRI. The results are shown in Table 8.4.

Once the table is prepared, it is easy to use any diagnostic test evaluation calculator. However, there are three important considerations:

1. All the cases must undergo both the screening test (or test for evaluation) and a confirmatory test. Remember that sensitivity and specificity are concurrent validity tests and therefore both the tests must be applied.
2. The *a, b, c, d* nomenclature (Table 8.1), depends on which cell does one name as *a, b, c, d*. As one notes, MedCalc uses different nomenclature than Table 8.1 and other epidemiology books (Porta, 2014).

Table 8.4 Diagnostic test evaluation of the research in question.

Test for evaluation—screen X scores	On the basis of confirmatory test—MRI		Total
	Disease present	*Disease absent*	
Test positive	72	96	168
Test negative	8	224	232
Total	80	320	400

3. Prevalence: The actual prevalence of the disease is extremely important for predictive values and diagnostic accuracy. The prevalence could be different than the local prevalence. In the case of our example, the prevalence is 20% (80/400). However, the local prevalence was 25%.

The steps in the application of diagnostic test evaluation are simple:

1. Open the online test calculator for diagnostic test evaluation. The MedCalc calculator is available at https://www.medcalc.org/calc/diagnostic_test.php (MedCalc Software, 2022). Fill in the boxes with the desired numbers from the study table (Table 8.4 and Fig. 8.4).

2. Enter the disease prevalence if it is different than the prevalence through the study table. In this example, it is 25% rather than 20% in the study sample.

3. Enter Test and the results are displayed in Fig. 8.5 .

3.2 Interpretation of results of diagnostic test evaluation

The results of the diagnostic test evaluation are straightforward and are shown in Fig. 8.5. A sensitivity or specificity of 80% is considered good. A likelihood ratio of >10 and <0.1 is considered good enough to rule in or rule out disease in any individual (Deeks & Altman, 2004).

The test has a high sensitivity at 90% (95% CI) and a slightly lower specificity at 70% (64.65%–74.97%). This shows that the test has reasonable concurrent validity and is a good screening test. There is a high chance that most diseased patients will be found to be positive with such a high sensitivity. Can this replace the investigative decisions on individual patients? With a negative predictive value of 95.45% (91.55%–97.60%)

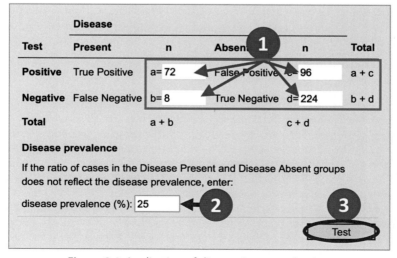

Figure 8.4 Application of diagnostic test evaluation.

Results

Statistic	Value	95% CI
Sensitivity	90.00%	81.24% to 95.58%
Specificity	70.00%	64.65% to 74.97%
Positive Likelihood Ratio	3.00	2.50 to 3.60
Negative Likelihood Ratio	0.14	0.07 to 0.28
Disease prevalence (*)	25.00%	
Positive Predictive Value (*)	50.00%	45.45% to 54.55%
Negative Predictive Value (*)	95.45%	91.55% to 97.60%
Accuracy (*)	75.00%	70.46% to 79.17%

(*) These values are dependent on disease prevalence.

Figure 8.5 Results of diagnostic test evaluation.

and a low negative likelihood at 0.14 (0.07−0.28), one thing is clear: *Those who test negative on this test are very unlikely to have the disease.* Thus, this test is the only test for patients who are negative. If the patients are negative on this test, they do not need to be referred for a confirmatory test. They can be sent home with detailed instructions for follow-up and consultation if any new symptom appears.

The test has a positive predictive value of 50% (45.45%−54.55%) with a positive likelihood ratio of 3.00 (2.50−3.60). This means that for the patients who test positive on the screening test, there is a little indication about whether they have the disease or not. They need to undergo further tests for confirmation of the disease. The results could be described as follows:

Screen X scores were evaluated for its screening and diagnostic test evaluation with MRI as a confirmatory test for disease X. The local prevalence of 25% was used as prevalence for predictive scores. MedCalc software was used for the estimation. The sensitivity, specificity and diagnostic accuracy were found to be 90% (81.24−95.58%), 70.00% (64.65−74.97%) and 75.00 (70.46−79.17%). The predictive values were higher for negative tests, with a negative predictive value at 95.45% (91.55−97.60%) and a positive predictive value at 50% (45.45%−54.55%). Further, with a likelihood ratio of 0.14 (0.07−0.28) for negative and 3.00 (2.50−3.60) for positive, the test stands as a good screening test and a negative test is strong enough to rule out the presence of the disease. However, a positive test must be confirmed through further investigations. Given the expenses and burden of the confirmatory test, Screen X should be used to test the patients as a screening tool and only positive ones may be sent for the confirmatory test (MRI).

4. Combining screening tests

In a world with imperfect tests where sensitivity and specificity is <100%, we require more decisive tests. Fortunately, two tests may be combined to improve sensitivity and specificity. This application is very useful in diagnosing conditions such as HIV/AIDS, where the screening test (based on ELISA) is nonexpensive, less resource intensive, and more accessible than the confirmatory test (based on Western Blot). Combining tests is done through two methods: series and parallel testing (Table 8.5). In series testing, one test is done first and then any other tests are done. This is done to improve specificity. In parallel testing, all the tests are done simultaneously and decisions are taken after the combined results are available. This is done to improve sensitivity.

Operationally series testing is considered more efficient as further tests are done only on the basis of the first test results, and not all the patients usually undergo the next test. For example, in HIV/AIDS diagnosis, the first test assay is a series test. If the first test assay is negative, the patient is given a negative report because the test has a high sensitivity, negative predictive value, and negative likelihood. In other words, it is a very good screening test where those who are negative are extremely unlikely to be diseased. However, if someone tests positive, they are sent for the second test assay. If the patient is positive in the second assay, the patient is reported as HIV/AIDS positive. By combining the positivity in both the tests, the combined specificity as well as positive predictive value increases. If someone tests negative in the second assay results, they undergo the third assay for the final report. Based on the protocol of the National AIDS Control Organization (National AIDS Control Organization (NACO), 2021), HIV/AIDS diagnosis strategy discussed earlier is shown in Fig. 8.6. While conceptually the tests are interpreted in this fashion, practically in NACO centers the first two kits are used simultaneously and the third kit is used only if needed.

Parallel testing is done when the clinician has two or more tests but without a very good sensitivity. To improve sensitivity, the clinician has to do all the tests at once and the combined specificity increases.

Calculating the combined sensitivity and specificity of series and parallel tests can be done through online tools such as epitools (Epitools, 2022). In series testing, the combined sensitivity is a product of the individual sensitivity of the two tests. In parallel

Table 8.5 Series and parallel testing.

S. No.	Test	Series testing	Parallel testing
1.	Test strategy	Sequential	Simultaneous
2.	Timing	One-by-one	All-at-one
3.	Effect on combined sensitivity	Decreases	Increases
4.	Effect on combined specificity	Increases	Decreases
5.	Operational efficiency	More efficient	Less efficient
6.	Overall cost	Lower	Higher

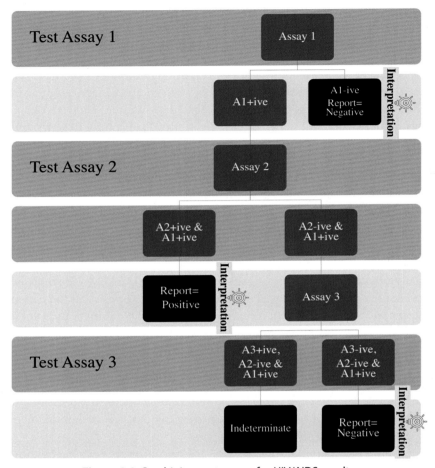

Figure 8.6 Combining test assays for HIV/AIDS results.

testing, the combined specificity is a product of the individual specificity of the tests. Therefore, in series testing sensitivity reduces, and in parallel specificity reduces. However, the focus of parallel tests is to improve sensitivity and for series, tests are to improve specificity. The formula for calculation is given in the following.

$$\text{Sensitivity in series} = \text{Sensitivity } 1 * \text{Sensitivity } 2 \text{ or,}$$

$$S_n\text{series} = S_{n1} * S_{n2}$$

$$\text{Sensitivity in parallel} = [\{1 - (1 - \text{Sensitivity1})\} * (1 - \text{Sensitivity2})] \text{ or,}$$

$$S_n\text{parallel} = [\{1 - (1 - S_{n1})\} * (1 - S_{n2})]$$

$$\text{Sensitivity in series} = [\{1 - (1 - \text{Sensitivity1})\} * (1 - \text{Sensitivity2})] \text{ or,}$$

$$S_p \text{series} = \left[\{1-(1-S_{p1})\}^* (1-S_{p2})\right]$$

$$\text{Specificity in parallel} = \text{Specificity } 1^* \text{ Specificity 2 or,}$$

$$S_p \text{ parallel} = S_{p1}^* S_{p2}$$

5. Continuous data and ROC curves

The diagnostic accuracy to differentiate diseased from normal in continuous data is evaluated through receiver operating characteristic (ROC) curve. Interpreting a dichotomous test such as test positive and test negative is straightforward. However, when the data are quantitative or even ordinal, the cut-off value for positivity affects sensitivity and specificity. Given the inverse relationship between sensitivity and specificity, an increase in sensitivity reduces specificity and vice versa. In such cases, the receiver operating characteristic curve is a beneficial tool used in health research. It is useful in predictions such as whether this cancer biomarker predicts cancer. If it does, at what value should be the cut-off point for positivity?

5.1 Understanding the ROC curve

Use of the ROC curve dates back to Second World War when radar operators were used to predict enemy objects (true positive result) or noise (false positive result). A long way since, it has been used in multiple fields including health research. ROC is a graphical representation that plots the true positive rate (sensitivity) against the false positive rate (1—specificity) at different threshold settings (Fig. 8.7). This helps to determine the

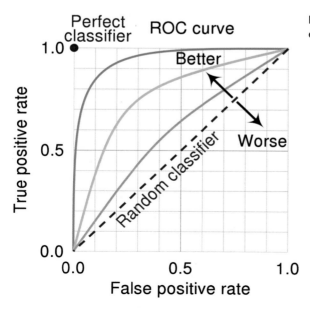

Figure 8.7 ROC curve versus random classifier.

cut-off value with optimum sensitivity and specificity. Another important aspect is the area under the curve (AUC). The AUC signifies the discriminating ability of the predictor in identifying the diseased state with the nondiseased. If the AUC is 0.5, then it means that the predictability is 50%, that is this predictor predicts disease versus nondisease 50% of the time. Predictability of 50% is worthless as even random probability between two events is 50% (disease vs. nondisease event). The curve starts becoming better as it moves toward the left as the true positive rate increases and the false positive rate decreases. The perfect classification is at a true positive rate of 1.0 with a false positive rate of 0.0 and an AUC of 1 (100%). However, it remains an ideal state as such a prediction is impossible in the real world.

5.1.1 Area under curve

The AUC provides useful information on diagnostic accuracy. The value of AUC ranges from 0 (perfectly inaccurate test) to 1 (perfectly accurate) and a value of 0.5 suggests no discrimination (Mandrekar, 2010). A 100% area under the curve has a value of 1 which means that the test can classify accurately 100% of the time. Needless to say, this never happens in real-world settings. A value of 0.5 is no better than random guessing as any random guesser would guess correctly among two options (disease or no disease) 50% of the time. An interpretative guideline for AUC indicates that an AUC of 0.7−0.8 is acceptable, 0.8−0.9 is excellent, and >0.9 is outstanding (Hosmer et al., 2013). The significance value of the AUC is also important. The software results mention the AUC with its significance or P-value calculated against a null hypothesis that the AUC is no better than a random classifier (H_0:AUC $= 0.5$). Sometimes, two or more screening tests need to be compared to find which AUC is better. This can be easily done through a ROC curve that plots and analyses them together.

5.1.2 Criteria for cut-off value

In most cases, choosing an appropriate cut-off value is very important for further analysis of test results. It is often based on sensitivity and specificity, and giving preference to one compromises the other. As the ROC curve plots Sensitivity against 1−Specificity, ROC curve analysis is helpful in locating the cut-off point. While both are important, the relative importance of sensitivity and specificity depends on the context of its application. In cases where the disease is dangerous or critical, sensitivity may be more important than specificity. The cut-off decision is usually based on one of the following points:

1. The cut-off point is when the sensitivity is equivalent to the specificity: Most frequently, this is an easy way to choose the cut-off value. It is one of the frequently used values (Fig. 8.8). On the ROC curve, this point intersects the perpendicular drawn from the diagonal reference line to the left upper corner (True positive rate-1.0). It can also be chosen from the table of coordinate points of ROC as we shall see later.

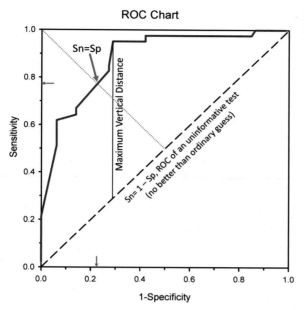

Figure 8.8 Identifying the cut-off value in an ROC curve.

2. Youden's index: Youden's index (*J*) is a point on the ROC curve with the highest vertical distance from the 45 degrees diagonal line and is calculated as, *J* = Sensitivity + Specificity—1. It measures the effectiveness of a diagnostic test as well as an optimal threshold value (the cutoff point) for the test. One disadvantage in using Youden's index as the cut-off point is that it automatically prefers sensitivity or specificity values with a higher score.

5.2 Applying the ROC curve

Before applying the ROC curve through SPSS, we must check for the main assumption. The "state" variable, which classifies the subjects into two groups (diseased/nondiseased) must be independent of the test of interest. The test measure is continuous and the state variable is a binary (nominal) variable.

For the application of ROC curve, we use a dataset (*8. Organ Failure.sav*) which measured bedside Index for severity in acute pancreatitis score (BISAP) to predict organ failure. The research question focuses on whether BISAP can predict organ failure or not.

The steps in the application of the ROC curve are as follows:

1. Open data file *8. Organ Failure.sav* and go to *Analyze > Classify > ROC Curve* (Fig. 8.9).
2. In the *ROC Curve* box > transfer *Bedside Index for severity in Acute Pancreatitis score (BISAP)* to *test variable* and> *Organ Failure* to *State variable*. The value of the *State variable* should be "*2*" as 2 codes for *Organ Failure* (the state we are interested in, 1 stands for no organ failure).

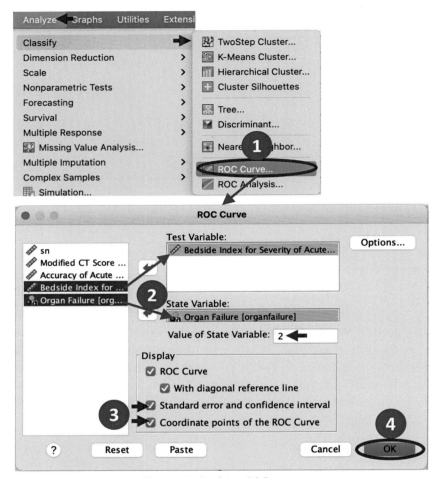

Figure 8.9 Applying ROC curve.

3. In the display tick all the options—*ROC Curve* (With diagonal reference line), *Standard error and confidence interval*, and *Coordinate points* of the ROC Curve.

4. Click *OK* to obtain the results.

5.3 Interpretation of the results of the ROC curve

The results of the ROC curve have four parts—the first is the case processing summary, followed by the ROC curve, the area under the curve, and the coordinates of the curve (Fig. 8.10).

1. ROC curve: As we can see, the curve is above the diagonal reference line. The Area under the curve shows that the Area is 0.89 (95% CI: 0.82—0.96). As discussed earlier, as per the interpretative guideline for AUC, an AUC of 0.7—0.8 is acceptable, 0.8—0.9 is excellent, and >0.9 is outstanding (Hosmer et al., 2013). Thus, the AUC is excellent. It is also significant with a *P*-value <.001.

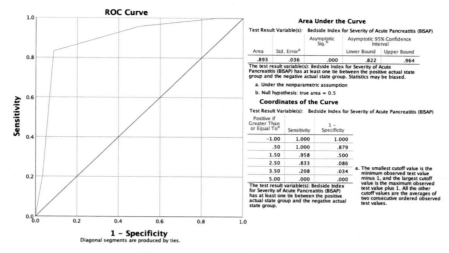

Figure 8.10 Results of ROC curve.

Table 8.6 Specificity and Youden's index from coordinates of the curve.

BISAP score	Sensitivity	1 - specificity	Specificity	Youden's index, $J = S_n + S_p - 1$
−1.00	1.000	1.000	0	0
0.50	1.000	0.879	0.121	0.121
1.50	0.958	0.500	0.500	0.458
2.50	0.833	0.086	0.914	0.747
3.50	0.208	0.034	0.966	0.174
5.00	0.000	0.000	1.000	0

2. **Cut-off value**: The cut-off value can be analyzed from the third table coordinates of the curve. Finding the right balance with good sensitivity and specificity is important. The Youden's index can also be calculated (Table 8.6). Sensitivity and specificity above 0.75 (75%) are reasonable. As we can see in Table 8.6, at the BISAP value of 2.50, the sensitivity is 0.83 and the specificity is 0.91. This is good sensitivity and specificity and aligns with Youden's index of 0.75. Moreover, any point below and beyond compromises either sensitivity or specificity. Please note that Youden's index is best used according to the situation.

Thus, the final result could be written as follows:

The Bedside Index for severity in Acute Pancreatitis score (BISAP) was analyzed to predict organ failure. The ROC curve for BISAP can be seen in Fig. 8.10 . The area under the curve was excellent with an area of 0.89 (95% CI: 0.82-0.96) and was significant with a p-value <0.001. The BISAP value at 2.50 was a good cut-off point with a sensitivity of 0.83 and a specificity of 0.91.

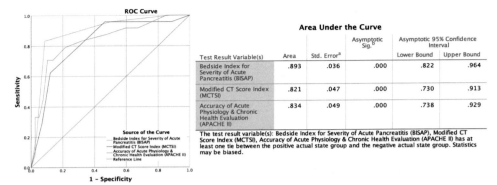

Figure 8.11 Comparing ROC curves and areas under the curve for multiple test variables.

5.4 Comparing multiple ROC curves

A similar procedure can be used to test more than one test variable. In the dataset (*8. Organ Failure.sav*), there are two other such scores besides BISAP. One is the modified computed tomography scan score index (MCTSI) and the other is Accuracy of Acute Physiology and Chronic Health Evaluation (APACHE II). We can use the same procedure for applying ROC with all three—BISAP, MCTSI, and APACHE II as test variables. All the results can then be compared. In Fig. 8.11, the ROC curve and area under the curve results are shown.

The interpretation of results is done similarly. As we can see from the ROC curve as well as the table of area under the curve, BISAP is the best predictor of organ failure with an area of 0.89 (0.82−0.96) followed by APACHE II at 0.83 (0.74−0.93), and, MCTSI at 0.82 (0.73−0.91). Additionally, the coordinates can be used to find cut-off values for each test variable.

References

Abramson, J., & Abramson, Z. H. (2011). *Research methods in community medicine: Surveys, epidemiological research, programme evaluation, clinical trials.* John Wiley & Sons.

Deeks, J. J., & Altman, D. G. (2004). Diagnostic tests 4: Likelihood ratios. *BMJ, 329*(7458), 168−169. https://doi.org/10.1136/bmj.329.7458.168

Epitools. (2022). *Diagnostic test evaluation and comparison.* https://epitools.ausvet.com.au/twoteststwo.

Fulton, L. V., Mendez, F. A., Bastian, N. D., & Musal, R. M. (2012). Confusion between odds and probability, a Pandemic? *Journal of Statistics Education, 20*(3). https://doi.org/10.1080/10691898.2012.11889647

Hiebert, J., Zubach, V., Charlton, C. L., Fenton, J., Tipples, G. A., Fonseca, K., & Severinia, A. (2021). Evaluation of diagnostic accuracy of eight commercial assays for the detection of measles virus-specific IgM antibodies. *Journal of Clinical Microbiology, 59*(6). https://doi.org/10.1128/JCM.03161-20

Hosmer, D. W., Jr., Lemeshow, S., & Sturdivant, R. X. (2013). *Applied logistic regression* (Vol 398). John Wiley & Sons.

Mandrekar, J. N. (2010). Receiver operating characteristic curve in diagnostic test assessment. *Journal of Thoracic Oncology, 5*(9), 1315−1316. https://doi.org/10.1097/JTO.0b013e3181ec173d

MedCalc Software. (2022). *MedCalc's diagnostic test evaluation calculator. MedCalc. Version 20.110.* https://www.medcalc.org/calc/diagnostic_test.php.

National AIDS Control Organization (NACO). (2021). *National guidelines for HIV care and Treatment.* National AIDS Control Organization. http://naco.gov.in/sites/default/files/National_Guidelines_for_HIV_Care_and_Treatment_2021.pdf.

Porta, M. (2014). *A dictionary of epidemiology.* Oxford University Press.

Schwartz, A. (2022). *Diagnostic test calculator (version 2010042101).* http://araw.mede.uic.edu/cgi-bin/test-calc.pl?DT=70&Dt=30&dT=45&dt=855&2x2=Compute.

Webb, M. P. K., & Sidebotham, D. (2020). Bayes' formula: A powerful but counterintuitive tool for medical decision-making. *BJA Education, 20*(6), 208–213. https://doi.org/10.1016/j.bjae.2020.03.002

CHAPTER 9

Reliability and agreement*

Our main business of life is not to see what lies dimly at a distance, but to do what lies clearly at hand

Thomas Carlyle.

1. Reliability and agreement

Reliability testing and agreement testing are integral to health research. The main objective of a research study could be to measure the reliability or agreement between raters using any instruments. While raters could be two or more individuals, instruments could mean tools/devices/methods/techniques. We will use the word instruments for the sake of brevity. For example, reliability and agreement between two independent raters of facial asymmetry after cosmetic dental surgery or two raters of hypopigmentation after using a cream. Apart from the main objective, reliability and agreement are also used as quality control to test consistency between two raters in larger diagnostic accuracy studies, clinical trials, epidemiological, or even patient satisfaction surveys (Kottner et al., 2011). For example, in an interventional trial for improvement in facial asymmetry, testing the three raters for reliability and agreement on the same set of subjects is a prerequisite.

1.1 Validity and reliability

There is a clear distinction between validity and reliability (Fig. 9.1). In measurement, validity is how well a measurement measures what it intends to measure. In this sense, validity is akin to accuracy. Whereas reliability refers to the stability or consistency of information, and is similar to reproducibility/repeatability (Abramson & Abramson, 2011). In this sense, reliability is akin to precision. While we use the dart example to explain validity and reliability, it is important to emphasize that without high reliability, a measure cannot have high validity as highlighted in Box 9.1 (Abramson & Abramson, 2011).

1.2 Reliability versus agreement

While reliability is often used synonymously with agreement; technically, they are different in meaning (Fig. 9.2). The proposed Guidelines for Reporting Reliability and Agreement Studies define the two concepts (Kottner et al., 2011):

---

*For datasets, please refer to companion site: https://www.elsevier.com/books-and-journals/book-companion/9780443185502

Biostatistics Manual for Health Research
ISBN 978-0-443-18550-2, https://doi.org/10.1016/B978-0-443-18550-2.00004-9

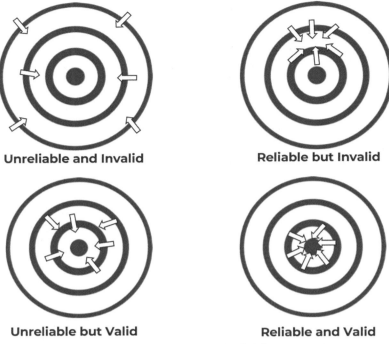

Unreliable and Invalid   **Reliable but Invalid**

Unreliable but Valid   **Reliable and Valid**

Figure 9.1 Validity and reliability.

BOX 9.1 Unreliable but valid?

The bull's eye figures demonstrate an example of valid (accurate) but unreliable measures. However, in truth, if the reliability is low, the measure cannot have high validity. Similarly, technically speaking, a measure with low reliability cannot have a good agreement.

Reliability: The ability of a measurement to differentiate between subjects or objects. In simpler terms, this is the capability of a rater or instrument to replicate the same order when measured twice on the same respondents (Berchtold, 2016).

Agreement: The degree to which scores or ratings are identical. In simpler terms, this is the capability of a measure/test to provide strictly identical results when measured twice on the same respondents (Berchtold, 2016).

While conceptually they are distinct, they are often used synonymously in health research. Specifically, reliability is a necessary but not sufficient condition to demonstrate agreement (Berchtold, 2016). This is also true for validity and reliability. Without a high reliability, a measure cannot have high validity (Abramson & Abramson, 2011). While

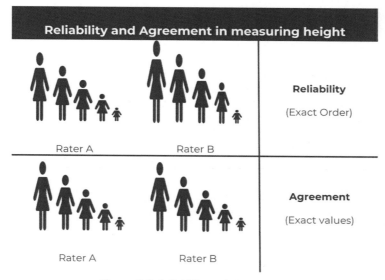

Figure 9.2 Reliability and agreement.

reliability and agreement can be used interchangeably, the problem arises when it is used in longitudinal studies. If the measurement error is larger than the change we want to detect, the measurement tool needs not only reliability but also agreement (Guyatt et al., 1987). Such a problem is uncommon in day-to-day research.

It is important to note that reliability and agreement are not necessarily static and may be affected by sources of variability other than the rater or instrument. These sources of variability during measurement could be (1) sample characteristics, (2) type and use of measurement/rating tool, (3) characteristics of the sample, (4) characteristics of the rater, and (5) statistical approaches including assumptions of the measurement levels and statistical models (Kottner et al., 2011). Therefore, sufficient information on the study design and conduct is vital along with a strictly documented protocol on the use of study tools with clear operational definitions.

1.3 Types of reliability

Reliability measures could be of different types on the basis of differences in raters or time (situation). Broadly, it is of two types—intrarater agreement/reliability and interrater agreement/reliability. The types of reliability are defined as follows:

Interrater reliability: Reliability between different raters assessing the same subjects.

Intrarater reliability: Reliability between the same raters assessing them at two different times (or situations).

Test—retest reliability: Same as intrarater reliability. However, the term is often restricted for use in instruments and not raters (Koo & Li, 2016).

2. Reliability methods for categorical variables

Reliability and agreement are measured through different methods depending on the type of outcome variable and number of raters. If the outcome is categorical (nominal), kappa (κ) test is used to measure agreement. If there are only two raters to be compared, Cohen's kappa (κ) test is used, whereas Fleiss kappa (κ) test is used when there is a comparison among more than two raters. If the outcome variable is ordinal and has to be compared with two raters, then Cohen's weighted kappa test is used. However, Fleiss' kappa (κ) test is valid for both nominal and ordinal tests when more than two raters are compared (Table 9.1).

If the outcome is continuous, the intraclass correlation coefficient (ICC) is used to assess agreement when there are two or more independent raters. The other most commonly used statistical test for reliability analysis is Cronbach's alpha (α). When there

Table 9.1 Methods to measure reliability in categorical variables.

S. No.	Objective	Scale	Applicable test
1.	Agreement between two raters (interrater reliability)	Nominal	Cohen's κ
2.	Agreement between the same rater at two different times/situations (intrarater reliability)	Nominal	Cohen's κ
3.	Agreement between the same instrument at two different times/situations (test—retest reliability)	Nominal	Cohen's κ
4.	Agreement between two raters (interrater reliability)	Ordinal	Weighted Cohen's κ
5.	Agreement between the same rater at two different times/situations (intrarater reliability)	Ordinal	Weighted Cohen's κ
6.	Agreement between the same instrument at two different times/situations (test—retest reliability)	Ordinal	Weighted Cohen's κ
7.	Agreement between >2 raters (interrater reliability)	Nominal/ordinal	Fleiss κ
8.	Agreement between the same rater at >2 different times/situations (intrarater reliability)	Nominal/ordinal	Fleiss κ
9.	Agreement between the same instrument at >2 different times/situations (test—retest reliability)	Nominal/ordinal	Fleiss κ

is a set of questions that measure different aspects of a composite variable such as quality of life, Cronbach's α helps in testing the reliability of this set of questions. It thus measures internal consistency. Table 9.1 highlights the methods to measure reliability in different circumstances.

3. Cohen's kappa test

Jacob Cohen introduced Cohen's kappa as a coefficient of agreement for nominal scales in 1960 (Cohen, 1960). Fleiss kappa, introduced later by Joseph L. Fleiss, is applicable for nominal as well as ordinal scales when >2 raters need to be compared for reliability. Whenever kappa is written alone, it stands for Cohen's kappa test. Kappa test coefficient calculates the misclassifications (differently rated) variables for the same set of patients. Kappa does not give any information on the source of misclassification/disagreement and is seldom comparable across diverse settings. Hence contextual information, strict protocol, and study design are of vital importance.

3.1 Assumption of Cohen's kappa test

The main assumption of the kappa test is that both the raters are independent of each other. As discussed earlier, any other source that could cause variability other than the raters in question, should be controlled. A clear protocol on the use of study tools and rating categories with clear operational definitions is a must. Kappa is written as κ.

Cohen's kappa test works in the following settings:

- The *outcome variable* is nominal with mutual exclusivity in categorization (either this or that—anemia or no-anemia).
- The *independent variable* or observations should be paired, that is, the ratings should be compared with the same set of patients. The observations should be independent and no rater should be able to influence each other while rating.
- The *subcategories of rating should be the same* for both raters. For example, if one rates in anemia and no-anemia (2 variables), the other should also rate in the same two variables (2 × 2 symmetricity). Similarly, if the subcategories are anemia, no-anemia, and polycythemia, then both raters should rate in the three subcategories (3 × 3 symmetricity).

3.2 Applying Cohen's kappa test

For the application of *Cohen's kappa test,* we take a dataset from a cosmetic dentistry Outpatient Department (OPD) screening. The screening of patients is done for facial asymmetry for patients for further referral. There are two raters who rate the patients in three nominal categories—facial asymmetry present, absent or undecided. As mentioned, both the raters have been thoroughly trained on the three categories and how to rate them. All the patients sit in a fixed position with the head in normal anatomical position, centric occlusion, and lips in the resting stage.

Research Question: Is there an agreement between Rater A and B on the facial asymmetry of patients? The dataset we use is named as *9. Kappa.sav*. The question can be tested based on the values of kappa and the following hypothesis could be used.

H_0: There is no agreement between Rater A and Rater B in detecting facial asymmetry in patients.

H_A: There is an agreement between Rater A and Rater B in detecting facial asymmetry in patients.

Steps in the application of Cohen's kappa test are as follows:

1. Open data file (*9. Kappa.sav*). Go to Analyze > Descriptive Statistics > Crosstabs (Fig. 9.3).
2. In the *Crosstabs* box, choose Row(s) > *Rater A* and Column(s) > *Rater B*.
3. Click *Statistics*, and a new dialog box named Crosstabs: Statistics opens up. Select *Kappa* in the Crosstabs: Statistics box.
4. We get the results after clicking *Continue* in the Crosstabs: Statistics box, followed by OK in the Crosstabs box.

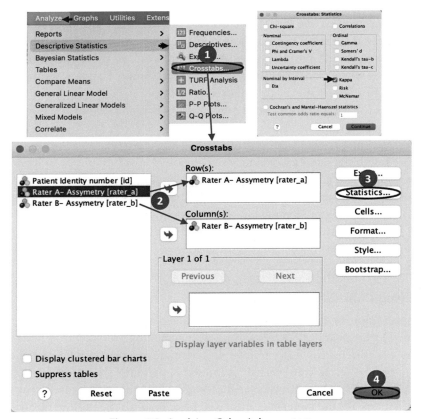

Figure 9.3 Applying Cohen's kappa test.

3.3 Interpretation of results of Cohen's kappa test

Kappa test has two important features: one is its significance and the other is its strength.

1. There are two tables of interest in the resulting output of Cohen's kappa test (Fig. 9.4): (1) Crosstabulation, (2) Symmetric measures.
2. Crosstabulation: This explains the statistics of individual ratings. Both raters agreed in most instances of Facial asymmetry with agreement on the presence of facial asymmetry in 46 cases, absence of facial asymmetry in 39 cases, and undecided in 5 cases. Thus, in 90/120 cases, the raters were in agreement.
3. The second table shows the symmetric measures and the results of the kappa test. The test statistic, that is, kappa $\kappa = 0.57$ with an asymptotic standard error of 0.06 and a P-value of $<.001$, which is significant. Thus, the null hypothesis is rejected; there is an agreement between rater A and B in detecting facial asymmetry in patients.
4. The other important point is the strength of this agreement. The $\kappa = 0.57$. There are many guidelines for the interpretation of strength, any of which may be followed. We will follow the guidelines as shown in Table 9.2 (Landis & Koch, 1977). As per the guidelines, this is a moderate agreement. One must note that to suggest a new screening tool/test/score to replace a standard/established tool/test/score source, we should prefer the coefficient to be at least 0.8 or more.
5. Thus, the null hypothesis is rejected, and the results can be written as follows. *The rating for the presence of facial asymmetry was compared between Rater A and B. Both raters agreed with their assessment of facial asymmetry in 90 out of 120 subjects, with the agreement of presence in 46 cases, absence in 39 cases, and undecided in 5 cases. On applying Cohen's kappa test, there was a moderate agreement which was significant, $\kappa = 0.57$, $P < .001$.*

Rater A– Assymetry * Rater B– Assymetry Crosstabulation

		Rater B– Assymetry			
		Facial Assymetry present	Facial Assymetry absent	Facial Assymetry undecided	Total
Rater A– Assymetry	Facial Assymetry present	46	20	1	67
	Facial Assymetry absent	1	39	2	42
	Facial Assymetry undecided	1	5	5	11
Total		48	64	8	120

Symmetric Measures

		Value	Asymptotic Standard Error[a]	Approximate T[b]	Approximate Significance
Measure of Agreement	Kappa	.572	.063	7.993	.000
N of Valid Cases		120			

a. Not assuming the null hypothesis.

b. Using the asymptotic standard error assuming the null hypothesis.

Figure 9.4 Results of Cohen's kappa test.

Table 9.2 Interpreting the strength of agreement.

κ value	Interpretation
<0.20	Poor agreement
0.21—0.40	Fair agreement
0.41—0.60	Moderate agreement
0.61—0.80	Good agreement
0.81—1.00	Very good agreement

To suggest a new screening tool/test/score against an established source the κ should be at least 0.8.

4. Weighted Cohen's kappa test

Cohen's kappa test measures agreement through differences in classifications between the two raters. In nominal variables such as the one above, any misclassification (whether 1 is rated 2 or 3), does not make a difference as the variables are nominal in nature. However, if the variables are ordinal, there is an inherent ranking or order between them. In ordinal variables, if 1 is graded as 2, this misclassification is not as bad as 1 categorized as 3. In other words, the level of individual disagreements is different in weightage. Hence, in ordinally graded measures of agreement, Cohen's kappa should not be used.

For ordinal variables agreement between two raters (interrater reliability) and between the same raters/instruments at two different times/situations (intrarater reliability or test—retest reliability), weighted Cohen's kappa test can be used (Table 9.1).

4.1 Assumption of weighted Cohen's kappa test

The main assumption of the kappa test, or any test of agreement, is that both the raters are independent of each other. As discussed above, any other source that could cause variability other than the raters in question should be controlled. A clear protocol on the use of study tools and rating categories with clear operational definitions is a must. Kappa is written as κ.

The weighted Cohen's kappa test works in the following settings:
- The *outcome variable* is ordinal.
- The *independent variable* or observations should be paired, that is, the ratings should be compared with the same set of patients. The observations should be independent and no rater should be able to influence each other while rating.
- The *subcategories of rating should be same* for both raters. For example, if one rates in anemia and no-anemia (2 variables), the other should also rate in 2 variables (2×2 symmetricity). Similarly, if the subcategories are anemia, no-anemia, and polycythemia, then both raters should rate in the three subcategories (3×3 symmetricity).

4.2 Applying weighted Cohen's kappa test

For the application of *Cohen's kappa test,* we take a dataset that compares pathology labs. Both pathology labs have graded the same tissue specimen in Grade 1, 2, 3, 4, and 5 based on a qualitative judgment of pathologists. Please note that the categorical grades are ordinal.

Research Question: Is there an agreement between the first and second pathology labs in grading the same tissue specimens? The dataset we use is named *9. Weighted Kappa.sav.* The question can be tested based on the values of kappa and the following hypothesis could be used.

H_0: There is no agreement between the first and second pathology laboratory in the grading of tissue specimens.

H_A: There is an agreement between the first and second pathology laboratory in the grading of tissue specimens.

4.2.1 Applying weighted Cohen's kappa test in SPSS version 27 and above

Steps for applying weighted Cohen's kappa are simple in SPSS version 27 and beyond.
1. Open data file (*9. Weighted Kappa.sav*). Go to *Analyze > Scale > Weighted Kappa.*
2. In the Weighted Kappa Box, select the variables to be tested in Pairwise raters. (patho_1 and patho_2).
3. Click Criteria, and a new dialog box named Weighted Kappa: Criteria opens up.
4. Select Linear Weights in the Weighted Kappa: Criteria box.
5. We get the results after clicking Continue in the Weighted Kappa: Criteria box, followed by OK in the Crosstabs box.
6. The results are similarly interpreted as they are for Cohen's kappa test. The only difference is that the weightage type must also be mentioned while writing about Cohen's kappa test.

4.2.2 Applying weighted Cohen's kappa test in SPSS version 26 and below

In SPSS 26, which is used in this book, weighting has to be done by creating a new variable for weighting cases. Steps in application of weighted Cohen's kappa test in SPSS version 26 or below can be divided into 1. Calculating weights, 2. Creating weight variable, 3. Applying weight and 4. Cohen's kappa analysis on weight dataset.

4.2.3 Calculating weights

In SPSS 26, which is used in this book, weighting can be done by creating a new variable for weighting cases. Applying weights helps us in giving relative weightage to the misclassifications in ordinal data. For example, grading 5 as 1 is considered worse than grading 5 as 4. Through weighting, such misclassifications are accorded relative importance in terms of their degree of misclassification. There are two types of weighting:

(1) linear weights and (2) quadratic weights. If the misclassification does not differentiate between lower and higher levels, then linear weights should be used. For example, if there is no difference between 1 graded as 2 or 4 graded as 5 (because the difference is 1), linear weights are applicable. However, if there is a difference, which means that misclassification at higher levels is considered more severe, then quadratic weights should be used. For example, 1 graded as 2 might be less severe than 4 graded as 5 (Such that stage 5 signifies an extremely fatal and incurable stage!). Quadratic weights accord higher importance and penalize harder at higher level misclassifications.

In the research question discussed earlier, the misclassifications are not more severe at higher levels and linear weights are applicable. As discussed, we need to calculate weights. The calculation of linear weights is done by the formula, $w_i = 1 - [i/(k - 1)]$; whereas, for quadratic weights the formula is $w_i = 1 - [i^2/(k - 1)^2]$. In the formulae, k stands for the number of categories and i for the disagreement difference. As the grades are from 1 to 5 in our question, the number of categories is 5. The calculation of the weights is shown in Table 9.3.

4.2.4 Creating the weight variable

Just beside the desired variables to be compared, the weights should be entered in a new variable. There are many ways to do this. One way is to compute a new variable (patho_1–patho_2) or look at the disagreements directly. Depending on the disagreement, enter the adequate weightage. If there is no disagreement, enter 1, if the difference is 2, enter 0.75, and so on as per Table 9.3.

Steps in creation of weights and selecting weighted data (Fig. 9.5):

1. Open the data file (*9. Weighted Kappa.sav*) and start entering the weights as per calculation (Table 9.3). We are using linear weights and since the absolute difference between two observations for serial no 1 case is 3 (1−4), enter 0.25 in the first row, as calculated in Table 9.3.
2. Finish all the entries based on the disagreement difference and weights calculated in Table 9.3. You can use *Compute Variable* function from the *Transform* tab for calculating absolute difference and then *Replace* function from the *Edit* tab, replacing difference with weights as per calculation in Table 9.3.

Table 9.3 Calculating linear and quadratic weights.

Difference in grading score between graders	Linear weight, $w_i = 1 - [i/(k - 1)]$	Quadratic weight, scores $w_i = 1 - [i^2/(k - 1)^2]$
0	$1 - [0/(5 - 1)] = 1$	$1 - [0^2/(5 - 1)^2] = 1$
1	$1 - [1/(5 - 1)] = 0.75$	$1 - [1^2/(5 - 1)^2] = 0.9375$
2	$1 - [2/(5 - 1)] = 0.5$	$1 - [2^2/(5 - 1)^2] = 0.75$
3	$1 - [3/(5 - 1)] = 0.25$	$1 - [3^2/(5 - 1)^2] = 0.4375$
4 (5 is graded as 1 by other)	$1 - [4/(5 - 1)] = 0$	$1 - [4^2/(5 - 1)^2] = 0$

	serno	patho_1	patho_2	Diff_1.2	Weight exercise	weight_lin
1	1	1	4	3	.25	.25
2	3	1	1		.	1.00
3	5	2	2	|patho_1 – patho_2|	1.00
4	7	2	2	.	.	1.00
5	9	3	2	.	.	.75
6	2	3	3	.	.	1.00
7	4	4	4	.	.	1.00
8	6	4	4	.	.	1.00
9	8	5	5	.	.	1.00
10	13	5	5	.	.	1.00
11	15	1	1	.	.	1.00
12	17	1	1	.	.	1.00
13	19	2	2	.	.	1.00
14	10	2	4	.	.	.50
15	11	3	3	.	.	1.00

Figure 9.5 Creating weight variable.

3. Make adequate changes in the data view such as name (weight_lin), label (linear weights), and measure (scale).
   Note: For ease, we have provided a readymade weight variable as the last column.

4.2.5 Applying weights
Steps in applying weights:
1. Open the data file (*9. Weighted Kappa.sav*). Go to *Data > Weight Cases* (Fig. 9.6).
2. In the Weight Cases box > Select Weight cases by, and transfer Linear Weights (weight_lin) under the Frequency variable. Click OK.

4.2.6 Applying Cohen's kappa test
The steps in the application of Cohen's kappa test are already shown in (Fig. 9.3).
1. After opening the data file, Go to *Analyze > Descriptive Statistics > Crosstabs*.
2. In the Crosstabs box, choose Row(s) > Patho_1 and Column(s) > patho_2.
3. Click Statistics, and a new dialog box named Crosstabs: Statistics opens up.
4. Select *Kappa* in the Crosstabs: Statistics box.
5. We get the results after clicking *Continue* in the Crosstabs: Statistics box, followed by OK in the Crosstabs box.

4.3 Interpretation of results of weighted Cohen's kappa test
Before we interpret the weighted kappa test, we must reensure that the data weighting has been applied before applying kappa test. While the kappa test outputs do not show

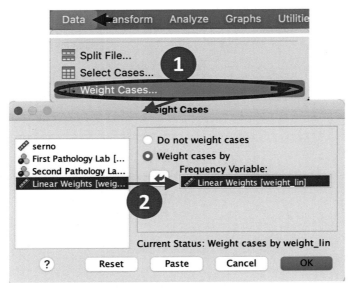

Figure 9.6 Applying weights.

whether it was weighted or not but a look at the crosstabulation results (Fig. 9.7) provides an idea. Kappa test has two important features: one is its significance and the other is its strength.

1. The two tables of interest in the result output of weighted Cohen's kappa test (Fig. 9.7) are 1. Crosstabulation, 2. Symmetric measures.

First Pathology Lab * Second Pathology Lab Crosstabulation

		Second Pathology Lab					
		1	2	3	4	5	Total
First Pathology Lab	1	3	0	0	0	0	3
	2	0	3	0	1	0	4
	3	0	1	3	0	0	4
	4	0	0	1	3	0	4
	5	0	0	0	0	3	3
Total		3	4	4	4	3	18

Symmetric Measures

		Value	Asymptotic Standard Error[a]	Approximate T[b]	Approximate Significance
Measure of Agreement	Kappa	.791	.111	6.661	.000
N of Valid Cases		18			

a. Not assuming the null hypothesis.

b. Using the asymptotic standard error assuming the null hypothesis.

Figure 9.7 Results of Cohen's kappa test.

2. Crosstabulation: This explains the statistics of weighted individual ratings. We can easily check whether the data is weighted or not by looking at this table. The total is only 18, instead of 20. This is due to differential ratings for misclassification, the total disagreements are rated as 0.

3. Both raters agreed completely in 15 cases and mildly disagreed in 3 cases. This much can be ascertained from the crosstabulation table, but we can't comment on the total disagreements as they are rated as 0 on weighting (considered nonagreement). Given the total number shown in crosstabulation as 18 instead of 20, one can presume that in two cases there was a total disagreement in ratings.

4. The second table shows the Symmetric measures and the results of the kappa test. The test statistic, kappa is, $\kappa = 0.79$ with an asymptotic standard error of 0.11 and a P-value of $<.001$, which is significant. Thus, the null hypothesis is rejected; there is an agreement between the first and second pathology labs in the grading of tissue specimens. The strength of this agreement as per the guidelines shown in Table 9.2 (Bartko & Altman, 1992; Landis & Koch, 1977) is a good agreement.

5. The results can be written as follows:

The grading of tissue specimens was compared between the first and second pathology labs. Both labs agreed completely on the grading of 15 specimens and partially on 3 specimens. On applying the weighted Cohen's kappa test, there was a good agreement which was significant, $\kappa = 0.79$, $P < .001$.

Note: The case of misapplication of Cohen's kappa on ordinal variables is shown in Box 9.2.

5. Fleiss kappa test

Fleiss kappa test measures agreement through differences in classifications between >2 raters. Unlike Cohen's kappa test, there is no weighting required for ordinal variables. Fleiss kappa test is applicable for nominal/ordinal variables between >2 raters (inter-rater reliability) and between the same raters/instruments at >2 different times/situations (intrarater reliability or test–retest reliability) (Table 9.1). A unique and beneficial feature

---

BOX 9.2 What happens when we apply kappa on ordinal variables?

It is wrong to apply kappa on ordinal variables unless the variables are weighted. Applying kappa on ordinal variables without weighting also reduces the value of kappa as it values all misclassifications equally. In ordinal variables, misclassifications are not equal and should be valued based on the extent of this misclassification. In our dataset, kappa without weighting is 0.69, whereas after weighting it is 0.79. This is a substantial difference. Kappa with quadratic weights may be applicable on continuous variables as well.

of Fleiss kappa is that it allows comparison in cases where different items are rated by different raters, as long as the total number of raters is fixed (Fleiss, 1971).

5.1 Assumptions of Fleiss kappa test

The main assumption of the Fleiss kappa test is that all the raters are independent of each other. As discussed with kappa tests, any other source that could cause variability other than the raters in question should be controlled. A clear protocol on the use of study tools and rating categories with clear operational definitions is a must. Kappa is written as κ.

A major principle of Fleiss kappa is that the raters should be nonunique. This means that for the same set of observations different raters are used to rate the observations.

For example, an Indian Medical College has 20 psychiatric consultants and it wants to determine the agreement between five specific psychosis diagnoses (Schizotypal disorder, Delusional disorder, brief psychotic disorder, schizophreniform disorder, and Schizophrenia). For each patient suffering from either of these five psychoses, any three psychiatrists may be randomly chosen (out of 20) to diagnose these patients. This makes them nonunique. If the same three psychiatrists are used to diagnose the whole set of patients, it makes them unique and Fleiss should not be applied. This is an example of the Fleiss test for nominal data as the five specific psychosis diagnoses are nominal in nature.

Another example is measuring an agreement of grading anemia as mild, moderate, and severe among a set of laboratory technical officers in an institute of diagnostics with 20 technical officers. Again for each sample observation, three randomly selected technical officers will grade the observations in mild, moderate, and severe anemia. In case, the same three are selected to grade they will be unique and Fleiss should not be applied.

The Fleiss kappa test works in the following settings:
- The **outcome variable** is nominal or ordinal with mutual exclusivity in categorization (there should be no confusion in categorization-the categories should be clear in definition and understanding)
- The **independent variable** or observations should be paired, that is, the ratings should be compared with the same set of patients. The observations should be independent and no rater should be able to influence each other while rating.
- The **subcategories of rating should be the same** for both raters. For example, if one rates in anemia and no-anemia (2 variables), the other should also rate in 2 variables (2 × 2 symmetricity). Similarly, if the subcategories are mild, moderate, and severe anemia, both raters should rate in the three subcategories (3 × 3 symmetricity).
- **Nonuniqueness of raters:** The raters should be nonunique for observations. This means that the three raters should not be the same for each observation as that makes them unique.

5.2 Applying Fleiss kappa test

For the application of Fleiss kappa test, we take the example discussed above. The Institute of Diagnostics, Aligarh wants to measure the agreement in mild, moderate, and severe anemia grading in the institute. The grading is done by either of its 20 laboratory technical officers from which any three will be randomly selected to grade the 100 samples for mild moderate and severe anemia. Kindly note that Fleiss kappa tests are only available in versions of SPSS 26.0 and beyond.

Research Question: Is there an agreement between the laboratory technical officers in grading anemia at the Institute of Diagnostics, Aligarh?

The dataset we use is named as *9. Fleiss Kappa.sav*. The question can be tested based on the values of kappa and the following hypothesis could be used.

H_0: There is no agreement between the laboratory technical officers in grading mild, moderate, and severe anemia at the Institute of Diagnostics, Aligarh.

H_A: There is an agreement between the laboratory technical officers in the grading of mild, moderate, and severe anemia at the Institute of Diagnostics, Aligarh.

The steps in the application of the Fleiss kappa test are as follows:

1. After opening the data file (*9. Fleiss Kappa.sav*), go to *Analyze > Scale > Reliability Analysis* (Fig. 9.8).
2. In the *Reliability Analysis* box, select the rating variables and enter them in *Ratings* box (*First, second and third raters*).

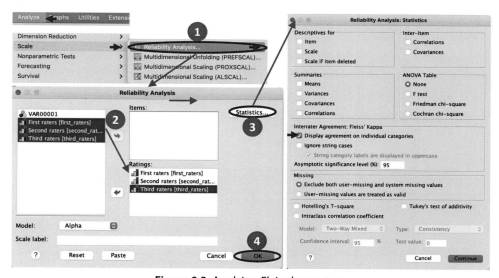

Figure 9.8 Applying Fleiss kappa test.

3. In the *Reliability Analysis* box, click *Statistics*, and a new dialog box named *Reliability Analysis: Statistics* opens up. Click *Display agreement on individual ratings*. This will give us the ratings for individual categories as well.

4. We get the results after clicking *Continue* in the Reliability Analysis: Statistics box, followed by *OK* in the Reliability Analysis box.

5.3 Interpretation of results of Fleiss kappa test

Fleiss kappa test has two important features: the first is its overall agreement and the second is about agreement on individual categories. The first is more important and the value of individual categories is of secondary importance (Fig. 9.9).

1. There are two tables of interest in the result output of Cohen's kappa test (Fig. 9.9): 1. Overall agreement, 2. Agreement on individual categories.

2. Overall agreement: This explains the overall agreement. The overall agreement on Fleiss kappa is $\kappa = 0.66$ (95% Confidence interval: 0.650–0.660) with an asymptotic standard error of 0.041 and a significant *P*-value <.001. The strength of agreement is good (Table 9.2).

3. The second table shows the agreement on individual categories. Often in health sciences, it is desirable to have higher agreement in detection of severe cases for prompt diagnosis and treatment. The agreement for Mild, Moderate and Severe can be seen against Rating category 1, 2, and, 3 respectively. The rating for Severe anemia is very good in strength with $\kappa = 0.84$ (95% CI: 0.83–0.84) followed by a good strength for mild anemia with $\kappa = 0.64$ (95% CI: 0.64–0.65) and moderate strength for moderate anemia at $\kappa = 0.52$ (95% CI: 0.515–0.523).

Thus, the null hypothesis is rejected, and the results can be written as follows.

The agreement between the laboratory technical officers in grading mild, moderate, and severe anemia at the Institute of Diagnostics, Aligarh was found to be good in strength on applying the

Fleiss Multirater Kappa **Overall Agreement**[a]

	Kappa	Asymptotic Standard Error	z	Sig.	Asymptotic 95% Confidence Interval Lower Bound	Upper Bound
Overall Agreement	.657	.041	16.037	.000	.655	.660

a. Sample data contains 100 effective subjects and 3 raters.

Agreement on Individual Categories[a]

Rating Category	Conditional Probability	Kappa	Asymptotic Standard Error	z	Sig.	Asymptotic 95% Confidence Interval Lower Bound	Upper Bound
1	.340	.643	.058	11.146	.000	.640	.647
2	.380	.519	.058	8.989	.000	.515	.523
3	.280	.835	.058	14.457	.000	.831	.838

a. Sample data contains 100 effective subjects and 3 raters.

Figure 9.9 Results of Fleiss kappa test.

Fleiss kappa test with κ = 0.66 (0.65–0.66), P < .001. The agreement on individual categories was very good for severe anemia with κ = 0.84 (95% CI: 0.83–0.84) followed by a good strength for mild anemia with κ = 0.64 (95% CI: 0.640–0.647) and moderate strength for moderate anemia at κ = 0.52 (95% CI: 0.515–0.523).

6. Agreement and concordance: which test to use?

Concordance is another measure of agreement. Kendall's tau is a correlation method for ranked data that can be applied through bivariate correlation. Kendall's coefficient of concordance is another test of concordance that is a nonparametric test for K variables. Table 9.4 serves as a guide for which test to use in different situations. Kindly note that an explanation of the terms correlation and concordance has been discussed in the chapter on correlations. While the chapter on correlation discusses concordance, for agreement and reliability testing, the final guide is given in Table 9.4.

7. Reliability for continuous variables: intraclass correlation

When the ratings are measured on a continuous scale, the agreement between any number of independent raters is done through intraclass correlation coefficient, commonly known as ICC. The reliability measures could be on the basis of differences in raters or time (situation). As already described in the beginning, reliability could be intrarater or interrater (including test–retest reliability). For continuous scales, Kappa statistics using quadratic weights may also be used.

Table 9.4 Agreement and concordance: tests.

Type of data	Test to apply for agreement/concordance
Scenario 1: Nominal data	Kappa test (if between two raters-Cohen's, >2-Fleiss's kappa)
Scenario 2: Ordinal data with two raters	Cohen's weighted kappa
Scenario 3: Ordinal data with >2 nonunique raters	Fleiss' kappa
Scenario 4: Ordinal data with two raters in which one is a standard rater/instrument	Cohen's weighted kappa + Kendall's tau (correlation)
Scenario 5: Ordinal data with >2 raters with known standard	Kendall's tau for each rater compared to known standard. For agreements between non-standard raters- Fleiss kappa or weighted kappa, as per assumptions.

The ICC measures the consistency or conformity of measurements made by multiple raters or the same raters on multiple occasions. However, the variability could be due to both interrater (between observers or raters) and intrarater (due to a certain patient's rating/observation). While the latter is what we are interested in, if fixed raters rate all the patients, their interrater variability could be a systematic difference that will affect ICC. This is because the ICC is meant to operate on principles of *exchangeable* measurements, which means that the observers are completely exchangeable. When they are fixed and systematic difference exists between them, the interpretation could become difficult. Fortunately, this problem can be solved by the selection of appropriate models within ICC. However, a low ICC could be due to a small number of subjects and raters. Experts suggest that for ICC, a minimum of 30 heterogeneous samples and 3 raters must be selected for reliability studies (Koo & Li, 2016).

7.1 Assumptions of ICC

The ICC is based on analysis of variance models and works in the following settings:
- The *outcome variable* is continuous.
- The *ratings* are independent, that is, the ratings of one should not influence the other.
- The basis of *ratings* should be the same for all the raters. Ideally, the raters should be trained in the operational definition and rating.

There are three models and two types for measuring ICC measures, which need to be specified while applying the ICC, which are also explained in Fig. 9.10. Further, in terms of measurement, ICC reliability is frequently applied when a single measure of a single rater is performed. However, reliability can also be applied to average measures where measures of k raters can be averaged for each subject.

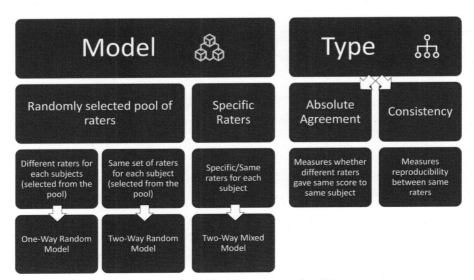

Figure 9.10 Models and types for ICC.

7.1.1 Models

There are three types of models that could be applicable in ICC calculation. If the raters are selected from a random pool of raters, then the model is random. If the raters are specific and not selected from a random pool, then the model is fixed and the model is a mixed model (Fig. 9.10). The variability of rating difference between subjects is the primary source of variability and this signifies the difference between one-way and two-way models. When different randomly selected raters rate the subjects, there is no systemic variability due to raters and a one-way random model is applicable. If the same set of raters rate each subject, but the raters were originally selected from a random pool, then their systematic variability (fixed bias) is also taken into account and a two-way random model is used. In the case of mixed models, since the same raters are used, the systematic variability (fixed bias) is always important and a two-way mixed model is applicable. This is shown in Fig. 9.10.

7.1.2 Type of agreement

There are two types of agreement: (1) absolute agreement and (2) consistency. Absolute agreement measures whether there is an agreement in the scoring of the same subjects between different raters. Consistency means whether the raters' score for the same group of subjects is consistent or correlated additively (ranking order and differences between subjects) (Liljequist et al., 2019). We refrain from further discussion on the models and types of ICC for which readers may refer to a paper by Koo and Li (2016) on intraclass correlation coefficients for reliability research (Koo & Li, 2016).

7.2 Applying ICC

Before applying ICC, three things should be clearly known and considered:

1. Type of reliability study: For intrarater reliability (or test—retest reliability) with the same raters, a two-way mixed model is applicable. For interrater reliability with different raters for each subject—one-way random model is applicable. For interrater reliability with the same raters from a randomized pool of raters, a two-way random model is used.
2. Applicable Model of ICC: One needs to decide this based on the raters and study settings among the three models available (Fig. 9.10).
3. Type of ICC measure: Absolute agreement between different raters is the only measure of interest in the case of the one-way random effect model. For two-way models, depending on the primary interest, absolute agreement and consistency may be applicable.

The research in which we apply ICC is based on interrater reliability of hemoglobin measure using technique X between three different raters. The raters are different for each observation and are randomly selected from a pool of 300 laboratory technologists in a medical university. The dataset we use is named *9. ICC.sav.*

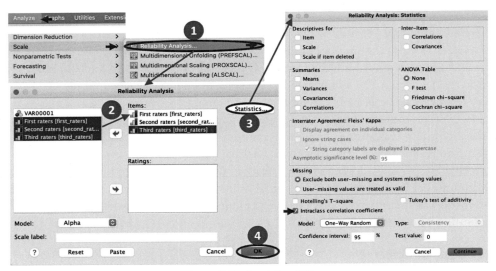

Figure 9.11 Applying ICC.

The steps in the application of ICC are already shown as follows:

1. After opening the data file (*9. ICC.sav*), go to *Analyze > Scale > Reliability Analysis* (Fig. 9.11).
2. In the *Reliability Analysis* box, select the Items and enter them in the Items box (*first raters, second raters and third raters*).
3. Click *Statistics*, and a new dialog box named *Reliability Analysis: Statistics* opens up. Click *Intraclass correlation coefficient* and choose the appropriate model and type. Since we are using different raters for each subject who is randomly selected from a pool (intrarater variability), the model is *One-Way Random*. In *One-Way Random*, the only type is absolute agreement. Kindly note that in case any other model is selected, an appropriate type must be selected.
4. We get the results after clicking *Continue* in the Reliability Analysis: Statistics box, followed by *OK* in the Reliability Analysis box.

7.3 Interpretation of results of ICC

Intraclass correlation coefficient interpretation is given in the second table.

1. There are two measures of ICC in the table (Fig. 9.12): (1) single measures and (2) average measures. The intraclass correlation coefficient is of our interest and is given in the Average measure table.
2. The average measures give us an idea about how the different raters agree on the rating of the subjects on an average. The ICC = 0.85 (95% CI: 0.72−0.92). An ICC <0.5 is graded as poor reliability, 0.50−0.74 as moderate, 0.75−0.90 as good, and >0.90 as excellent reliability (Koo & Li, 2016).

Reliability Statistics

Cronbach's Alpha	N of Items
.930	3

Intraclass Correlation Coefficient

	Intraclass Correlation	95% Confidence Interval		F Test with True Value 0			
		Lower Bound	Upper Bound	Value	df1	df2	Sig
Single Measures	.818	.758	.867	14.461	99	200	.000
Average Measures	.931	.904	.951	14.461	99	200	.000

One-way random effects model where people effects are random.

Figure 9.12 Results of ICC.

3. Thus, the results may be stated as follows: *The agreement between three different raters, randomly selected for each subject from a pool of 300 laboratory technologists in the medical university measured hemoglobin levels using technique X. A One-Way random model for absolute agreement Intraclass Correlation Coefficient (ICC) was calculated. The average agreement was found with an ICC = 0.85 (95% CI: 0.72–0.92), which is a good agreement based on guidelines* (Koo & Li, 2016).

8. Cronbach's alpha

The most commonly used statistical test for scale reliability analysis is Cronbach's alpha (α). It is a measure of internal consistency, that specifies how closely related are a set of items as a group. Cronbach's alpha measures the reliability estimates of indices (Cronbach, 1951). An index is a composite measure based on a set of questions. An easy example is asking a set of questions that measure different aspects of a composite variable such as quality of life. Cronbach's α tests the reliability of these sets of questions which are added to measure the quality of life.

A measuring instrument (such as a composite scale) must have good validity and reliability. However, unless an instrument has high reliability, it cannot be valid in a particular setting (Tavakol & Dennick, 2011). Thus, reliability must be measured in each research that uses the instrument regardless of its validity.

8.1 Applying Cronbach's alpha

Before applying Cronbach's alpha, one must be sure of its applicability. The Cronbach's alpha is applied to one composite question presuming that all the individual and interrelated questions affect that. If there are multiple constructs in some composite measure or index, Cronbach's alpha should be applied to each individual construct (Tavakol & Dennick, 2011). Essentially, the presumption is that the set of questions is homogenous, equally important, interrelated and together, they constitute the index together.

To understand the application of Cronbach's alpha, we will use a research where we measured the dermatological quality of life index (DQLI) computed on the basis of a standardized ten-question measure in patients of Tinea (Mushtaq et al., 2020). Put simply, we wanted to measure the internal consistency or reliability of the dermatological quality of life index (DQLI). The dataset is based on the published research with a few changes (Mushtaq et al., 2020).

This is based on dermatology research which measured dermatological quality of life (DLQI—a 10-question measure) in patients of Tinea. If one were to measure the internal consistency or reliability, Cronbach's alpha testing is done. A dataset (*9. DLQI_Cronbach.sav*) was developed for this example.

The presumption check for Cronbach's alpha: Are all the questions homogenous, equally important, interrelated, and validated to measure the same index? Yes, all 10 questions are homogenous, equally important, interrelated, and validated to measure DLQI (Finlay & Khan, 1994).

The steps in the application of Cronbach's alpha test are as follows:

1. After opening the data file (*9. DLQI_Cronbach.sav*), go to *Analyze > Scale > Reliability Analysis* (Fig. 9.13).
2. In the *Reliability Analysis* box, select the Items and enter them in the *Items* box. In this case, all the 10 DLQI questions (DLQIQuestion1, 2 … 10) are the items and must be sent to this box.
3. In the *Reliability Analysis* box, click *Statistics*, and a new dialog box named Reliability Analysis: Statistics opens up. Select *Descriptives* for *Scale and Scale, if item deleted*. This will help us understand the scale as well as the impact on the scale if an individual question is deleted.

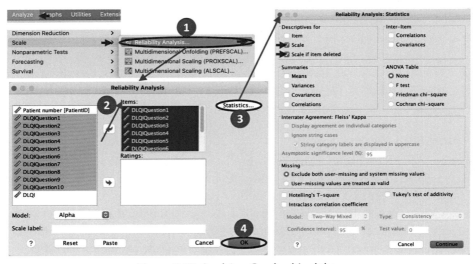

Figure 9.13 Applying Cronbach's alpha.

4. We get the results after clicking *Continue* in the Reliability Analysis: Statistics box, followed by *OK* in the Reliability Analysis box.

8.2 Interpretation of results of Cronbach's alpha

The Cronbach's alpha results has three tables of interest: (1) Reliability Statistics, (2) Item-Total Statistics, and (3) Scale Statistics (Fig. 9.14).

1. The first thing to note is the Reliability Statistics. The Cronbach's alpha is 0.87 for the 10 items (The 10 DLQI questions). The Cronbach's alpha measures as an interpretation of internal consistency are shown in Table 9.5 (George & Mallery, 2019). Thus, Cronbach's $\alpha = 0.87$ signifies a "good" internal consistency.

2. The next table—Item-Total—is important to understand the impact of deletion of any item. So, if DLQI question nine is deleted, Cronbach's alpha would be 0.853. In this table, we do not find any significant rise in Cronbach's alpha if any item is deleted. However, in practice, some research could have a significant rise in Cronbach's alpha if any item is deleted. In those cases, the items may be deleted to have higher reliability in the research. In case the reliability is already high, this is not warranted.

3. A low Cronbach's alpha is due to poor homogeneity or interrelatedness of questions. It could also be due to the lower number of questions on the scale. The opposite is

Reliability Statistics

Cronbach's Alpha	N of Items
.866	10

Scale Statistics

Mean	Variance	Std. Deviation	N of Items
13.55	53.343	7.304	10

Item–Total Statistics

	Scale Mean if Item Deleted	Scale Variance if Item Deleted	Corrected Item–Total Correlation	Cronbach's Alpha if Item Deleted
DLQIQuestion1	11.20	48.586	.381	.867
DLQIQuestion2	11.74	43.417	.607	.851
DLQIQuestion3	12.17	43.138	.590	.852
DLQIQuestion4	12.09	42.597	.639	.848
DLQIQuestion5	12.40	42.103	.708	.843
DLQIQuestion6	12.92	46.579	.396	.867
DLQIQuestion7	11.90	42.590	.592	.853
DLQIQuestion8	12.55	42.847	.643	.848
DLQIQuestion9	12.77	43.970	.586	.853
DLQIQuestion10	12.24	42.681	.636	.849

Figure 9.14 Results of Cronbach's alpha.

Table 9.5 Interpreting Cronbach's alpha.

Cronbach's α	Interpretation of internal consistency
≥ 0.9	Excellent
0.8–0.89	Good
0.7–0.79	Acceptable
0.6–0.69	Questionable
0.5–0.59	Poor
<0.5	Unacceptable

true for a high Cronbach's alpha. Similarly, some experts warn against a Cronbach's alpha beyond 0.9, as it could be due to a large number of redundant questions measuring the same thing (Streiner, 2003).

4. The third table shows the Scale statistics. The total DLQI has a mean of 13.53 and a standard deviation of 7.304.

5. Thus, the results of internal consistency may be stated as follows: *The Dermatological Life Quality Index (DLQI) was measured for internal consistency in the study setting. With Cronbach's α at 0.87, the internal consistency was good as per the established criterion. The deletion of any item does not lead to a significant rise in Cronbach's alpha. Therefore, all the 10 questions were retained to have a reliable and internally consistent measure of DLQI.*

References

Abramson, J., & Abramson, Z. H. (2011). *Research methods in community medicine: Surveys, epidemiological research, programme evaluation, clinical trials.* John Wiley & Sons.

Bartko, J. J., & Altman, D. G. (1992). Practical statistics for medical research. *Journal of the American Statistical Association, 87*(419), 907. https://doi.org/10.2307/2290246

Berchtold, A. (2016). Test—retest: Agreement or reliability? *Methodological Innovations, 9.*

Cohen, J. (1960). A coefficient of agreement for nominal scales. *Educational and Psychological Measurement, 20*(1), 37—46. https://doi.org/10.1177/001316446002000104

Cronbach, L. J. (1951). Coefficient alpha and the internal structure of tests. *Psychometrika, 16*(3), 297—334. https://doi.org/10.1007/BF02310555

Finlay, A. Y., & Khan, G. K. (1994). Dermatology Life Quality Index (DLQI)—a simple practical measure for routine clinical use. *Clinical and Experimental Dermatology, 19*(3), 210—216. https://doi.org/10.1111/j.1365-2230.1994.tb01167.x

Fleiss, J. L. (1971). Measuring nominal scale agreement among many raters. *Psychological Bulletin, 76*(5), 378—382. https://doi.org/10.1037/h0031619

George, D., & Mallery, P. (2019). *IBM SPSS statistics processes for PC* (pp. 8—25). Informa UK Limited. https://doi.org/10.4324/9780429056765-2

Guyatt, G., Walter, S., & Norman, G. (1987). Measuring change over time: Assessing the usefulness of evaluative instruments. *Journal of Chronic Diseases, 40*(2), 171—178. https://doi.org/10.1016/0021-9681(87)90069-5

Koo, T. K., & Li, M. Y. (2016). A guideline of selecting and reporting intraclass correlation coefficients for reliability research. *Journal of Chiropractic Medicine, 15*(2), 155—163. https://doi.org/10.1016/j.jcm.2016.02.012

Kottner, J., Audige, L., Brorson, S., Donner, A., Gajewski, B. J., Hróbjartsson, A., Roberts, C., Shoukri, M., & Streiner, D. L. (2011). Guidelines for reporting reliability and agreement studies (GRRAS) were proposed. *International Journal of Nursing Studies, 48*(6), 661—671. https://doi.org/10.1016/j.ijnurstu.2011.01.016

Landis, J. R., & Koch, G. G. (1977). The measurement of observer agreement for categorical data. *Biometrics, 33*(1), 159—174. https://doi.org/10.2307/2529310

Liljequist, D., Elfving, B., & Roaldsen, K. S. (2019). Intraclass correlation—a discussion and demonstration of basic features. *PloS One, 14*(7).

Mushtaq, S., Faizi, N., Amin, S. S., Adil, M., & Mohtashim, M. (2020). Impact on quality of life in patients with dermatophytosis. *Australasian Journal of Dermatology, 61*(2), e184—e188. https://doi.org/10.1111/ajd.13191

Streiner, D. L. (2003). Starting at the beginning: An introduction to coefficient alpha and internal consistency. *Journal of Personality Assessment, 80*(1), 99—103. https://doi.org/10.1207/S15327752JPA8001_18

Tavakol, M., & Dennick, R. (2011). Making sense of Cronbach's alpha. *International Journal of Medical Education, 2*, 53—55. https://doi.org/10.5116/ijme.4dfb.8dfd

CHAPTER 10

Survival analysis*

On a long enough timeline, the survival rate for everyone drops to zero

Chuck Palahniuk

1. Time to event as a variable

Commonly biostatistics considers two types of variables—categorical and continuous. Regardless of the type, the variables are assessed for significant associations or impact in inferential statistics. However, *time to an event* is an important area of health research. Such measures are useful for any event's incidence, survival rates, morbidity events, time to complication events, etc. This also helps in understanding the pattern of change with respect to time.

With advances in healthcare, it is often desirable to show how rapidly an intervention works, in addition to its clinical significance (strength) and statistical significance (chance elimination). In oncology and chronic diseases, many clinicians are more interested in how something changes with respect to time, rather than just the significance of the association. For example, the natural history of disease documenting events concerning time, etiology of mental illness, the prognosis of chemotherapy, etc.

Time to event can be considered as a hybrid variable of two characteristics—time duration and occurrence of an event. Complete information- while ideal- is uncommon in time-to-event studies as some subjects are lost during follow-ups (censoring). Follow-up losses are also inevitable if subjects develop alternate events that could conflict with the research in question and need to be dropped from the study. For example, in a study on the 5-year survival of carcinoma, if the subject dies due to road traffic accidents or develops pernicious behavioral risk factors, they will be excluded. The survival variable does not follow statistical approaches like the assumption of normality of distributions, as they are always positive and often positively skewed distributions. With the advances in biostatistics, many powerful techniques have been developed to study the dynamics of change. A lot of these techniques are based on multivariate analysis and regression, which will be introduced in the next chapter. Among them, hierarchical linear models, time series analysis, and survival analysis are commonly employed techniques for assessing change. While hierarchical linear models and time series analysis are used when the change is measured on a

---

*For datasets, please refer to companion site: https://www.elsevier.com/books-and-journals/book-companion/9780443185502

Biostatistics Manual for Health Research
ISBN 978-0-443-18550-2, https://doi.org/10.1016/B978-0-443-18550-2.00010-4

quantitative scale, for example, change in blood glucose due to oral hypoglycaemic drugs over time in a subject with Type II diabetes. The latter—survival analysis—is used when the change is measured qualitatively, for example, death after the cancer diagnosis, development of cirrhosis of the liver in alcoholics, pacemaker failure, etc. (Luke & Homan, 1998). In this chapter, we will introduce the concept of survival analysis and understand when and how can it be utilized to understand the dynamics of change.

2. Survival analysis

Survival analysis is a technique for time-to-event analysis, to study the time taken for an event/outcome to occur. Time to an event refers to the time from enrollment in a study until the occurrence of specific event. Death used to be the event that was commonly analyzed, and thus this technique came to be known as survival analysis. In our first example, death after cancer, we observe the survival time between two points—exposure and outcome. While the exposure is when the diagnosis of cancer in a patient is established, the outcome is the event of interest, which in this case is death.

Apart from the exposure and outcome, information on independent variables with an impact on the outcome is also essential, especially if they can potentially prepone or postpone the event.

2.1 Applications in health research

- Cancers or any other disease studies where we observe the probability of death such as 5-year survival rates. We can also add an independent variable, an intervention like drug or surgery, or dietary restriction, and measure whether they can change the survival time.
- Contraceptive failure rate using life-table analysis, a basic type of survival analysis.
- Dementia and occurrence of its complications.
- Time to failure of the procedure or medical device used in the patient. For example, pacemaker or knee replacement failure. This can also be compared among different groups.
- Time to relapse in case of substance use
- Age of first substance use and its covariates
- Time to suicide in high-risk personalities
- Dropping out from the school or any other program
- The benefit of a new treatment for any chronic disease in terms of prolonging life or delaying complications.

As the time to death or any event of interest is of short duration in acute infectious diseases like COVID-19, survival analysis is less useful. In survival analysis, we not only focus on an event but also model the length of time to the event. Whereas in traditional biostatistics, we analyze and comment on who (type of person) is more likely to die (association), survival analysis is helpful to know how soon that person (type of person) dies (Luke & Homan, 1998).

2.2 Terminology

Survival time/time to event: The time between the entry of the subject into a study and the event occurrence. Due to the differential occurrence of an event and censoring, survival time varies and is thus used to predict the risk of the event. It is considered the dependent variable in survival analysis. It has characteristics that are always positive, and thus the distributions are often skewed toward the right.

Censoring: Loss to follow-up before the occurrence of an event of interest is censoring. In such cases, we cannot ascertain whether or when the event occurred, and therefore such subjects are censored. Sometimes, there could be censoring by competing risks such as the death of a study subject in a 5-year survival study of cancer due to a road traffic accident (Porta, 2014).

Survival function: Probability of surviving (not having the event) longer than any particularly defined time. The dictionary of epidemiology defines survival function as follows: "A function of time, usually denoted by S(t), that starts with a population 100% well at a particular time and provides the percentage of the population still well at later times. Survival functions may be applied to any discrete event; for example, disease incidence or relapse, death, or recovery after the onset of disease (Porta, 2014)."

Hazard function: "A theoretical measure of the probability of occurrence of an event per unit time at risk (Porta, 2014)." It is actually a rate, not a probability. It is like velocity and signifies how likely an individual is to witness the event at that particular time (instantaneous death rate).

Hazard ratio: It is an equivalent of the risk ratio and helps in interpreting the effect of how a covariate changes the actual risk of an event. Mathematically, it is calculated as = Hazard of exposed/Hazard of not exposed.

2.3 Types of survival analysis

Within the realm of survival analysis, there are a handful of techniques where we can analyze time to an event. Similar to traditional statistical tests, they too are divided into parametric, nonparametric, and semiparametric. Some of these are as follows:
- Kaplan—Meier survival method
- Life table analysis
- Cox proportional hazards regression
- Exponential and Weibull Survival Analysis
- Log-rank test and Frailty models

2.3.1 Kaplan—Meier survival method

The Kaplan—Meier survival method is a nonparametric test used to estimate survival or time of an event occurrence such as death, surgical interventions, symptom/complication-free periods in diseases, etc. It is based on estimating the survival time when an event occurs or at censoring. An intuitive graphical presentation of survival time is drawn, known as Kaplan—Meier survival curve. The symbols on the curve represent censoring, while the curve swings down when the event of interest occurs. Kaplan—Meier's estimate is also helpful in comparing two groups of participants, a control group and a treatment group, to assess whether they differ in survival time.

2.3.2 Life table analysis

Similar to Kaplan—Meier, life table analysis is also a nonparametric test and examines the time-to-event rate of two or more treatment groups. The difference from Kaplan—Meier is that the observations of survival are done at regular intervals. Its usefulness in medical science is limited due to the assumption that the likelihood of an occurrence of the event only depends on time. The subjects who enter the study at different times may act differently, where life table analysis is not appropriate.

2.3.3 Cox proportional hazards regression

The Cox regression is a semiparametric procedure that utilizes modeling to study the relationship between time to a specified event and covariates. Unlike Kaplan—Meier survival method, which draws the survival curve, the Cox regression model gives us a hazard ratio, that helps estimate the effect size. This model can accommodate both discrete and continuous measures of event times.

2.3.4 Exponential and Weibull survival analysis

They are the parametric tests used to predict survival. Exponential survival analysis is the purest of them and is based on the assumption that the Hazard ratio is constant throughout the study. Weibull survival analysis employs modeling to examine data in which the Hazard Ratio increases or decreases over time.

2.3.5 Log-rank test and frailty models

Log-rank test and frailty models are considered parametric survival analysis methods. Log-rank test is a one-way ANOVA substitute for survival analysis where we compare the significance of two or more groups in Kaplan—Meier curves. Frailty models are complex analyses of survival time utilized when there are multiple covariates and heterogeneity in the distributions, which are accounted for, by including random effects in the model. In the proceeding sections of this chapter, we will learn about the Kaplan—Meier curve and Cox proportional hazards regression in detail.

The difference between Kaplan—Meier, Cox regression, and exponential survival analysis techniques is shown in Table 10.1.

Table 10.1 Kaplan—Meier, Cox regression, and exponential survival analysis techniques.

Kaplan—Meier	Cox regression	Exponential
Nonparametric method	Semiparametric method	Parametric method
Simple to perform and interpret. Can estimate survival but cannot estimate hazard ratio and effect size	Can estimate hazard ratio and effect size but cannot estimate survival function accurately. The hazard ratio can fluctuate with time	Can estimate survival function hazard ratio and effect size
Cannot describe the shape of the curve in the form of an equation	Cannot describe the shape of the curve in the form of equation	Although not always reliable, it can describe the shape of the curve
Only categorical variables can be included, and multiple predictors cannot be added	Multiple predictors can be used for both categorical and continuous variable	Multiple predictors can be used for both categorical and continuous variable
Useful in a situation where we need to predict the probability of survival beyond a certain time	Useful in a situation where we need to assess the relationship of covariates to survival time and to estimate how a new drug/technique improves survival in relation to other (effect size)	Weibull modeling allows the hazard ratio to increase with time or decreases with time

3. Kaplan—Meier survival method

The Kaplan—Meier survival method or product-limit method is a commonly employed technique to describe survival or time to event. Kaplan Meier is a nonparametric method where only categorical variables are included. It is most useful in situations where the primary objective is to predict survival probability beyond a certain time.

3.1 Assumptions of the Kaplan—Meier survival method

- Independence of participants and groups: Each participant appears only once in one group.
- Dichotomous event status: Event status should be dichotomous and consist of mutually exclusive categories-censored or event, and all the participants should fall under at least one of these states.
- Clearly defined and precisely measured event status: Event or censorship should be clearly defined and measured precisely with the information on exactly when they occurred with respect to time. For example, in a 5-year follow-up study, measuring events at yearly intervals would not be precise; recording them in days, weeks, or months would be required.

- No left censoring: All the participants must be event-free when they enroll in the study.
- Independence of censoring and the event: Those participants who were censored (dropout or end of the study) should not be at a higher or lower risk of the occurrence of the event.
- No secular trends: The survival rate or event occurrence rate should remain constant in the population. If there are fluctuating trends of events' occurrence or fatality/survival, then that trend could introduce a bias. As participant enrollment occurs at different time periods and it may take several months to recruit estimated samples, secular trends will introduce bias.
- A similar pattern and amount of censorship: To test statistical differences between groups, censoring should be similar in all the groups.

These assumptions for the Kaplan—Meier method must be met. Failure to do this may result in bias and wrong conclusions. If assumptions are violated, the Kaplan—Meier method should be avoided, and other survival analysis techniques should be used instead. If secular trends are observed with variables related to survival time, the Cox regression procedure should be used.

3.2 Applying the Kaplan—Meier survival method

The data we will use to understand the application of the Kaplan—Meier survival method is a fictitious data provided in this book (*10.cancer_survival.sav*). A drug manufacturer claims the therapeutic benefit of its new drug "drug X," which extends the life of lung cancer patients. To confirm their claim, we conducted a study on two similar patients group, one with conventional therapy and the other receiving the drug X. We conducted a time-to-death analysis by Kaplan—Meier method to compare overall survival rates.

3.2.1 Datasheet for Kaplan—Meier survival

The data should have different variables as columns and rows corresponding to a particular case/patient response. For Kaplan—Meier survival analysis in SPSS, we need at least three variables in the datasheet: survival time variable, event status, and comparing group. The dependent variable is time to event (survival time variable), which must be continuous (numeric type). In contrast, the independent variable (comparing group) should be categorical but entered as a numeric type with coding representing the categorical outcomes (dummy coded). Event status variables can be continuous or categorical (dummy coded).

In our dataset, 20 patients were randomly allotted into two categories, receiving standard therapy and new drug X. The dependent variable *time* is continuous, and independent variables- *intervention* is categorical with standard treatment coded as 1, and new drug X coded as 2. The event status variable is dichotomous, with death (event of interest) coded as 1 and censored coded as 2.

H$_0$: The survival time for standard therapy and new drug X in lung cancer patients is the same.

H$_A$: The survival time for new drug X in lung cancer patients differs from standard therapy.

Steps in the application of Kaplan–Meier survival method are as follows:

1. Open *10.cancer_survival.sav*. *Time* is the dependent variable, and *intervention* is the independent variable. Go to *Analyze > Survival > Kaplan–Meier* (Fig. 10.1).
2. In the new dialog box of Kaplan–Meier, shift *time* variable in *Time*, *status* variable in *Status*, *Intervention* variable in *Factor* box, and *id* variable to *Label case by: id*. The latter would help you identify the case in the survival table.
3. When the *Status* box is filled, the *Define event* box gets activated. Click it to provide information to SPSS that our event of interest "*died*" is coded as 1, and enter the same in a *single value* and click *Continue*.

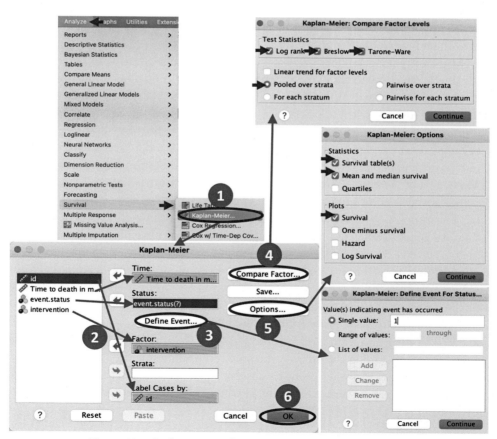

Figure 10.1 Performing Kaplan–Meier survival analysis in SPSS.

4. Click *Compare Factor,* and a new dialog box will open. Here it is preferred to check all three test statistics (*Log-rank, Breslow, and Tarone-Ware*), leave the rest as it is, and click *Continue.*

5. Now select *Option* in the Kaplan–Meier dialog box to open the new dialog box. Tick *Survival table(s)* and *Mean and median survival* checkboxes and *Survival* checkbox under Plots and click *Continue.*

6. Finally, click *OK* to run it.

3.3 Interpretation of results of the Kaplan–Meier analysis

There will be four tables and a Kaplan–Meier curve in results output.

1. **Survival table and its estimates:** The first table in the output shows the case processing summary. The second and third table shows survival table and estimates the survival time for each intervention group along with their 95% CI. The survival table lists the time to event for both groups and calculates the probability of surviving at each time. Means and medians estimate along with standard error and 95% confidence interval of estimates are provided for survival time. The mean survival for standard therapy was 20.48 and for drug X it was 18.63 (Fig. 10.2).

2. **Group comparison.** The overall comparisons table provides chi-square statistics for three tests we chose to study the difference in survival time, log rank (Mantel–Cox), Breslow (Generalized Wilcoxon), and Tarone-Ware statistic. This is the test of equality of survival distributions for the different levels of intervention. All are nonsignificant ($P > .05$), so we can conclude that there is no significant difference in survival of lung cancer patients taking drug X with respect to standard treatment. Which test to report? This depends on the shape of the intervention group survival function plot. The log-rank (Mantel–Cox) test considers the null hypothesis of no difference in the overall survival distributions among the intervention groups and calculates a χ^2 statistic. The assumption of the log-rank test is that the survival function plot of the groups should remain parallel and not cross each other. In our example, the survival plot of the two intervention crosses (Fig. 10.3), thus log-rank test in our example would have reduced power and should be substituted by Breslow or Tarone-Ware test (Hosmer & Lemeshow, 1999). We want to reiterate that SPSS does not give any effect size estimate for the Kaplan–Meier test.

3. The cumulative survival proportion, as listed in Survival Table, is plotted against time for each study group in the form of the Kaplan–Meier curve (Fig. 10.3). The horizontal interjunction on the curve represents censoring while the fall represents death (event of interest). Another point to observe in the plot is whether the curves cross each other, which in turn affects the power of the statistical tests. This curve can

Survival Table

intervention		ID	Time	Status	Cumulative Proportion Surviving at the Time		N of Cumulative Events	N of Remaining Cases
					Estimate	Std. Error		
Std therapy	1	7	6.000	Died	.900	.095	1	9
	2	15	9.000	Died	.800	.126	2	8
	3	1	12.000	Died	.700	.145	3	7
	4	17	15.000	censored	.	.	3	6
	5	12	16.000	censored	.	.	3	5
	6	19	20.000	Died	.560	.171	4	4
	7	20	22.000	Died	.420	.176	5	3
	8	13	25.000	Died	.280	.164	6	2
	9	2	30.000	censored	.	.	6	1
	10	4	30.000	censored	.	.	6	0
Drug X	1	14	6.000	Died	.900	.095	1	9
	2	5	7.000	Died	.800	.126	2	8
	3	8	7.000	censored	.	.	2	7
	4	16	9.000	censored	.	.	2	6
	5	9	10.000	Died	.667	.161	3	5
	6	10	16.000	Died	.533	.176	4	4
	7	6	17.000	censored	.	.	4	3
	8	11	18.000	Died	.356	.186	5	2
	9	18	19.000	censored	.	.	5	1
	10	3	30.000	censored	.	.	5	0

Means and Medians for Survival Time

intervention	Mean[a]				Median			
	Estimate	Std. Error	95% Confidence Interval		Estimate	Std. Error	95% Confidence Interval	
			Lower Bound	Upper Bound			Lower Bound	Upper Bound
Standard therapy	20.480	2.731	15.127	25.833	22.000	2.519	17.064	26.94
Drug X	18.633	3.323	12.119	25.147	18.000	4.795	8.603	27.40
Overall	19.288	2.103	15.167	23.409	20.000	3.064	13.994	26.01

a. Estimation is limited to the largest survival time if it is censored.

Overall Comparisons

	Chi-Square	df	Sig.
Log Rank (Mantel–Cox)	.267	1	.606
Breslow (Generalized Wilcoxon)	.353	1	.552
Tarone–Ware	.356	1	.551

Test of equality of survival distributions for the different levels of intervention.

Figure 10.2 Results of Kaplan–Meier survival analysis in SPSS.

calculate the probability of survival at a particular time. So, the 20 month survival for the participant on standard therapy is 56%, while for drug X is 36%. We can also make out that most of the time, standard therapy had slightly better survival. One can also comment on the median survival time (at 0.5 cum survival), which was 18 months for drug X and 22 months for standard therapy.

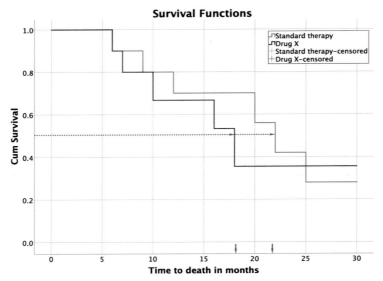

Figure 10.3 Graphs in the output of linear regression analysis.

3.4 Writing the results of the Kaplan—Meier

Thus, the null hypothesis is retained as drug X and standard therapy are not significantly different in their survival time among lung cancer patients. The results can be expressed as follows:

The results of the Kaplan—Meier survival analysis indicate that the median survival time for drug X and standard therapy for patients with lung cancer was 18 and 22 months, respectively. The difference in survival time is not statistically significant between drug X and standard therapy among patient with lung cancer χ^2 Breslow (1, N = 20) = 0.353, P = .552.

4. Cox regression survival method

The Cox regression method is another commonly employed technique that builds a predictive model for time to event. In this section, we discuss the application of the Cox regression method.

4.1 Assumptions of Cox regression

- Independence of observations
- Proportional hazards assumption: Hazard ratio between two groups should remain constant over time. This can be tested by examining the log minus log plots (and scatterplots of residuals for continuous variables) and checking whether they are parallel

or not. If one curve drops while the other plateaus, then the hazards are not proportionate. It can also be tested by the scaled Schoenfeld residuals test, which the SPSS currently does not support. We can still calculate the assumption statistically by running Cox with the time-dependent covariates procedure (explained later).

- Linearity: The relationship between continuous independent (X) variables and logit transformation of the hazard variable should be linear. It is checked by residuals.
- Multiplicative risk
- Random censoring: Censoring in the data should be random.

If the proportional hazards assumption is not met, we may use the Cox with time-dependent covariates procedure (Therneau et al., 2017). The Kaplan—Meier procedure is applicable to only one categorical covariate. If the sample lacks censored data (all cases experienced the event), the linear regression procedure can be used to observe the relationship between predictors and time to event. If the assumption of linearity is violated, data transformation of independent (X) variables can be considered.

4.2 Applying Cox regression

The data that we will use to understand the Cox regression method is the same as we used in the Kaplan—Meier survival method (*10.cancer_survival.sav*). It is a fictitious data of new drug "drug X" which claims to prolong the life of lung cancer patients. It contains data of two similar patients group- one with traditional therapy and the other receiving the drug X- along with their time to death and censoring.

4.2.1 Datasheet for Cox regression

For Cox regression analysis in SPSS, we need at least three variables in the datasheet-survival time variable, event status, and comparing group. The dependent variable is time to event (survival time variable), which may be continuous or discrete (numeric type), while the independent variable (comparing group) can be continuous or categorical. If categorical, they should be entered as Numeric types with coding representing the categorical outcomes (dummy-coded). Event status variables can be continuous or categorical (dummy-coded).

In our dataset, 20 patients were randomly allotted into two categories—receiving standard therapy and new drug X. The dependent variable *time* is continuous, and independent variables *intervention* is a categorical type variable with standard therapy coded as 1 and new drug X coded as 2. The event status variable is dichotomous with death (event of interest) coded as 1 and censored coded as 2.

H_0: The survival time for standard therapy and new drug X in lung cancer patients is the same.

H_A: The survival time for new drug X in lung cancer patients is different than standard therapy.

Steps in the application of the **Cox regression** survival method are as follows:

1. Open *10.cancer_survival.sav*. *Time* is dependent variable and *intervention* is independent variable. Go to *Analyze > Survival > Cox Regression* (Fig. 10.4).

2. In the new dialog box of Cox regression, shift *time* variable in *Time*, *status* variable in *Status*, and *Intervention* variable in *Covariate* box, by dragging them or with the use of the right arrow button.

3. When the *Status* box is filled, *Define Event* box gets activated. Click it to provide information to SPSS that our event of interest "*died*" is coded as 1, and enter the same in *single value* and click *Continue*.

4. The covariate we have entered (intervention) is categorical variable and we need to inform this to SPSS. For this, click the *Categorical* box, which will open the new dialog box. Drag the covariate which you want to label as categorical, (in our case *intervention*) to *Categorical* Covariate space. As soon as the reference category is activated, the reference category is assigned as last by default in SPSS. In the *intervention* group, 1 is

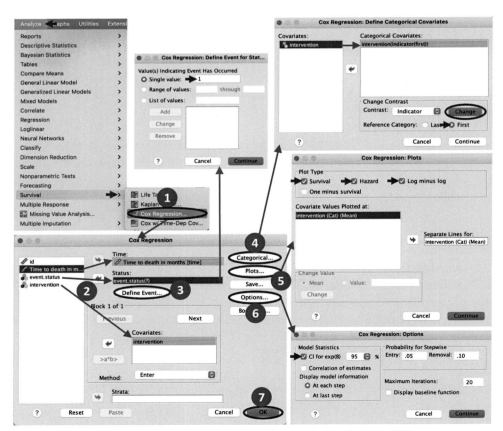

Figure 10.4 Performing Cox regression survival analysis in SPSS.

labeled as standard treatment and 2 as drug X. We want to observe the drug X with respect to standard treatment, so change the reference category by clicking the *First* and confirm it by clicking *Change*. Click *Continue* to return to the Cox regression dialog box.

5. Click *Plots* and the new dialog box will open. Check boxes against *Survival*, *Hazard*, and *Log minus log*. Under *Covariate Value Plotted at:*, shift the main Covariate (*intervention*) to *Separate Lines for* and click *Continue*.

6. Now select *Option* in the Cox regression dialog box to open a new dialog box. Tick *CI for exp(B)* checkboxes and click *Continue*.

7. Finally, click *OK* to run it.

4.3 Interpretation of results of the Cox regression analysis

There will be six tables and four curves in the results output (Fig. 10.5).

1. **Descriptive:** Initial tables in the output show case processing summary and categorical coding. Drug X is coded as 1 (code for predictor) and standard treatment is 0 (code for reference).

2. **Omnibus test** of model coefficient without any covariate is given under Block 0, while after adding covariates is shown in Block 1. We are interested in the Block 1 table as it describes how well the predicted model fits our dataset. The omnibus test in block 1 is nonsignificant, so the predicted model fit is not good. This should

Case Processing Summary

		N	Percent
Cases available in analysis	Event[a]	11	55.0%
	Censored	9	45.0%
	Total	20	100.0%
Cases dropped	Cases with missing values	0	0.0%
	Cases with negative time	0	0.0%
	Censored cases before the earliest event in a stratum	0	0.0%
	Total	0	0.0%
Total		20	100.0%

Omnibus Tests of Model Coefficients

−2 Log Likelihood
52.247

Categorical Variable Codings[a]

		Frequency	(1)
intervention[b]	1=Standard therapy	10	0
	2=Drug X	10	1

This is being assessed

Covariate Means and Pattern Values

		Pattern	
	Mean	1	2
intervention	.500	.000	1.000

Omnibus Tests of Model Coefficients[a]

−2 Log Likelihood	Overall (score)			Change From Previous Step			Change From Previous Block		
	Chi−square	df	Sig.	Chi−square	df	Sig.	Chi−square	df	Sig.
51.987	.264	1	.608	.259	1	.611	.259	1	.611

a. Beginning Block Number 1. Method = Enter

Variables in the Equation

	B	SE	Wald	df	Sig.	Exp(B)	95.0% CI for Exp(B)	
							Lower	Upper
intervention	.320	.626	.262	1	.609	1.378	.404	4.699

Figure 10.5 Results of Cox regression survival analysis.

alarm the statistician since decisions based on ill-fitting models could be badly misleading.

3. **Variables in the equation:** This is the most informative table. It provides estimates of the model parameter along with each predictor's significance and odds ratios with their confidence intervals. In the first column, B is the *logistic coefficient*. The *logistic coefficient* of the predictor indicates the influence and the direction of the effect. The closer the logistic regression coefficient is to zero, the lesser is its effect. At the same time, a positive value shows an increasing effect, and a negative value shows that probability decreases with an increase in the predictor's value. In our model, its value is 0.320, which means that with a unit increase in intervention variable (standard treatment—1 to drug X—2), there would be an increased risk of death among patients with lung cancer. The table also displays the Wald statistic, which tests the significance of the logistic coefficient being different from zero. Cox regression analyzing the time to death with intervention groups in our study did not result in significant changes by covariates. Thus, drug X therapy does not add any benefits to standard treatment. The estimated Hazard ratio can be observed in the table given (under Exp(B)) below as 1.378 (95% CI 0.404, 4.699) was again nonsignificant with a *P*-value of .609. A hazard ratio of more than 1 indicates that patients receiving drug X are more likely to die. This can also be interpreted as the percentage by subtracting from 1. So the risk of dying is increased by 37.8% [(1.378 − 1)*100)] with the change of treatment from standard to drug X.

4. The cumulative survival is plotted against time for the average participant and each study group in the form of a survival curve (Fig. 10.6). Similar to the Kaplan–Meier curve, a fall represents death (event of interest). We can also observe that the curves of covariates (drug X and standard treatment) in survival, hazard function, and log minus log plot are almost parallel, having a minimum difference between them. We get some idea that the proportional hazards assumption is met since both the curves are almost parallel, except at a few points where they meet. This may be further tested by Cox regression with a time-dependent covariate. Drug X had slightly lower survival and slightly better hazard ratio.

4.4 Cox regression with a time-dependent covariate

If there is uncertainty about the assumptions of proportional hazards, the covariate can be run in time-dependent methods.

Steps in the application of **Cox regression with a time-dependent covariate** are as follows:

1. Open *10.cancer_survival.sav. Time* is the dependent variable and *intervention* is the independent variable. Go to *Analyze* > Survival > Cox w/Time-Dep Cov (Fig. 10.7).

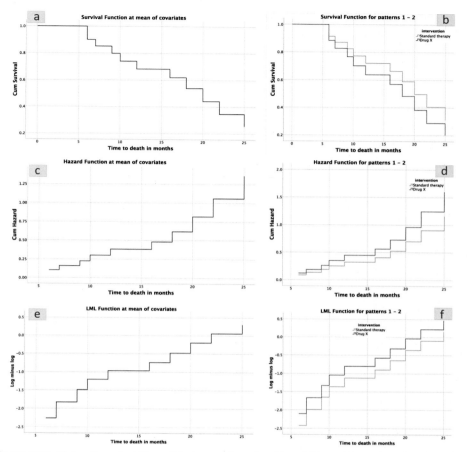

Figure 10.6 Plots of survival (A and B), hazard function (C and D), and log minus log (E and F).

2. In the new dialog box of time-dependent covariate, shift the *Time [T_]* variable to the *Expression for T_COV_* box. From the symbols below, click "*" (used as a multiplication sign) to transfer it to *T_COV_* box. Now shift the covariate you want to convert as time-dependent (*intervention*) to the same box. Click *Model.* To open the Cox regression dialog box.

3. In the new dialog box of Cox regression, shift time-dependent covariate created in the previous step *T_COV_* to *Covariate* box. Perform all the steps of Cox regression as usual, including shifting *time* variable in *Time, Intervention* variable in *Covariate* box, and *status* variable in *Status* along with entering coding of the event in *Define Event* box.

4. In the *Categorical* box, drag the covariate which you want to label as categorical, (in our case *intervention*) to the categorical covariate space. Change the reference category

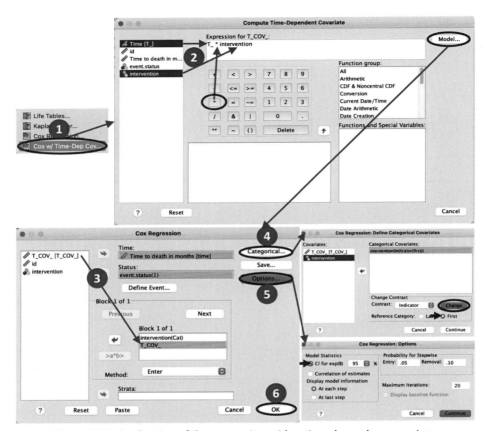

Figure 10.7 Application of Cox regression with a time-dependent covariate.

by clicking the *First* radio button and confirm it by clicking *Change*. Click *Continue* to return to the Cox regression dialog box.

5. Now select *Option* in the Cox regression dialog box to open a new dialog box. Tick *CI for exp(B)* checkbox and click *Continue*.
6. Finally, click *OK* to get the results in the output window.

4.4.1 Interpretation of results of the Cox regression with a time-dependent covariate

You will observe similar tables as seen in simple Cox regression output. We are interested in the Table of Variable in the Equation which would be the second last table. Only a new variable of the interaction of T_COV_ with covariate is observed to assess the proportionality of hazards, which in our case is nonsignificant. Thus the time-dependent covariate of intervention does not have a significant effect on the model, and the proportional hazards assumption would be met. We can use the results of simple Cox regression output (Fig. 10.8).

Variables in the Equation

	B	SE	Wald	df	Sig.	Exp(B)	95.0% CI for Exp(B) Lower	Upper
intervention	.839	1.509	.309	1	.578	2.313	.120	44.551
T_COV_	-.040	.105	.141	1	.707	.961	.782	1.182

Figure 10.8 Output of Cox regression with a time-dependent covariate.

4.4 Writing the results of Cox regression

Thus, the null hypothesis is retained as drug X and standard therapy are not significantly different in their survival time among lung cancer patients. The results can be expressed as follows:

The Cox regression survival analysis was used to assess the difference in hazard function of death among patients with lung cancer who received new drug X in comparison to standard treatment. The predicted model was prepared after the covariate met the assumption of Proportional hazards. It was found that the patients receiving drug X had 1.378 times more likelihood of dying because of lung cancer as compared to standard treatment but it was not significant (HR = 1.378; 95% CI [0.404, 4.699], P = .609).

References

Hosmer, D. W., & Lemeshow, S. (1999). *Applied survival analysis.* Wiley.

Luke, D. A., & Homan, S. M. (1998). Time and change: using survival analysis in clinical assessment and treatment evaluation. *Psychological Assessment, 10*(4), 360–378. https://doi.org/10.1037/1040-3590.10.4.360

Porta, M. (2014). *A dictionary of epidemiology.* Oxford University Press.

Therneau, T., Crowson, C., & Atkinson, E. (2017). Using time dependent covariates and time dependent coefficients in the cox model. *Survival Vignettes, 2*(3), 1–25.

CHAPTER 11

Regression and multivariable analysis*

Statisticians, like artists, have the bad habit of falling in love with their models.

—*George Box.*

1. Regression and multivariable analysis

Regression is an analytical method that studies the change in a variable corresponding to a change in the other. The outcome variable is also known as the dependent or response variable, whereas the explanatory or exposure variable is also called the independent variable. In terms of regression, the outcome/response/dependent variable is also called *Regressand,* and the explanatory/independent variable is called *Regressor.* The synonymous terms and their mathematical conventions are shown in Table 11.1. In terms of analytical value, regression is a step ahead of correlation. Regression predicts the value of the dependent/outcome variable with respect to the changes in the explanatory/response/independent variable. This is different from correlation, which is simply a measure of a symmetric relationship where one variable is related to the other variable.

Table 11.1 Terms and conventions for response and explanatory variables.

Categories	Outcome variable	Exposure variable
Synonyms/alternative terms		
Dependence effect	Dependent variable	Independent variable
Investigation based	Response variable	Explanatory variable
Intervention based	Outcomes	Treatment group
Regressions	Regressand	Regressor
		Covariates (continuous) & Factors (categorical)
Case-control design	Case-control groups	Risk factors
Conventions		
Mathematical/regression equations	Left-hand side	Right-hand side
Tables	Columns	Rows
Graphs	y-variable	x-variable
	Vertical	Horizontal

*For datasets, please refer to companion site: https://www.elsevier.com/books-and-journals/book-companion/9780443185502

Biostatistics Manual for Health Research
ISBN 978-0-443-18550-2, https://doi.org/10.1016/B978-0-443-18550-2.00011-6

Correlation does not assign which variable is dependent and which is not, as it is symmetric in nature (Pagano & Gauvreau, 2000). Sometimes, we are more interested in finding the actual change in the outcome with a change in the explanatory variable and not mere strength of correlation. Another difference is that unlike correlation, in which only two variables can be assessed at a time, regression can predict the change in the presence of multiple variables, including confounders. The simplest regression equation is $Y = a + bX$, where Y is the outcome variable and X is the explanatory variable. Mathematically, regression is about this exact equation. The key differences between correlation and regression are highlighted in Fig. 11.1.

In inferential statistics discussed in the book up until now, we focused on statistical significance and strength of association of one independent variable with the dependent variable. However, multiple independent variables affect the dependent variable. Sometimes, the association could be confounded by the presence of another independent variable. For example, in one research discussed earlier, we studied the effect of the clinical stage of HIV/AIDS on predicting whether the patient is depressed or not. The independent/explanatory variable is the clinical stage of HIV/AIDS and the dependent variable is depression. However, the presence of other explanatory variables could also have an impact on depression. Some of these variables are age, gender, family support, stigma, and discrimination. Suppose that we find statistically that most patients at a severe stage of HIV/AIDS are depressed significantly. We also find that poor family support is also markedly associated with depression. Many severe-stage patients tend to have poor family support. How do we ascertain that the clinical stage, even in the presence of poor family support is affecting depression? We can do this through regression techniques where two (or more) independent variables are studied together for their effect on the dependent

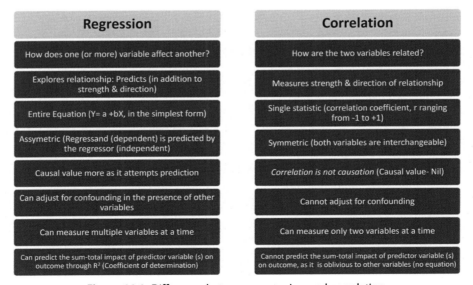

Figure 11.1 Difference between regression and correlation.

variable. The procedure is called *adjustment,* as in our example, the clinical stage of HIV/AIDS has a statistically significant association with depression even after adjustment for the family support. Commonly this is known as multivariable analysis as opposed to univariable analysis, where only one dependent and independent variable are studied. The wrong usage of these terminologies in the health research literature continues unabated despite appeals (Peters, 2008; Tsai, 2013).

1.1 Univariate, univariable and multivariable: terminologies

The use of the terminologies such as univariate, bivariate, multivariate, univariable and multivariable is confusing due to multiple interpretations. Attempts at building consensus and restricting researchers to use the correct terminology continue to be unsuccessful due to conventional usage in epidemiology and terms used in the software (Hidalgo & Goodman, 2013; Peters, 2008; Tsai, 2013). We will discuss the meaning of these words as well as their popular usage along with the terms used in SPSS.

Let us start with the meaning of the terms - uni, bi, and multi. Uni means one, bi means two, and multi means more than two. Statistically speaking, *"variate"* is a term used for the outcome or dependent variable, *univariate* is a single outcome and *multivariate* is multiple outcomes (Peters, 2008). In this sense, most health research is concerned with univariate analysis, for example, ANOVA, *t*-test, Mann—Whitney test, or chi-square tests. Multivariate tests are about multiple outcomes, as in trials with multiple end-points. Examples of such multivariate tests are multivariate analysis of variance (MANOVA) or principal component analysis, which are less common in biomedical research. On the other hand, *"variable"* is a term for explanatory or independent variables. *Univariable* means only one explanatory variable and *multivariable* means many explanatory variables. Thus, the univariate analysis could be univariable univariate analysis (single explanatory variable-single outcome) or multivariable univariate analysis (multiple explanatory variables-single outcome). Therefore, multivariable and multivariate are not exchangeable terms, as is often seen in research articles (Tsai, 2013).

However, tests such as *t*-test and ANOVA tests are sometimes called bivariate on the premise that they have two variables (Tsai, 2013). However, both these tests are univariate analysis as it has a single outcome. In many health research papers on adjusted factors, the Odds ratio is specified as univariate and multivariate. Whereas univariate here means univariate univariable analysis, while multivariate here denotes univariate multivariable analysis (still single outcome but multiple explanatory variables). Ideally, univariable and multivariable terms must be used. However, the multivariate analysis continues to conventionally stand for multivariable analysis in many health research articles. As discussed earlier, the consensus frequently fails; however, our readers should try their best to adhere to the terms univariable and multivariable (variable stands for explanatory) instead of the misappropriate use of univariate and multivariate (variate stands for outcome) (Box 11.1).

> **BOX 11.1 Multiple regression and multivariate regression**
> Misleading use of "multivariate" as a term is common. *Variate* is related to the dependent variable. If there is more than one dependent variable, it is called multivariate regression, which are uncommon. More commonly, simple linear regression and multiple regression are used. Simple stands for one independent variable and multiple stands for more than one independent variable, which is actually a multivariable analysis.

1.2 Dependence and interdependence methods

While we concentrate on health research, where there is a common use of a dependent or outcome variable, other research areas have limited or no application of dependence. Based on whether dependence is present or not, multivariate analysis techniques are divided into two types—dependence and interdependence (Fig. 11.2).

The dependence methods are employed when the dataset has been divided into the independent and dependent variables. This method observes the association and studies cause–and–effect relationships by making assumptions about the variables. Multiple logistic and linear regression, MANOVA, linear probability models, conjoint analysis, multiple discriminant analysis, structural equation modeling, and canonical correlation analysis are some of the dependence methods used in biomedical and more recently in machine learning.

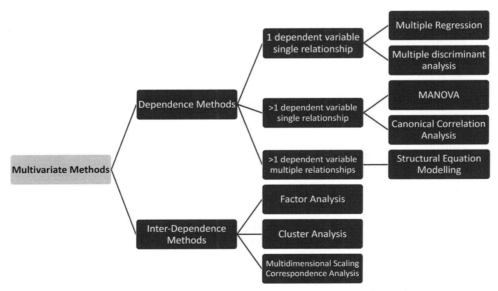

Figure 11.2 Multivariate methods of dependence and interdependence.

Interdependence methods handle datasets without making many assumptions about the variables. They help in understanding underlying patterns within the dataset. Thus, structural makeup and interdependent relationship are examined and analyzed to give meaning to the variables, either by grouping them or segregating them. Factor analysis, cluster analysis, multidimensional scaling, and correspondence analysis are some of the common methods. We will not go into the details of most of these methods because of their limited application in health research.

1.3 Other applications of regression

The process for performing multivariable analysis is determined by the techniques used and the objective of the analysis. We usually conduct multivariable analysis to achieve one of the following objectives:
1. Hypothesis testing
2. Data reduction
3. Classification or grouping
4. Investigation of dependents among variables.
5. Prediction

1.3.1 Hypothesis testing

Most commonly in health research, regression techniques are used for multivariable analysis to investigate the relationship between a dependent variable and several independent variables, along with its nature and strength of association. This helps in adjusting the variable for confounders. Regression analysis is a collection of techniques used to predict and assess the relationship between variables. Linear and logistic regression are covered in detail in the subsequent sections of this chapter.

1.3.2 Data reduction

In this type of analysis, several variables are combined to form one or few simple measures. For example, a dataset may contain data about a person's income, education, occupation, and residence. Expectedly many of them would have a high degree of correlation among themselves and could be combined to form a single variable—socioeconomic status. Similarly, the Human Development Index is a composite of multiple measures combined to form one variable considered to have a better interpretation than the original measures. Thus, composite variables can be derived from different related variables through reduction techniques.

Data reduction also helps us when it is difficult to find patterns in the dataset due to too many variables. Also, it is preferred to perform data reduction when we have too many variables before regression because a model with many variables is susceptible to overfitting. Among the type of data reduction analysis, the most commonly used are factor analysis and principal component analysis. The definitions of the same based on the Dictionary of Epidemiology are as under (Porta, 2014):

Factor analysis is "a set of statistical methods for analyzing the correlations among several variables in order to estimate the number of fundamental dimensions that underlie the observed data and to describe and measure those dimensions." Factor analysis is commonly used in scoring systems, rating scales, and questionnaires.

Principal component analysis is "a statistical method to simplify the description of a set of interrelated variables. Its general objectives are data reduction and interpretation; there is no separation into dependent and, independent variables, and the original set of correlated variables is transformed into a smaller set of uncorrelated variables called the principal components. Often used as the first step in factor analysis."

1.3.3 Grouping and classification

Grouping analyzes the data distribution in a sample and looks for patterns. Grouping can be done on similar themes, objects, or study participants. So in a dataset, we can use physiological variables to prepare a group of alcoholics and nonalcoholics. Among the type of Grouping and classification analysis, the most commonly used are:

Clustering analysis (or K mean clustering): Cluster analysis divides a dataset into groups of similar elements, known as clusters. Participants in one cluster are more similar to those in other clusters. So, there is homogeneity within the cluster, while there is heterogenicity between the two clusters.

Hierarchical clustering: In this, we form a tree with branches, and individuals can be considered as the leaves on branches, which share similar elements. The closer the branches are to one another, the closer the individuals on that branch to the individuals on the other, thus depicting similarity.

1.3.4 Investigation of dependents among variables

This is a type of interdependence method of multivariate analysis where we use an exploratory analysis technique to examine underlying patterns and structural makeup in an interdependent relationship.

1.3.5 Prediction and forecasting

If we have a large dataset from different geographies and times, we can predict the value of a dependent variable by analyzing the relationship between independent and dependent variables. For example, by assessing the different risk factors, we can predict whether a person could get a myocardial infarction.

Regression analysis, explained in detail later, and time series analysis (TSA) are frequently used for prediction. TSA is the foundation for prediction and forecasting in time-based problems, where data points that occurred in successive order over a period of time are collected and analyzed.

2. Regression analysis

Regression analysis is a technique used to predict the relationship between a dependent (aka outcome) variable and an independent (aka predictor) variable (s) in terms of a mathematical equation called a model. It has broad applicability, and medical science is just one of the fields where we can utilize its power in prediction. The mathematical model prepared after regression analysis provides a modeling line or curve where all the data points are at a minimal distance to this line. This line can be understood as the type of line in a scatter plot while correlating two variables (Figs. 11.3 and 11.4). There are many types of regression analysis, but the most important and commonly used are as follows:

1. Linear regression: When the outcome/dependent variable is continuous.
2. Logistic regression: When the outcome/dependent variable is categorical.

2.1 Approaching regression and multivariable analysis

The approach to regression and multivariable analysis is more complicated than other inferential statistics. We need to pay attention to the variables, choice of regression technique, methods of entering variables as well as fitness of the model. In addition, the assumptions of regression are also essential. Regression is a powerful technique for analysis and therefore, its assumptions and models should also be verified before interpreting the results. We will discuss the details later when we discuss different regression techniques. Fig. 11.5 provides a summarized approach to applying regression. One must keep this approach in mind while applying any type of regression.

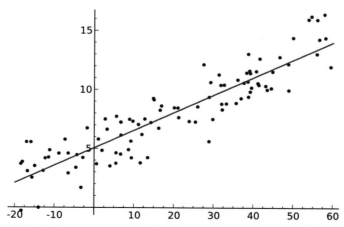

Figure 11.3 Simple linear regression with one outcome and one explanatory variable.

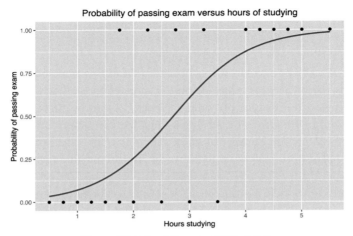

Figure 11.4 Logistic regression curve.

3. Linear regression

Linear regression uses the modeling technique to predict the relationship between the dependent variable (y) and one or more independent variables (x) in the best fit straight line (Fig. 11.3). When we predict the relationship between one dependent (outcome) and one independent (predictor) variable, then the technique is known as simple linear regression, and if two or more predictor variables are used then it is called multiple linear regression. Given the nature of this book, we will restrict ourselves from using complex mathematical equations. However, the best fit line or regression line can be best understood through the regression equations, which we will discuss later. Depending on the number of independent variables, linear regression can be of two types:

1. Simple linear regression
2. Multiple linear regression

3.1 Terminologies in linear regression

Equation: The regression line is a straight line, based on the following equation:

$$Y = a + bX + e \qquad \text{(equation A1)}$$

where Y is the dependent variable, a is the intercept, b is the slope of the line, X is the independent variable, and e is the error term.

In multiple linear regression, the regression equation would look like this:

$$Y = a + b_1X_1 + b_2X_2 + e, \qquad \text{(equation A2)}$$

where b_1, b_2, ... is the slope of the lines, X_1, X_2, ... are independent variables and e is the error term.

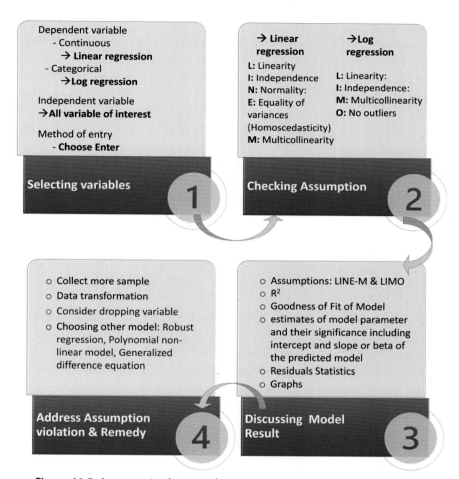

Figure 11.5 A summarized approach to regression and multivariable analysis.

Least square regression: The most common technique of fitting explanatory variables on a regression line is least-square regression. The vertical deviations from the line for each observed data (if it is on the line, the vertical distance is 0) are squared and summed to calculate the best-fitting line.

Intercept: It is the value of Y when $X = 0$. So it is the y value on the regression line when it crosses the y-axis.

Slope: It is the ratio of the change in Y over the change in X between any two points on the line.

Error: Represented by **e**, it is an unobservable error component, which is the gap between the true and observed realization of Y and accounts for the failure of data to lie on a straight line.

Residual: It is the error in each independent variable, not explained by the regression line. It is measured by the distance of the independent variable from the regression line. They are positive as well as negative summing up to zero.

Coefficient of determination (R^2): R-squared measures the proportion of variation in the dependent variable or outcome through the selected independent variable(s) in the equation. It can range from 0 to 1. For example, a value of 0.75 would mean that 75% of the variation in the dependent variable/outcome can be explained through the selected independent variables.

Goodness of fit/line of best fit: This indicates how well the model fits the observed data by summarizing the difference with expected values under the model.

3.2 The assumptions for linear regression

Linear regression works in a setting where the dependent and independent variables are continuous. There are four essential assumptions if one independent variable is used, which is remembered by the acronym LINE (Fig. 11.6). An additional assumption of Multicollinearity must also be met if more than one independent/explanatory variables are used (LINE-M).

1. *Linearity:* The relationship between the dependent (*Y*) variables and the independent variable (*X*) should be linear.
2. *Independence:* The variables should not be paired; their observations must be independent and separate so that there is the independence of errors.
3. Normality: The residuals should follow a normal distribution.

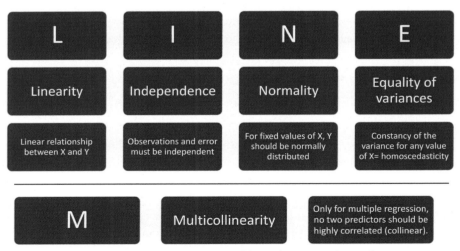

Figure 11.6 The assumptions of linear regression (LINE-M).

4. *Equality of variance (homoscedasticity):* The residuals at each level of predictors should have the same variance.

5. *Multicollinearity*: There should be an absence of multicollinearity among independent variables, they cannot be highly correlated.

Despite all these assumptions, we can perform the regression analysis with some modifications in SPSS:

- SPSS can perform linear regression even when independent (X) variables are categorical in nature, provided they are binary (only two categories). If you have more than two categories, you may use staircase coding and create multiple dummy variables.
- If the significance and confidence interval of the model is questionable (violation of homoscedasticity), we can still calculate them by bootstrapping.
- If homogeneity of variance is in doubt, then the model can rerun standard errors of heteroscedastic residuals.
- If model parameters have some issues, then robust regression can be used instead.

4. Simple linear regression analysis

As described earlier, simple linear regression involves one independent variable, which is used to predict one dependent variable. All the assumptions for linear regression should be fulfilled before applying the analysis.

4.1 Applying the simple linear regression

The data we will use to understand the application of simple linear regression are based on the following hypothesis from a paper on the association of serum vitamin D level and patient's age and gender. We would be using the dataset provided along with this book (*6.Vit D_PTH.sav*), which consists of age and gender of 102 patients along with their serum vitamin D level. Vitamin D level is the dependent variable, while we are trying to predict it using independent variables (predictors) age and gender. However, for simple linear regression, we are restricting our independent variable to just one: the age of the patients.

Applying linear regression in SPSS, the dependent variable must be continuous (numeric type), while the independent variable may be continuous (numeric type) or categorical (numeric type with dummy-coding). In our dataset, the dependent variable *vit_D* is continuous, and independent variables *Age* is continuous and *Gender* variable is categorical with Male coded as 1 and Female coded as 2.

H_0: There is no association of patient's age with serum level of vitamin D.

H_A: Age of patient is associated with serum level of vitamin D.

Steps in the application of simple linear regression are as follows:

1. Open *6.Vit D_PTH.sav*. Vitamin D level is the dependent variable and the age of the patient is the independent variable. Go to *Analyze > Regression > Linear* (Fig. 11.7).

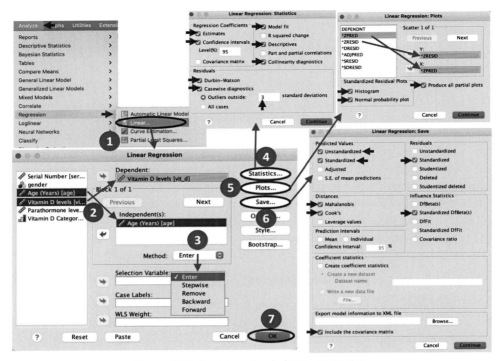

Figure 11.7 Applying simple linear regression.

2. In the linear regression dialog box, select the dependable variable (vitamin D levels) and transfer it to the box labeled as dependent. Similarly, transfer independent variable (age) in the space labeled as independent(s).

3. After the independent variable is transferred, the *Method* box becomes activated, and by default, Enter is selected. Keep it as it is. Similarly, the *Next* box under Block 1 of 1 is activated. We have only one variable in simple regression, so we can ignore it.

4. Click the box labeled as *Statistics* to open a new dialog box. By default, only *Estimate and Model fit* as selected. We also advise selecting *Confidence interval, Descriptives, collinear diagnostics,* and *Durbin—Watson*. In Outliers outside under *Casewise diagnostics,* change it to two standard deviations from default 3, for more potential identification of outliers. Click *continue.*

5. Click *Plot* to open a new dialog box where we need to provide the command to SPSS to test our assumptions. We need to prepare a plot with *ZRESID* versus *ZPRED* as *Y* and *X*-axis, respectively for assessing the assumption of linearity and homogeneity of variance. Similarly to assess the normality of residual, we need to select a *Histogram* and *Normal probability plot.* Click *continue* to return to the main regression box.

6. For other assumptions of linear regression, we have to calculate some factors for our data. To do that, click *Save* in the main dialog box and tick the boxes against *Unstandardized, Standardized Predictive value, Mahalanobis and Cook's distances, Standardized Residuals, Standardized DfBeta, and Covariance matrix.* Click *Continue*.

7. Click *OK* for detailed analysis in the output window of SPSS.

4.2 Interpretation of results of the simple linear regression

There will be about nine tables in the simple linear regression results output (Fig. 11.8).

1. **Descriptive statistics, correlations, model summary, and ANOVA:** In the initial tables including Descriptive Statistics and Correlations, the mean and standard deviation of dependent and independent variables and Pearson correlations are shown. These tables gives an idea of whether or not the two variables are significantly correlated. The table of Model Summary gives R^2 and adjusted R^2, while the ANOVA table gives F statistics. The R^2 measures how much variability in outcome (dependable variable) is accounted for by the predictor (independent variable). The

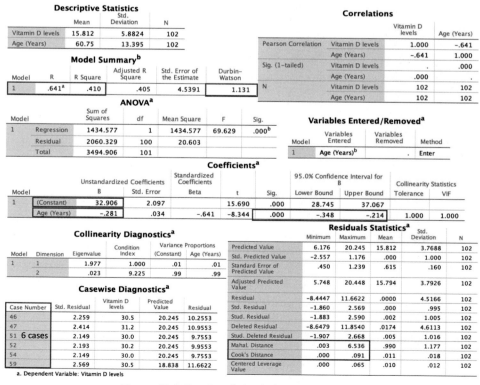

Figure 11.8 Results of simple linear regression.

R^2 with age as a predictor is 0.410, which means that the age of the patients accounts for 41% of the variability in vitamin D levels. The adjusted R^2 explains how well our model would perform in population. Another thing to note is the Durbin–Watson value, which is used to assess the assumption of independence of error. A value beyond 1–3 is considered as residuals having a high correlation and is a cause for concern (Field, 2018).

2. **Coefficients:** The most informative table in the output of regression analysis is the table of Coefficients, which provides estimates of the model parameter and their significance. In our model, the intercept a is 32.906 (B for constant), b (slope or beta) is −0.281 (B for Age variable), while e (error term) cannot be calculated but predicted from R^2. The b value represents the unit change in the dependent variable (vit D level) associated with a unit change in the predictor (Age of patient). Thus, b value of −0.281 indicates that with each year (unit of predictor) increase in the patient's age, the serum vitamin D value will decrease by 0.281, as predicted by our model. This coefficient table also gives us the significance and confidence interval of the model. The significance of the model can be observed under the column Sig. in the row of our predictor variable age, which is 0.000 (<0.001), while the 95% confidence interval for predictor variable b is −0.348 to −0.214. Notably, this 95% CI does not cross 1, indicating that the model's beta would be significant in the population. As discussed earlier, the significance and confidence interval of the model could be questionable if the assumption of homoscedasticity is violated, which we will check in the proceeding section. In the form of an equation, this is what is signified:

$$\text{Vitamin D level} = 32.906 + (-0.281)\text{Age}$$

3. **Collinearity diagnostics and casewise diagnostics:** These tables assess the assumption and validity of our model by providing collinearity diagnostics and residuals statistics. Along with the Collinearity Statistics from the previous table of coefficients, the table of Collinearity Diagnostics helps us to establish Collinearity between two independent variables. As there is only one explanatory variable, the multicollinearity assumption is not applicable and this table is of no use here. The Casewise Diagnostics and Residuals statistics table would reveal bias in the model. We need to look for standard residuals (Std. Residual) of more than 2. Given the total cases (102), we expect 95% of cases to have standardized residuals within 2, and those with values greater than 3 are probably outliers. In other words, no more than five cases (5% of 102) should have standard residuals of greater than 2, as they are potential outliers. In our model, there are six cases outside two standard deviations, which need to be investigated by other measures of outliers. Note that if we had not changed the default outlier limit from 3 to 2, you would not get the Casewise Diagnostics table in the output, as none of our cases are outside the three standard residuals value. Kindly

note that the default standard limit in SPSS is 3 which is the absolute limit, keeping it at 3 is perfectly fine.

4. **Residuals Statistics:** Look for Cook's and Mahalanobis distance in the Residuals statistics table. The maximum limit for Cook's Distance is one, and Mahalanobis distance is 15 (small sample) to 25 (large sample, 500 or more). Our model meets these two conditions, so none of the cases has an undue influence on our model. Remember we also have selected unstandardized and standardized predictive values, standardized residuals, standardized and DfBeta, which SPSS computed in the data-view tab as a new variable. They also help in diagnosing outliers and high influencing points. We discuss this more when we discuss assumptions in the multiple linear regression section.

5. **Graphs** (Fig. 11.9): At last, we need to take care of the assumptions of the normality of residuals, linearity, and homoscedasticity. The normality of residuals can be predicted by observing the histogram and P—P plot of standardized residuals. The ideal histogram approximates a bell shape and in the P—P plot, the dots and line should be hugging each other. Although both these are not in perfect alignment, we may consider them reasonable given our small sample size. Linearity and homoscedasticity are observed by the scatterplot of standardized predictors and standardized residuals. If the dots have any pattern like a curve, then the assumption of linearity is probably unrealistic. If the points are randomly and evenly distributed without any pattern and no funneling, our assumption of homoscedasticity is satisfied. In our results, although there is no curve pattern, there is some funneling as many values are constricting around +1 values. Thus, the assumption of homoscedasticity is doubtful.

4.3 Applying the robust linear regression model

In case of violation of the assumption of linear regression, we may still use it after some adjustment. In our example, the assumption of homoscedasticity is doubtful.

Heteroscedasticity refers to unequal dispersion of residuals or error terms. This is a serious problem as significance and confidence interval are predicted based on the assumption of homoscedasticity and constant variance. This misleadingly increases the

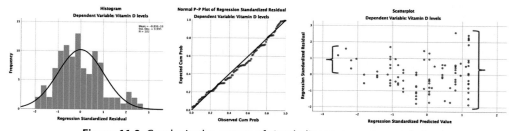

Figure 11.9 Graphs in the output of simple linear regression analysis.

likelihood of obtaining a statistically significant *P*-value. Despite the biomedical research data being prone to heteroscedasticity, researchers often ignore it when performing linear regression. We recommend that researchers observe this in the output and report it. As mentioned earlier, we usually test homoscedasticity by visually assessing scatterplots. In addition, Breusch—Pagan and White's test can also confirm this.

If one fails to meet the assumption of homoscedasticity by any of the above methods, we have the option of transforming the dependent variable (log transformation, rate transformation), or performing Robust linear regression (Hayes & Cai, 2007). Alternatively, we can also calculate the confidence interval by performing bootstrapping.

Steps in applying the robust linear regression model:

1. Open *6.Vit D_PTH.sav*. Go to Analyze > General Linear Model > Univariate (Fig. 11.10).
2. In the Univariate dialog box, transfer the dependable variable (vitamin D levels) to the box labeled as Dependent and transfer the independent variable (age) under the space labeled as Covariates(s).
3. Click the Options box to open a new dialog box. Select parameter estimates, modified Breusch—Pagan test, and White's test for heteroskedasticity. Check parameter estimates with robust standard errors, and keep HC3 selected as default. Click Continue to return.
4. Click OK for obtaining parameter estimates with robust analysis in the output window of SPSS.

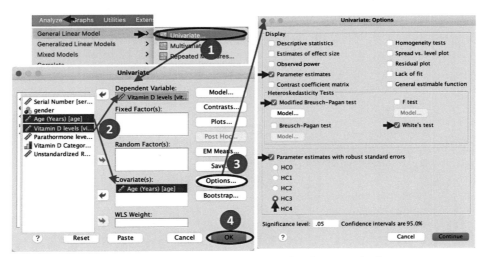

Figure 11.10 Linear regression analysis with robust standard errors.

4.4 Interpretation of results of the simple linear regression with robust standard errors

There will be five tables in the results output of linear regression with Robust estimates (Fig. 11.11).

1. **Homoscedasticity:** Our data seem to violate the assumption of homoscedasticity visually on scatter plots, which can be confirmed by a the significant modified Breusch—Pagan test and White's test.

2. **Model summary and coefficients parameters** including ANOVA, R^2, and adjusted R^2 are the same values as in linear regression output. But the significance and confidence interval of beta cannot be trusted as the data has heteroskedasticity, so we calculate parameters with robust estimates.

3. **Robust estimated parameters:** These are calculated by heteroskedasticity-consistent standard errors—3 (HC3 methods), which gives the most accurate estimates (Hayes & Cai, 2007). Even after corrections with Robust Standard errors, the analysis is significant and the equation can be used with robust standard errors.

White Test for Heteroskedasticity[a,] [b,c]

Chi–Square	df	Sig.
7.986	2	.018

Modified Breusch–Pagan Test for Heteroskedasticity[a,b,c]

Chi–Square	df	Sig.
5.222	1	.022

b. Tests the null hypothesis that the variance of the errors does not depend on the values of the independent variables.

Tests of Between–Subjects Effects

Source	Type III Sum of Squares	df	Mean Square	F	Sig.
Corrected Model	1434.577[a]	1	1434.577	69.629	.000
Intercept	5071.724	1	5071.724	246.161	.000
age	1434.577	1	1434.577	69.629	.000
Error	2060.329	100	20.603		
Total	28996.120	102			
Corrected Total	3494.906	101			

a. R Squared = .410 (Adjusted R Squared = .405)

Parameter Estimates

Parameter	B	Std. Error	t	Sig.	95% Confidence Interval Lower Bound	Upper Bound
Intercept	32.906	2.097	15.690	.000	28.745	37.067
age	-.281	.034	-8.344	.000	-.348	-.214

Parameter Estimates with Robust Standard Errors

Parameter	B	Robust Std. Error[a]	t	Sig.	95% Confidence Interval Lower Bound	Upper Bound
Intercept	32.906	2.350	14.004	.000	28.244	37.568
age	-.281	.036	-7.853	.000	-.352	-.210

a. HC3 method

Figure 11.11 Results of linear regression with robust estimated parameters.

4.5 Bootstrapping in linear regression

Bootstrapping is a procedure in which the dataset from the population is resampled "n" number of times to estimate population parameters including standard errors and confidence intervals with accuracy. This method for calculating parameters will always work as it does not rely on any assumptions about data distribution. Violation of the assumption of homoscedasticity makes significance and confidence interval calculated by the conventional technique unreliable. Bootstrapping can be used instead.

Performing and interpreting bootstrapping in linear regression (Fig. 11.12).

- Rerun the Simple linear regression as listed in the 4.1 section, omitting step 6 of *Save* variables. Instead, Click *Bootstrap* button to open its dialog box (Fig. 11.7). Check to Perform bootstrapping to activate confidence interval and sampling boxes. Select Bias corrected accelerated in Confidence interval instead of percentile for a more accurate confidence interval (Efron & Tibshirani, 1993). Click Continue to return to the Regression dialog box and click OK to run.

Figure 11.12 Bootstrapping in linear regression.

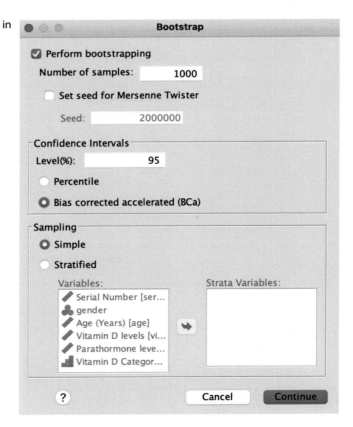

- In the output, you will get all the tables observed in the output of linear regression, along with a 95% confidence interval of all the statistics.
- There would be an additional table bootstrapping for coefficients, just below the coefficients table, that we are interested in Fig. 11.13.
- So it can be observed that after bootstrapping, the 95% confidence interval of b (beta) is -0.354 to -0.219, which does not include zero, along with $P = .001$. As the bootstrap confidence interval is calculated for the population rather than the current dataset, we can be assured that the relationship observed in our dataset would also be significant, even if it fails the assumptions of normality or homoscedasticity.

4.6 Writing the results of the simple linear regression

Thus, the null hypothesis is rejected as the age of the patient is significantly associated with serum level of vitamin D. The results can be expressed as follows:

Simple linear regression analysis was used to test whether the age of the patient significantly predicted participants' serum vitamin D levels. This model failed in the assumption of homoskedasticity as the scatterplot of standardized predictor and standardized residuals had a funneling pattern with values constricting, so we used heteroskedasticity-consistent standard errors—3 (HC3 methods) to calculate robust parameters. The results of the regression showed that the age of the patient explained 41% of the variance ($R^2 = 0.41$, $F(1.100) = 69.629$, $P < .001$). It was found that with an increase in the patient's age by 1 year, the serum vitamin D decreased by 0.281 ($\beta = -0.281$; 95% CI $[-0.352, -0.210]$, $P < .001$) as predicted by our model. So, the regression equation can be written as: Vit D level $= 32.906 - 0.281$(age of the patient).

5. Multiple linear regression analysis

Multiple linear regression analysis is performed when more than one independent variable is used to predict one dependent variable. The dataset should meet all the assumptions of linear regression enlisted before, as well as multicollinearity (LINE-M, Fig. 11.6).

Bootstrap for Coefficients

Model		B	Bias	Std. Error	Bootstrap[a] Sig. (2–tailed)	BCa 95% Confidence Interval Lower	Upper
1	(Constant)	32.906	.068	2.247	.001	28.517	37.630
	Age (Years)	−.281	−.001	.034	.001	−.354	−.219

a. Unless otherwise noted, bootstrap results are based on 1000 bootstrap samples

Figure 11.13 Bootstrapping coefficients in linear regression.

The dependent variable is continuous, whereas the independent variables may be continuous or even categorical.

5.1 Entering predictors into the model

Multiple logistic regression is the ideal choice for most health research as there are several predictors and confounders. However, there are two major considerations before the application of multiple linear regression:

5.1.1 Finalizing the list of predictors/explanatory variables

Should all explanatory variables be included in the model or only the significant ones (significant in univariate univariable regression or tests)? The safe answer is 'all variables of interest'. The existing literature and theoretical knowledge on the research question are helpful in guiding the variables of interest. However, this safe answer is not so helpful because the choice of predictors is highly subjective and contextual. While in economics, authors tend to include all the explanatory variables, there is a tendency among health researchers to include only the significant variables. This is because most health researchers are interested in adjusted significance and eliminating confounding, where it makes little sense to include the variables that had negligible influence on univariable analysis. However, significance is not a measure of strength, importance, or interest. Moreover, the most important variables are those that can be justified by theory and context. Depending on the context, the explanatory variable could theoretically be unrelated to the outcome and need not be measured in the first place.

Another useful way to evaluate the final variable selection is to use the value of R^2. A higher R^2 is better, provided the variables make subject-specific sense. In health research, some experts recommend performing a univariate univariable analysis (simple linear regression) with each selected variable. The variables with a predetermined limit (significance <0.2 or even <0.05) are then taken up for the multiple regression. Most health researchers, including us, are inclined toward the latter, but the final decision rests in the hands of the researcher's context and the subject of research (Field, 2018; Ranganathan et al., 2017).

5.1.2 Method—order of variable entry in the model

The second issue with multiple linear regression is the order in which the variables are included in the model. As shown in Step 3 of performing simple Linear regression (Fig. 11.7), there are five different methods to enter variable: enter, stepwise, remove, backward, and forward. In the Enter method, all variables are entered into the block together, while in other methods, the software keeps adding or removing the variables depending on the method chosen. Most researchers, including us, recommend the default—Enter method as the appropriate method for biomedical research. However, we suggest using this option with caution as it may have unacceptable consequences (Field, 2018; Ranganathan et al., 2017).

5.2 Applying the multiple linear regression

The data we will use to understand the application of multiple linear regression are the same as the one used in simple linear regression (*6. Vit D_PTH.sav*). Vitamin D level is the dependent variable, while we are trying to predict it using two independent variables (predictors)—age and gender. Simple linear regression analysis has found that age and gender are significantly associated with vitamin D level ($P < .05$), so we selected both predictors for our multiple linear regression.

H_0: There is no association of age and gender of the patient with serum level of vitamin D.

H_A: Age and gender of the patient are associated with serum level of vitamin D.

Steps in the application of multiple linear regression:

The steps in applying the multiple linear regression test are the same as for the simple linear regression explained above Fig. 11.7. In the linear regression dialog box (Step 2), select and transfer the dependable variable to the box labeled as dependent and transfer all independent variables under the space labeled as independent(s). Remember that only binary categorical variables can be entered. Otherwise, perform all the steps shown in Fig. 11.7. A summary of assumption checks in multiple regression is shown in the box below and a snapshot in Fig. 11.14 and Box 11.2.

5.3 Interpretation of results of the multiple linear regression

The output of the multiple linear regression results should have nine tables and five figures (Fig. 11.15).

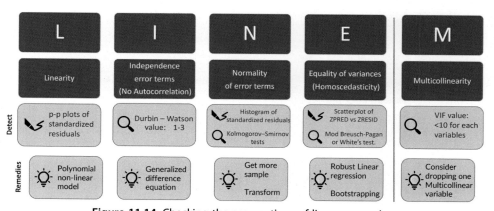

Figure 11.14 Checking the assumptions of linear regression.

BOX 11.2 Checking for outliers and highly influential points: residual statistics in linear regression

Ideally, the dataset should not contain outliers and highly influential points. In the Data view tab, new variables must be created after the linear regression analysis. Look for:

- Cook's distance should be <1 (absolute value). A large Cook's value indicates an influential observation. The size-adjusted threshold is obtained from the formula *4n-k-1*, where n = sample size, k = number of predictors (Gray & Fox, 1998). This formula is more sensitive in detecting influential cases.

- Leverage value: An observation with a high leverage pulls the regression line toward it. The size-adjusted threshold is given by formula 3(k + 1)/n, where n = sample size, k = number of predictors.

- Normalized residual (ZRE_1) should not be >3.0 (absolute value), and not more than 5% of the sample be >2. We expect 95% of cases to have a standard residual within ±2 while no more than 1% of cases within ±2.5.

- DFBeta of all variables (under DFB1_1, DFB2_1 and so on) should not be >1 (absolute value). The size-adjusted threshold should be below 2/√n, where n = sample size (Pedhazur, 1997).

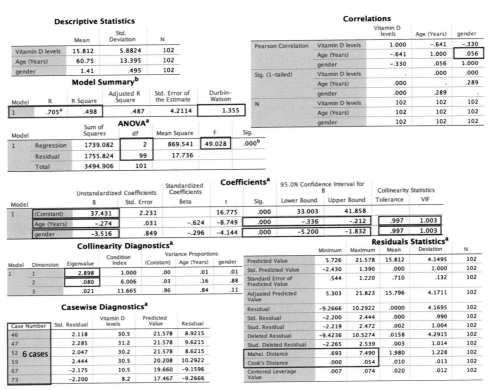

Figure 11.15 Results of the multiple linear regression.

1. **Descriptive statistics, correlations, model summary, and ANOVA:** In initial tables, including descriptive statistics and correlations, you can see the mean and standard deviation of dependent and independent variables and Pearson correlations. You can get an idea of whether the two are significantly correlated or not from these tables. The correlation coefficient between two independent variables is 0.056. The table of model summary contains R^2 and adjusted R^2 along with Durbin—Watson value while ANOVA table contains the F statistics. The R^2 with age and gender as predictors is 0.498, which is improved from the previous model of just age as a predictor (0.410 in Fig. 11.8). Thus, age and gender together account for 49.8% of the variability in vitamin D levels. ANOVA is also significant with $F = 49.028$. The Durbin—Watson value is also in the acceptable range (between 1 and 3).

2. **Coefficients:** The most important table in output, the table of coefficients, provides estimates of model parameters and the significance of each predictor. In our model, the intercept a is 37.431 (B for constant), b1 (beta for first variable—age) is -0.271 95% CI $[-0.336, -0.212]$ and b2 (beta for second variable—Sex) is -3.516 95% CI $[-5.200, -1.832]$. These predictors are significant ($P < .001$) for predicting vitamin D level in this model. Thus this new model with two predictors predicts that with an increase in the patient's age by 1 year, the serum vitamin D level decreases by 0.271, and we are 95% sure that the beta of age will lie between -0.336 and -0.212. Notably, this 95% CI does not cross1, indicating that the model's beta would be significant in population. Gender variable is categorical with values 1—Male and 2—Female. This model predicts unit change in the predictor's effect on the outcome. Thus, we can say that if the gender changes from male to female for the same age, the serum vitamin D level decreases by 3.516. As discussed earlier, the significance and confidence interval of the model could be questionable if the assumption of homoscedasticity is violated. In the form of an equation, this is what is signified: Vitamin D level $= 37.431 + (-0.274)$ Age $+ (-3.516)$ Gender.

3. **Collinearity:** Multicollinearity should not be present between any two variables when multiple predictors are present. Assessment of collinearity detects collinearity between two independent variables. The correlation matrix gives us an idea of correlationship between independent variables. The value of correlation coefficient r greater than 0.9 should ring a bell in favor of multicollinearity. It can also be estimated from the coefficients table, tolerance, and variance inflation factor (VIF). A tolerance <0.2 or a VIF >10 or average VIF (calculated by adding all VIF values divided by the number of predictors) substantially greater than 1 indicates that the assumption for multicollinearity is violated.

4. **Casewise diagnostics:** Casewise diagnostics provides the list of variables that are potential outliers and detects bias in the model. Five percent of the sample can be outside 2 standard deviations, while any value more than 3 is considered a potential outlier. In our model, there are six cases that fall outside 2 standard deviations, that need to be

investigated by other measures of outliers. Note that if you have not changed the default cutoff for outlier from 3 to 2, you may not get the casewise diagnostics table in the output, as none of our cases are outside the 3 standard residuals value. Kindly note that the default standard cutoff in SPSS is 3 which is the absolute limit. Therefore, keeping the default cutoff of 3 is fine as well.

5. **Residuals statistics:** In the Residuals statistics table, look for Cook's and Mahalanobis distance. The maximum limit for Cook's Distance is 1, and Mahalanobis distance is between 15 (small sample) and 25 (large sample, 500 or more). Our model meets these two conditions, so probably none of the cases have an undue influence on our model.

6. **Normality of residuals, linearity, and homoscedasticity:** At last, we need to look for assumptions about the normality of residuals, linearity, and homoscedasticity. You will see three graphs at the end of the output (Fig. 11.16) and their interpretation is similar to the simple linear regression discussed earlier. The normality of residuals can be predicted by observing the histogram and the P—P plot of standardized residuals. The ideal histogram approximates a bell shape and in the P—P plot the dots and lines should be hugging each other. In our sample, neither graph perfectly matches the description, but we may consider them reasonable given the small sample size. Linearity and homoscedasticity are observed by the scatterplot of standardized predictor and standardized residuals. If the dots have any pattern in them like a curve, then the assumption of linearity is probably unrealistic. If the points are randomly and evenly distributed without any pattern and no funneling, our assumption of homoscedasticity is met. In our results, although there is no curve pattern, there is some funneling as many values are constricting around +1 values. Thus, the assumption of homoscedasticity is doubtful. You may have to take help of Robust estimated parameters.

7. **Managing heteroskedasticity:** The scatterplot confirms that there was heteroskedasticity. The steps for performing and interpreting a robust regression method are

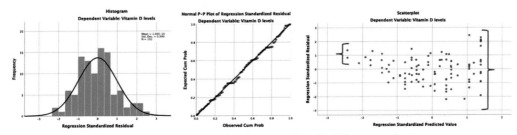

Figure 11.16 Graphs in the output of multiple linear analysis.

Modified Breusch–Pagan Test for Heteroskedasticity[a,b,c]

Chi-Square	df	Sig.
9.899	1	.002

Parameter Estimates with Robust Standard Errors

Parameter	B	Robust Std. Error[a]	t	Sig.	95% Confidence Interval Lower Bound	Upper Bound
Intercept	37.431	2.640	14.176	.000	32.192	42.670
age	−.274	.033	−8.413	.000	−.339	−.209
gender	−3.516	.784	−4.482	.000	−5.073	−1.960

Figure 11.17 Results of the multiple linear regression with robust standard errors.

described in Sections 4.3 and 4.4. Fig. 11.17 is from the output after performing the robust linear regression model. The violation of the assumption of homoscedasticity is confirmed by a significant modified Breusch–Pagan test, thus standard errors and confidence intervals calculated by the robust linear regression model should be used (Fig. 11.17).

5.4 Writing the results of the multiple linear regression

Thus, the null hypothesis is rejected as the age and gender of the patients are significantly associated with serum levels of vitamin D. The results can be expressed as follows:

Multiple linear regression analysis was used to test whether the age and gender of the patient significantly predicted participants' serum vitamin D levels. A scatterplot of the standardized predictors and standardized residuals showed that this model had a problem of heteroskedasticity, so we used HC3 estimators to calculate robust parameters. The results of the regression showed that the age and gender of the patient together explained 49.8% of the variance ($R^2 = 0.498$, $F(1.99) = 49.028$, $P < .001$). It was found that with the increase of the patients' age by one year, serum vitamin D level decreased by 0.274 ($\beta = -0.274$; 95% CI $[-0.339, -0.209]$, $P < .001$), and when gender changes from male to female for same age, the serum vitamin D value will decrease by 3.516 ($\beta = -3.516$; 95% CI $[-5.073, -1.960]$, $P < .001$) as predicted by our model. Thus, the regression equation can be written as: Vit D level = 37.431 − 0.274(age of the patient) − 3.516(gender).

6. Logistic regression analysis

Many dependent variables are categorical and not continuous. Like linear regression, logistic regression uses the modeling technique to predict the relationship between categorical dependent variables and one or more independent variables. The difference lies in the character of the dependent variable, which is not a continuous variable but categorical with two or more outcomes, such as pass or fail, improvement postintervention versus no improvement postintervention, grades of cancer, etc. Since the outcome is not continuous, the regression line is drawn using log techniques. Unlike linear regression, the log regression equation is not a straight line but a sigmoid–shaped curve (Fig. 11.4). Binary logistic regression is used when we are trying to predict a dependent variable with only two outcomes (dichotomous variable), for example, positive or negative. When the dependent variable has more than two categories, multinomial logistic regression is used. If the dependent variable has ordered categories, ordinal logistic regression is employed.

Regardless of whether we predict the relationship between one dependent dichotomous variable and one or more independent variables, it is still called binary logistic regression (or multinomial when outcome variable has more than two categories). Statistically, one explanatory variable means a univariate univariable test, whereas more than one explanatory variable means a univariate multivariable test. This has been discussed elsewhere as well. However, many research papers they are misleadingly referred to as multivariate logistic regression instead of multivariable logistic regression. We recommend that our readers understand this misuse and try their best to use the correct terms.

Given the limitations of this book, we refrain from discussing in detail the derivation of the regression equation in logistic regression. However, we will try to understand this superficially. In case you do not want, feel free to skip to the next section.

Let us recall that the mathematical equation for regression line in linear regression as

$$\mathbf{Y} = \mathbf{a} + \mathbf{b_1 X_1} + \mathbf{b_2 X_2} + \mathbf{e}, \qquad \text{(equation A3)}$$

However, Y was a continuous outcome in linear regression, but in binary logistic regression, it can take only two values (either 0 or 1). On the other hand, the probability exists from 0% to 100%. Therefore, the equation can be written as follows:

$$\textbf{Probability}(\mathbf{Y}) = \mathbf{1/1 + e}^{-(\mathbf{b0+b1x})} \qquad \text{(equation A4)}$$

where $b0$ denotes intercept, $b1$ is the slope, x is an independent variable, and e is the error term (see Section 3.1). The resultant curve will be an "S" shaped or sigmoid curve instead of a straight line in linear regression (Fig. 11.4).

Odds means a ratio of the probability of the event (P) to the probability of nonevent $(1-P)$. Thus, this can also be expressed on the scale of Log Odds of Y as follows:

$$\mathbf{Ln[P(Y) / 1 - P(Y)]} = \mathbf{b0 + b1x} \qquad \text{(equation A5)}$$

6.1 The assumptions of logistic regression

The logistic regression works in the setting where the dependent variable is categorical. In binary logistic regression, the variable should be binary/dichotomous. The independent variables can be either categorical or continuous. There are four essential assumptions that you can remembered by the acronym LIMO (Fig. 11.18). The four assumptions are (Stoltzfus, 2011):

1. *Linearity:* The relationship between continuous independent (X) variables and the logit transformation of the dependent variable should be linear.

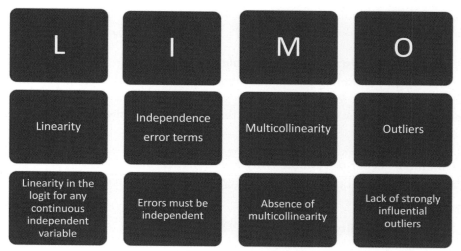

Figure 11.18 The assumptions of logistic regression.

2. *Independence:* The variables should not be paired, their observations must be independent and separate so that there is the independence of errors.

3. *Multicollinearity*: There should be an absence of multicollinearity among independent variables, they cannot be highly correlated.

4. *Outliers:* There should be lack of strongly influential outliers as they affect the model.

Thus key assumptions of linear regression, including homogeneity of variance and normality are not required in logistic regression. Thus, logistic regression can be considered if assumptions of linear regression fail even after data transformation.

7. Multiple logistic regression analysis

Logistic regression can be binary or multinomial depending on whether the outcome variable has two or more categories. We can conduct a univariable logistic regression when there is only one independent variable or multivariable logistic regression when there are more than one independent variable. The steps for application are the same except for testing the multicollinearity assumption when there are more than one independent variables.

7.1 Entering predictors into the model

The majority of biomedical research associations are complex concepts and are likely influenced by multiple factors. Logistic regression provides a way to understand how these variables correlate with each other and their relevance and relative importance in predicting binary outcomes in patients. As with multiple linear regression, there are two major considerations before the application of multiple linear regression (For a detailed discussion please refer Section 5.1):

7.1.1 Finalizing the list of predictors/explanatory variables

We recommend performing a univariate univariable analysis (simple logistic regression) with each selected variable. All the variables with a predetermined limit (significance <0.2 or at least <0.05) are then taken up for the multivariable logistic regression.

7.1.2 Method—order of variable entry in the model

We recommend using Enter method. The regression equation in multiple logistic regression would look like this

$$\textbf{Probability}(\textbf{Y}) = \textbf{1}/\textbf{1} + \textbf{e}^{-(\textbf{b0}+\textbf{b1x1}+\textbf{b2x2}+...)}$$ (equation A6)

where Y is the dependent variable, $\textbf{b0}$ denotes intercept, $\textbf{b1}, \textbf{b2}, ...$ are the slope of the lines, $x_1, x_2, ...$ are independent variables, and e is the error term.

7.2 Applying the multiple logistic regression

For ease of understanding and comparison, the dataset we will use to understand the application of multiple logistic regression is the same as that used in multiple linear regression (*6.Vit D_PTH.sav*). Instead of a continuous dependent variable of vitamin D level, we would use a dichotomous variable—vitamin D deficiency (either present or absent). We will predict our dependent variable using two independent variables (predictors): age and gender. Preliminary analysis has found age and gender are significantly associated with vitamin D deficiency ($P < .05$), so we selected both predictors for our multivariable logistic regression.

For applying logistic regression in SPSS, the dependent variable must be dichotomous with dummy coding with two numeric values representing each of the two dichotomous outcomes. In our dataset, the dependent variable *vit_D_cat* is dichotomous with Not Deficient coded as 1 and Deficient coded as 2. While performing logistic regression, by default SPSS predicts the membership of the highest value. Thus, in our dataset, logistic regression will predict the probability of vitamin D deficienct (coded as 2). The *Age* variable is continuous and *Gender* variable is categorical with Male coded as 1 and Female as 2.

H_0: There is no association of age and gender of patients with vitamin D deficiency.
H_A: Age and gender of the patient are associated with vitamin D deficiency.

The steps in the application of multiple logistic regression are as follows:

1. Open *6.Vit D_PTH.sav*. The dependent variable is *vit_D_cat*, *age* of the patient and *gender* are the independent variables. Go to *Analyze > Regression > Binary Logistics* (Fig. 11.19).

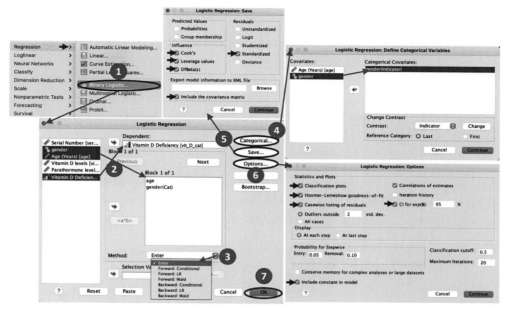

Figure 11.19 Applying the multiple logistic regression.

2. In the logistics regression dialog box, select the dependent variable (vitamin D Deficiency) and transfer it to the box labeled as *Dependent*. Similarly, transfer independent variables *Gender* and *Age* under the space labeled as *Block*.

3. After independent variables are transferred, the *Method* field activates, and by default, *Enter* is selected. Keep it as it is.

4. If the dataset has categorical variables, we need to inform SPSS about them. This is done by Clicking *Categorical*, which will open a new dialog box. Transfer the categorical variable to the field labeled as *Categorical Covariates*. Observe that *Contrast* and *Reference* categories are activated. It is advisable to keep Contrast as an *Indicator* and choose Reference categories according to the dataset. In our dataset *Gender* variable, Male is coded as 1 and Female as 2, so Female (Last) will be kept as the reference category.

5. To check for assumptions, we need to observe some statistics about our data. To do this, click *Save* in the main dialog box and tick the boxes against *Cook's, Leverages value* and *DfBeta(s)* under *Influence, Standardized Residuals*, and Include *covariance matrix*. Click *Continue*.

6. Click the *Options* box to open a new dialog box. We advise checking against *Classification plots, Hosmer–Lemeshow goodness of fit*, and *Casewise listing of residuals* with *2 std. dev., Iteration history,* and *Confidence interval (CI for expB)*. Keep selected *Include contrast* in the model and Click *Continue*.

7. Click *OK* for detailed analysis in the output window of SPSS.

7.3 Interpretation of results of the multiple logistic regression

The output of the logistic regression results of our dataset would contains about 13 tables and one plot (Fig. 11.20). It would be divided into three sections, Descriptive, Block 0, and Block 1. All of the information we need for reporting is in Block 1 tables.

1. Descriptive information: The initial tables include the *Case Processing Summary* table—which gives an overview of the missing cases, the *Dependent Variable Encoding* table—which confirms Deficient (higher value) is predicted and the *Categorical Variables Coding* table—which tells us that Male category (1.000) Odds ratio is calculated keeping Females (.000) as reference. This table is particularly useful in interpreting the odds ratio of categorical predictors. The category mentioned as .000 is the reference category while Odds ratio is calculated for the category mentioned as 1.000.

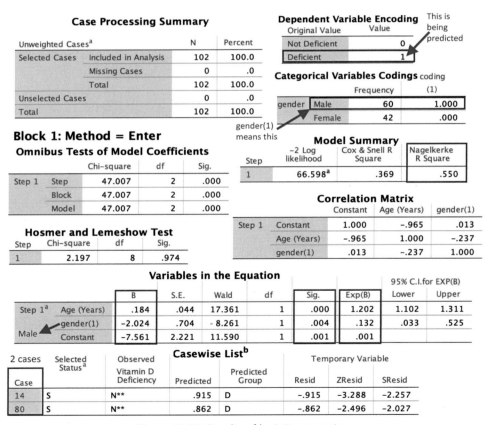

Figure 11.20 Results of logistic regression.

2. Block 0 is our null model. It provide little information. Since we used Enter method, all the predictors were added simultaneously in one Block, resulting in Block 1 only.

3. Model fit and pseudo R^2: *Omnibus Tests of Model Coefficients*, and *Hosmer and Lemeshow Test* tell us how well the predicted model fits our dataset. For a good fit, the Omnibus test must be significant and the Hosmer and Lemeshow test should be non-significant. The significance in Omnibus Tests of Model Coefficients is <0.001, indicating a good fit. On the other hand, Hosmer and Lemeshow's goodness of fit is non-significant, which indicates that the predicted model fits our data better than the null model. The *Model Summary* table gives log likelihood ratio and pseudo R^2. As *Nagelkerke R Square* value varies from 0 to 1, it is preferred to report pseudo R^2. So we can say that gender and age together predict 56.6% of the variance in vitamin D deficiency. Comparing the *Classification table* of Block 0 and Block 1, the percentage correct prediction has increased from 75.5% to 84.3%, which also shows that our model is better than the null model.

4. Variables in the equation: This is the most informative table. It contains the estimates of the model parameters along with the significance, and odds ratios of each predictor with their confidence intervals. In the first column, B is the *logistic coefficient*, which is the *beta* equivalent of linear regression. The interpretation of the logistic regression coefficient is complicated and cumbersome because we are talking in terms of probability and logit. However, the slope of the predictor gives a pretty good idea of its influence and the direction of the effect. The closer the logistic regression coefficient is to zero, the lesser is its effect. While a positive value indicates an increasing effect, a negative value shows a decreasing effect with an increase in the value of the predictor. In our model, the intercept a is −7.561 (B for constant). The slopes of age and gender are 0.184 and −2.024, indicating that as the age increase, the probability of being vitamin D deficient increases. Similarly, with the increase in gender variable unit (Male—1 to Female—2), the probability of a person being vitamin D deficient decreases. The table also displays the Wald statistic, tests the significance of the logistic coefficient being different than zero. Both predictors are significant ($P < .01$) in this model in predicting vitamin D deficiency.

5. Odds ratio: Exp(B) is the odds ratio (OR) of the predictor. This is a more effective way of to express the relationship between our predictor variables and the outcome. OR indicate the change in Odds of outcome in terms of per unit change in the predictor. As our OR of age is 1.202 with 95% CI [1.102, 1.311], it means that with each year increase in age, the odds of a person classified as vitamin D deficient increase by 1.202 after adjusting for gender. Similarly, OR of gender is 0.132. with 95% CI [0.033, 0.525] can also be expressed as males have a 0.132 times chance of being Vit D deficient in comparison to females after controlling for individual differences in age. In other words, males are less likely to have vitamin D deficiency. So, OR = 1 implies no difference in chance, OR < 1 implies a negative difference or reduced risk, and OR > 1 implies a positive difference or increased risk. We can also predict significance from the confidence interval of OR. If 95% CI does not contain 1, then it is a significant relationship. Notably, OR less than 1 is less intuitive to report, which can be inversed to make it more than 1, along with inverting the reference category. So $1/0.132 = 7.576$, which can be interpreted as the odds of a female being Vit D deficient are 7.576 times higher than those of a male after adjusting for age. This can also be done by rerunning the logistic regression, changing the reference category of *gender* to male.

6. **Collinearity:** The assumption of the absence of collinearity must be tested in multi-variable logistic regression. We get an idea of correlationship between independent variables from the correlation matrix; a value of correlation coefficient greater than 0.9 should ring the bell for multicollinearity. Unfortunately, unlike linear regression, logistic regression does not calculate bivariate correlation, tolerance or VIF. However, the correlation coefficient can be obtained by performing *Analyze > corelate > bivariate*, which in our dataset between age and gender was 0.056, meaning no correlation. Tolerance and VIF can be reliably estimated by running multiple linear regression with the same independent and dependent variable and selecting *Collinearity Diagnostics* from the *Statistics* tab (Lomax & Hahs-Vaughn, 2013).

7. **Case-wise diagnostics:** Casewise Diagnostics lists cases that the model incorrectly classified. It also provides information on residuals outside two standard deviations, which are potential outliers. Our model had 2 cases out of 102 (<2%) whose residuals were outside two standard deviations, which is tolerable.

8. **Residuals statistics:** In the residuals statistics table, look for Cook's distance. The maximum limit for Cook's distance is 1. Our model satisfies this condition, so it is unlikely that any of the cases have an undue influence on our model.

The assumptions of logistic regression and their checking is summarized in Fig. 11.21, whereas the case of linearity in logistic regression is shown in Box 11.3.

7.4 Writing the results of the multiple logistic regression

Thus, the null hypothesis is rejected as the age and gender of the patient are significantly associated with vitamin D deficiency. The results can be expressed as follows:

Multiple logistic regression analysis was used to test whether the age and gender of the patient significantly predicted participants' being vitamin D deficient. There was no multicollinearity and high influential observations in the predicted model. The results of the regression showed that the age and gender of the patient together explained 56.6% of the variance (Nagelkerke $R^2 = 0.566$, χ^2 Omnibus (2102) = 47.007, $P < .01$). It was found that with each year increase in age, the odds of a person being classified as vitamin D deficient increases by 1.202 after adjusting for gender (OR = 1.202; 95% CI [1.102, 1.311], $P < .001$). Similarly, the odds of a male being

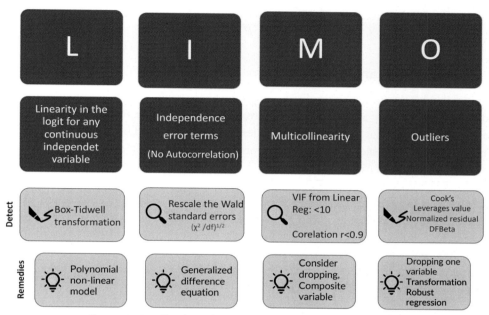

Figure 11.21 Checking the assumptions of logistic regression.

BOX 11.3 Assumptions of linearity in logistic regression

Since the dependent variable is categorical, logistic regression makes the assumption of linearity between continuous independent variables and the logit of the dependent variable. This is a little tricky, but the model fit and the pseudo R2 can help you estimate. A nonsignificant Hosmer and Lemeshow test and sufficiently large pseudo R^2 are a reliable indication that the linearity assumptions are met. Another technical approach to testing the linearity is to use the Box—Tidwell transformation. For this, first we need to transform all of our continuous independent variables to log function and its multiple. This is done by *Transform > Compute variable*, which opens a Compute variable dialog box. A name to new target variable (e.g., log.age) is given in *Target variable* box, and in *Numeric Expression* section write: LN( )*( ) and shift the variable of interest between bracket, for example, LN(age)*(age). This is the Box—Tidwell transformation. LN represents the log function, while * stands for multiplication. This will create a new variable at the last column of your dataset. Perform these steps for all continuous independent variables. Now you need to rerun the logistic regression analysis with the previously selected independent variables along with all the newly created Box—Tidwell transformation variables. Observe the significance of newly created variables. If none of them is significant, it indicates that there is no linear relationship between continuous- independent variables and the logit of the dependent variable.

vitamin D deficient are 0.132 times those of a female after adjusting for age (OR = 0.132; 95% CI [0.033, 0.525], $P < .001$).

8. Multivariable analysis

In many health research, the key focus of applying regression is to determine the adjusted odds ratio, commonly and incorrectly referred to as multivariate analysis. If one independent variable is associated with the dependent variable, it could be due to confounding. To eliminate this problem, we adjust for potential confounders. For clarity, let us take an example. In the univariable analysis, poverty has a significant association with poor immunization coverage. On the other hand, there is also a significant association between illiteracy and poor immunization. Illiteracy and poverty confound each other, as they both influence each other as well as the outcome. In multivariable analysis, these two independent variables are put together to adjust for each other and then significance is calculated. So, the univariable odds ratio is adjusted. The application of the regression technique and its assumption remain the same. However, the presented tables for this particular objective could be improved.

Based on the example and calculations above (Fig. 11.20), we are interested in finding the Odds ratio of vitamin D deficiency with relation to age and gender. In the univariable analysis, the age was found to be significant with OR of 1.188 (95%CI - 1.097—1.286) and the male gender had an OR of 0.195 (95%CI - 0.061—0.623) with females as a reference. In the multivariable analysis, adjusting for both age and gender, the adjusted ratios were found to be significant for both age and gender. The Nagelkerke R^2 with age and gender as the predictors was 0.57. The adjusted OR for age was found to be 1.202 (1.102—1.311) and for males with females as a reference—0.132 (0.033—0.525). The results are shown in Table 11.2.

Table 11.2 Multivariable odds ratio for age and gender for Vitamin D deficiency.

Independent variable		Odds ratio with CI	Adjusted odds ratio[a]
Age		1.188 [1.097, 1.286]	1.202 [1.102, 1.311]
Gender	Male	0.195 [0.061, 0.623]	0.132 [0.033, 0.525]
	Female	Reference	Reference

[a]Adjusted for age of the patient and gender with Nagelkerke $R^2 = 0.566$.

References

Efron, B., & Tibshirani, R. (1993). *An introduction to the bootstrap*. Chapman & Hall.

Field, A. (2018). *Discovering statistics using IBM SPSS statistics* (5th ed.). Sage Publication.

Gray, J. B., & Fox, J. (1998). Applied regression analysis, linear models, and related methods. *Technometrics, 40*(2), 156. https://doi.org/10.2307/1270653

Hayes, A. F., & Cai, L. (2007). Using heteroskedasticity-consistent standard error estimators in OLS regression: An introduction and software implementation. *Behavior Research Methods, 39*(4), 709—722. https://doi.org/10.3758/BF03192961

Hidalgo, B., & Goodman, M. (2013). Multivariate or multivariable regression? *American Journal of Public Health, 103*(1), 39—40. https://doi.org/10.2105/AJPH.2012.300897

Lomax, R. G., & Hahs-Vaughn, D. L. (2013). An introduction to statistical concepts. In *An introduction to statistical concepts* (3rd ed., pp. 1—822). Taylor and Francis Inc. https://doi.org/10.4324/9780203137819

Pagano, M., & Gauvreau, K. (2000). *Principles of biostatistics*.

Pedhazur, E. J. (1997). *Multiple regression in behavioral research: An explanation and prediction* (3rd ed.). Harcourt Brace Publication.

Peters, T. J. (2008). Multifarious terminology: Multivariable or multivariate? Univariable or univariate? *Paediatric and Perinatal Epidemiology, 22*(6), 506. https://doi.org/10.1111/j.1365-3016.2008.00966.x

Porta, M. (2014). *A dictionary of epidemiology*. Oxford University Press.

Ranganathan, P., Pramesh, C., & Aggarwal, R. (2017). Common pitfalls in statistical analysis: Logistic regression. *Perspectives in Clinical Research, 8*(3), 148—151. https://doi.org/10.4103/picr.PICR_87_17

Stoltzfus, J. C. (2011). Logistic regression: A brief primer. *Academic Emergency Medicine, 18*(10), 1099—1104. https://doi.org/10.1111/j.1553-2712.2011.01185.x

Tsai, A. C. (2013). Achieving consensus on terminology describing multivariable analyses/Hidalgo and Goodman respond. *American Journal of Public Health, 103*(6), E1.

CHAPTER 12

Annexures

1. Annexure 1: Choice of statistical tests (Fig. 12.1).

2. Annexure 2: Notes on data used in the book

The book has many datasets for hands-on practice. The screenshots of the application and results are based on these datasets. Some of the datasets have been modified from actual published research. However, the datasets are not the same as the ones used in the research as they have been modified to serve the purpose of this book. While we have cited the research with reference to the dataset, it is only meant to understand the research question, background, or interpretation (Table 12.1).

3. Annexure 3: Guidelines for statistical reporting in journals: SAMPL guidelines

3.1 Background

Reporting guidelines and checklists are useful aids to guide scientific accuracy in reporting, and improve the application, analysis, interpretation, and replication of the studies. A repository of the standard guidelines for different types of studies is available at Equator Network (http://www.equator-network.org). The most comprehensive guideline on statistical reporting is the Statistical Analyses and Methods in the Published Literature or SAMPL guidelines (Lang & Altman, 2013, pp. 175–182). SAMPL guidelines are based on the two foundational principles, based on the International Committee of Medical Journal Editors standards (*emphasized as per SAMPL guideline document*):

1. Describe statistical methods with enough detail to enable a knowledgeable reader with access to the original data to verify the reported results.
2. Provide enough detail so that the results can be incorporated into other analyses.

Both in the research protocol and methods section, a mention of the statistical plan is immensely important for replication and verification. A clear mention of the statistical plan includes the tests that are proposed to be used with their assumptions and alternatives

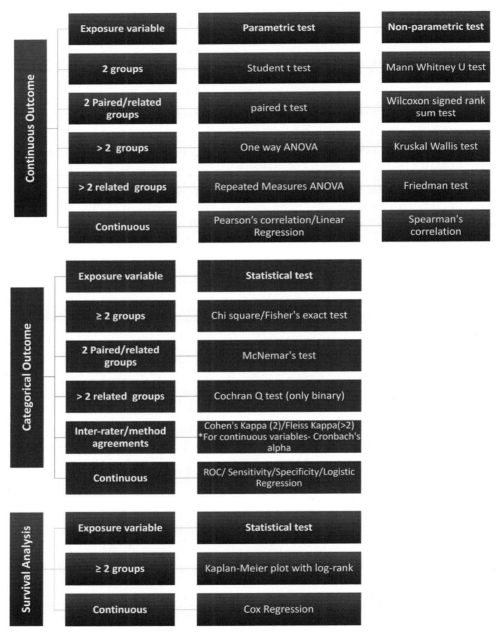

Figure 12.1 Choice of statistical tests.

Table 12.1 Datasets used in the book.

S. No.	Name of the dataset	Details
1.	2. TBreg_data.xlsx	A tuberculosis registration data with registration number, patient's demographic, and diagnostic variables.
2.	3. Adolescents_BMI.sav	The dataset has the body mass index (BMI) of adolescents with diet and lifestyle-related variables. The important variables used for assessment are as follows: (1) BMIZ—BMI for age Z score: the adolescents are less than 18 years of age and therefore their BMI for age Z-score is used as cut-off for overweight/obesity assessment. (2) sleep_night—sleep duration at night: categorized as adequate or inadequate sleep duration at night—ASDN and IASDN, respectively. (3) breakfast_freq—frequency of breakfast intake categorized as rarely, irregularly, and regularly.
3.	3. Fluorides_Dental.sav	The dataset compares fluoride release after the application of different fluoridating agents—sodium fluoride (NaF), stannous fluoride (SnF2), and acidulated phosphate fluoride (APF) with time. The time intervals are as follows: after 1 h, 1 week, and 1 week of application.
4.	5. Keto_Diet.sav	The dataset compares the preintervention weight with the postintervention weight after ketogenic diet.
5.	6. VitD_PTH.sav	The dataset compares vitamin D and parathormone (PTH) levels. It also has vitamin D categories variable—deficient, insufficient, and sufficient.
6.	6. Raters.sav	Three raters—Amar, Akbar, and Anthony grade the same student papers independently.

Continued

Table 12.1 Datasets used in the book.—cont'd

S. No.	Name of the dataset	Details
7.	7. HIV_Depression.sav	The dataset is of HIV/AIDS patients on treatment with their demographic and treatment-related variables. The important variables used in the analysis in the book are as follows: (1) clinical staging (initial, 1 year ago, and current): categorized into symptomatic and asymptomatic, (2) depression status: categorized into yes and no, (3) WHO clinical staging, and (4) depression grading.
8.	8. Organ Failure.sav	The dataset has organ failure as the outcome and three types of scores to determine an association with it. The three scores are as follows: (1) BISAP—Bedside Index for Severity in Acute Pancreatitis Score, (2) MCTSI—Modified Computed Tomography Scan Score Index (MCTSI), and (3) APACHE II—Accuracy of Acute Physiology and Chronic Health Evaluation.
9.	9. Kappa.sav	Two raters (Rater A and B) rate the facial symmetry of patients independently.
10.	9. Weighted Kappa.sav	Two pathology labs grade the same tissue specimens independently.
11.	9. Fleiss kappa	Three laboratory technical officers rate the same specimens into mild, moderate and severe anemia independently. (Different/nonunique raters)
12.	9. ICC.sav	Three raters measure hemoglobin from the same samples independently.
13.	9. DLQI_Cronbach.sav	The dataset has measures of the Dermatological Life Quality Index (DLQI) and its 10 questions from patients suffering from tinea.

in case the data does not fulfill the assumptions. Before discussing the SAMPL guidelines, we reiterate the following precautions while reporting *P*-values:

1. Clearly mentioning the difference between statistical and clinical significance, as the New England Journal of Medicine clearly recommends (Harrington et al., 2019). *Significance,* whenever used alone stands for statistical significance and nothing else.
2. *P*-values should always be two-tailed unless required by the study design (noninferiority trials).
3. Exact *P*-values must be mentioned unless *P*-value is <.001. All the latter values can be written as <.001.
4. As discussed in detail elsewhere, effect sizes and confidence intervals must accompany statistical significance reporting. For details, please refer to Chapter 3.

The SAMPL guidelines for reporting statistical methods and results are reproduced with minor textual modifications (in italics), wherever needed (Lang & Altman, 2013, pp. 175—182).

3.2 SAMPL guidelines for reporting statistical methods

3.2.1 Preliminary analyses

Identify any statistical procedures used to modify raw data before analysis. Examples include mathematically transforming continuous measurements to make distributions closer to the normal distribution, creating ratios or other derived variables, and collapsing continuous data into categorical data or combining categories.

3.2.2 Primary analyses

1. Describe the purpose of the analysis.
2. Identify the variables used in the analysis and summarize each with descriptive statistics.
3. When possible, identify the smallest difference considered to be clinically important.
4. Describe fully the main methods for analyzing the primary objectives of the study.
5. Make clear which method was used for each analysis, rather than just listing in one place all the statistical methods used.
6. Verify that data conformed to the assumptions of the test used to analyze them. In particular, specify that (1) skewed data were analyzed with nonparametric tests, (2) paired data were analyzed with paired tests, and (3) the underlying relationship analyzed with linear regression models was linear.
7. Indicate whether and how any allowance or adjustments were made for multiple comparisons (performing multiple hypothesis tests on the same data).
8. If relevant, report how any outlying data were treated in the analysis.
9. Say whether tests were one- or two-tailed and justify the use of one-tailed tests.
10. Report the alpha level (e.g., 0.05) that defines statistical significance.
11. Name the statistical package or program (*with version*) used in the analysis.

3.2.3 *Supplementary analyses*

1. Describe methods used for any ancillary analyses, such as sensitivity analyses, imputation of missing values, or testing of assumptions underlying methods of analysis.
2. Identify post hoc analyses, including unplanned subgroup analyses, as exploratory.

3.3 SAMPL guidelines for reporting statistical results

3.3.1 *Reporting numbers and descriptive statistics*

1. Report numbers—especially measurements—with an appropriate degree of precision. For ease of comprehension and simplicity, round as much as is reasonable. For example, mean age can often be rounded to the nearest year without compromising either the clinical or the statistical analysis. If the smallest meaningful difference on a scale is five points, scores can be reported as whole numbers; decimals are not necessary.
2. Report total sample and group sizes for each analysis.
3. Report numerators and denominators for all percentages.
4. Summarize data that are approximately normally distributed with means and standard deviations (SD). Use the form: mean (SD), not mean $\pm$ SD.
5. Summarize data that are not normally distributed with medians and interpercentile ranges, ranges, or both.
6. Report the upper and lower boundaries of interpercentile ranges and the minimum and maximum values of ranges, not just the size of the range.
7. Do NOT use the standard error of the mean (SE) to indicate the variability of a data set. Use standard deviations, interpercentile ranges, or ranges instead.
8. Display the data in tables or figures. Tables present exact values, and figures provide an overall assessment of the data (Lang, 2010; Schriger et al., 2006).

3.3.2 *Reporting risk, rates, and ratios*

1. Identify the type of rate (incidence rates; survival rates), ratio (odds ratios; hazards ratios), or risk (absolute risks; relative risk differences), being reported.
2. Identify the quantities represented in the numerator and denominator (e.g., the number of men with prostate cancer divided by the number of men capable of having prostate cancer).
3. Identify the time period over with each rate applies.
4. Identify any unit of population (that is, the unit multiplier: for example, $\times 100$; $\times 10,000$) associated with the rate.
5. Consider reporting a measure of precision (a confidence interval) for estimated risks, rates, and ratios.

3.3.3 *Reporting hypothesis tests*

1. State the hypothesis being tested.
2. Identify the variables in the analysis and summarize the data for each variable with the appropriate descriptive statistics.
3. If possible, identify the minimum difference considered to be clinically important.
4. For equivalence and noninferiority studies, report the largest difference between groups that will still be accepted as indicating biological equivalence (the equivalence margin).
5. Identify the name of the test used in the analysis.
6. Report whether the test was one- or two-tailed and for paired or independent samples.
7. Confirm that the assumptions of the test were met by the data.
8. Report the alpha level (e.g., 0.05) that defines statistical significance.
9. At least for primary outcomes, such as differences or agreement between groups, diagnostic sensitivity, and slopes of regression lines, report a measure of precision, such as the 95% confidence interval.
10. Do NOT use the SE to indicate the precision of an estimate. The SE is essentially a 68% confidence coefficient: use the 95% confidence coefficient instead.
11. Although not preferred to confidence intervals, if desired, P values should be reported as equalities when possible and to one or two decimal places (e.g., $P = .03$ or $.22$ not as inequalities: e.g., $P < .05$). Do NOT report "NS"; give the actual P value. The smallest P value that need be reported is $P < .001$, save in studies of genetic associations.
12. Report whether and how any adjustments were made for multiple statistical comparisons.
13. Name the statistical software package used in the analysis (*with the version of the software, wherever applicable*).

3.3.4 *Reporting association analyses*

1. Describe the association of interest.
2. Identify the variables used and summarize each with descriptive statistics.
3. Identify the test of association used.
4. Indicate whether the test was one- or two-tailed.
5. Justify the use of one-tailed tests.
6. For tests of association (e.g., a chi-square test), report the P value of the test (because the association is defined as a statistically significant result).
7. For measures of association (i.e., the phi coefficient), report the value of the coefficient and a confidence interval. Do not describe the association as low, moderate, or high unless the ranges for these categories have been defined.

8. Even then, consider the wisdom of using these categories given their biological implications or realities.
9. For primary comparisons, consider including the full contingency table for the analysis.
10. Name the statistical software package used in the analysis (*with version of the software, wherever applicable*).

3.3.5 Reporting correlation analyses

1. Describe the purpose of the analysis.
2. Summarize each variable with the appropriate descriptive statistics.
3. Identify the correlation coefficient used in the analysis (e.g., Pearson, Spearman).
4. Confirm that the assumptions of the analysis were met.
5. Report the alpha level (e.g., 0.05) that indicates whether the correlation coefficient is statistically significant.
6. Report the value of the correlation coefficient. Do not describe correlation as low, moderate, or high unless the ranges for these categories have been defined. Even then, consider the wisdom of using these categories given their biological implications or realities.
7. For primary comparisons, report the (95%) confidence interval for the correlation coefficient, whether or not it is statistically significant.
8. For primary comparisons, consider reporting the results as a scatter plot. The sample size, correlation coefficient (with its confidence interval), and P value can be included in the data field.
9. Name the statistical software package used in the analysis (*with version of the software, wherever applicable*).

3.3.6 Reporting regression analyses

1. Describe the purpose of the analysis.
2. Identify the variables used in the analysis and summarize each with descriptive statistics.
3. Confirm that the assumptions of the analysis were met. For example, in linear regression indicate whether an analysis of residuals confirmed the assumptions of linearity.
4. If relevant, report how any outlying values were treated in the analysis.
5. Report how any missing data were treated in the analyses.
6. For either simple or multiple (multivariable) regression analyses, report the regression equation.
7. For multiple regression analyses: (1) report the alpha level used in the univariate analysis; (2) report whether the variables were assessed for (a) colinearity and

(b) interaction; and (3) describe the variable selection process by which the final model was developed (e.g., forward–stepwise; best subset).

8. Report the regression coefficients (beta weights) of each explanatory variable and the associated confidence intervals and P values, preferably in a table.

9. Provide a measure of the model's "goodness-of-fit" to the data (the coefficient of determination, r^2, for simple regression and the coefficient of multiple determination, R^2, for multiple regression).

10. Specify whether and how the model was validated.

11. For primary comparisons analyzed with simple linear regression analysis, consider reporting the results graphically, in a scatter plot showing the regression line and its confidence bounds. Do not extend the regression line (or the interpretation of the analysis) beyond the minimum and maximum values of the data.

12. Name the statistical software package used in the analysis (*with version of the software, wherever applicable*).

3.3.7 Reporting analyses of variance or covariance

1. Describe the purpose of the analysis.

2. Identify the variables used in the analysis and summarize each with descriptive statistics.

3. Confirm that the assumptions of the analysis were met. For example, indicate whether an analysis of residuals confirmed the assumptions of linearity.

4. If relevant, report how any outlying data were treated in the analysis.

5. Report how any missing data were treated in the analyses.

6. Specify whether the explanatory variables were tested for interaction, and if so how these interactions were treated.

7. If appropriate, in a table, report the P value for each explanatory variable, the test statistics, and, where applicable, the degrees of freedom for the analysis.

8. Provide an assessment of the goodness of fit of the model to the data, such as R^2.

9. Specify whether and how the model was validated.

10. Name the statistical software package used in the analysis (*with version of the software, wherever applicable*).

3.3.8 Reporting survival (time-to-event) analyses

1. Describe the purpose of the analysis.

2. Identify the dates or events that mark the beginning and the end of the time period analyzed.

3. Specify the circumstances under which data were censored.

4. Specify the statistical methods used to estimate the survival rate.

5. Confirm that the assumptions of survival analysis were met.

6. For each group, give the estimated survival probability at appropriate follow-up times, with confidence intervals, and the number of participants at risk for death at each time. It is often more helpful to plot the cumulative probability of not surviving, especially when events are not common.
7. Reporting median survival times, with confidence intervals, is often useful to allow the results to be compared with those of other studies.
8. Consider presenting the full results in a graph (e.g., a Kaplan—Meier plot) or table.
9. Specify the statistical methods used to compare two or more survival curves.
10. When comparing two or more survival curves with hypothesis tests, report the *P* value of the comparison.
11. Report the regression model used to assess the associations between the explanatory variables and survival or time-to-event.
12. Report a measure of risk (e.g., a hazard ratio) for each explanatory variable, with a confidence interval.

3.3.9 Reporting Bayesian analyses
1. Specify the pretrial probabilities ("priors").
2. Explain how the priors were selected.
3. Describe the statistical model used.
4. Describe the techniques used in the analysis.
5. Identify the statistical software program used in the analysis.
6. Summarize the posterior distribution with a measure of central tendency and a credibility interval
7. Assess the sensitivity of the analysis to different priors.

   Although SAMPL guidelines broadly cover all aspects related to data management, it does not include data quality-related statements. In data entry without double data entry, matching, and validation, the data quality is often a problem (Faizi et al., 2018). However, with the increasing use of mobile and tablet-based data collection, data collection automatically leads to data entry (data capture = data collection + entry), automatically ensuring data entry quality. More information is provided in Chapter 2.

4. Annexure 4: Standards for reporting of diagnostic accuracy: STARD guidelines

The standards for reporting of diagnostic accuracy (STARD) guidelines deal predominantly with diagnostic accuracy (Bossuyt et al., 2003) and should complement the guidelines for reporting reliability and agreement studies (GRRAS), if the latter is also applicable (Kottner et al., 2011). An easy-to-use checklist, flow diagram, and guideline are available at the Equator Network (http://www.equator-network.org). They were proposed to improve the adequacy of information in such studies. Table 12.2 is a reproduction of the checklist.

Table 12.2 The STARD checklist.

Section	No.	Item
Title	1	Identification as a study of diagnostic accuracy using at least one measure of accuracy (such as sensitivity, specificity, predictive values, or AUC)
Abstract	2	Structured summary of study design, methods, results, and conclusions
Introduction	3	Scientific and clinical background, including the intended use and clinical role of the index test
	4	Study objectives and hypotheses
Study design	5	Whether data collection was planned before the index test and reference standard were performed (prospective study) or after (retrospective study)
Participants	6	Eligibility criteria
	7	On what basis potentially eligible participants were identified (such as symptoms, results from previous tests, inclusion in registry)
	8	Where and when potentially eligible participants were identified (setting, location and dates)
	9	Whether participants formed a consecutive, random or convenience series
Test methods	10a	Index test, in sufficient detail to allow replication
	10b	Reference standard, in sufficient detail to allow replication
	11	Rationale for choosing the reference standard (if alternatives exist)
	12a	Definition of and rationale for test positivity cut-offs or result categories of the index test, distinguishing prespecified from exploratory
	12b	Definition of and rationale for test positivity cut-offs or result categories of the reference standard, distinguishing prespecified from exploratory
	13a	Whether clinical information and reference standard results were available to the performers/readers of the index test
	13b	Whether clinical information and index test results were available to the assessors of the reference standard

Continued

Table 12.2 The STARD checklist.—cont'd

Section	No.	Item
Analysis	14	Methods for estimating or comparing measures of diagnostic accuracy
	15	How indeterminate index test or reference standard results were handled
	16	How missing data on the index test and reference standard were handled
	17	Any analyses of variability in diagnostic accuracy, distinguishing prespecified from exploratory
	18	Intended sample size and how it was determined
Results participants	19	Flow of participants, using a diagram
	20	Baseline demographic and clinical characteristics of participants
	21a	Distribution of severity of disease in those with the target condition
	21b	Distribution of alternative diagnoses in those without the target condition
	22	Time interval and any clinical interventions between index test and reference standard
Test results	23	Cross-tabulation of the index test results (or their distribution) by the results of the reference standard
	24	Estimates of diagnostic accuracy and their precision (such as 95% confidence intervals)
	25	Any adverse events from performing the index test or the reference standard
Discussion	26	Study limitations, including sources of potential bias, statistical uncertainty, and generalisability
	27	Implications for practice, including the intended use and clinical role of the index test
Other information	28	Registration number and name of registry
	29	Where the full study protocol can be accessed
	30	Sources of funding and other support; role of funders

5. Annexure 5: Guidelines for reporting reliability and agreement studies: GRRAS guidelines

5.1 Background

The GRRAS were proposed to improve the adequacy of information while reporting reliability and agreement studies (Kottner et al., 2011). In health research, the primary objective could be reliability and agreement testing. In addition, agreement and reliability testing are also part of larger diagnostic accuracy studies, and reliability assessments as well as a measure of quality control. The STARD guidelines deal predominantly with diagnostic accuracy and are discussed earlier (Bossuyt et al., 2003).

5.2 Salient features of the guidelines

The STARD guidelines have 15 items under six heads—(1) Title and Abstract (1 item), (2) Introduction (4 items), (3) Methods (5 items), (4) Results (3 items), (5) Discussion (1 item), and (6) Auxiliary Material (1 item) (Bossuyt et al., 2003).

In the title and abstract of reliability and agreement studies, a clear mention of interrater or intrarater reliability/agreement must be mentioned. This helps in evidence searching and detection which is difficult if the paper is a part of larger studies. In the introduction, there are four important items: (1) name and description of the diagnostic/measurement device, (2) specification of subject population of interest, (3) specification of rater population of interest, and (4) description of rationale as well as previous reliability and agreement studies on the same. For categorical measures, the total number of categories must be stated, whereas in continuous, the range of measures must be stated along with the categorical cut-offs. As discussed in detail earlier, the subject population details—settings of patient care, their stage, age, and other attributes—affect the interpretation and must be mentioned. Similarly, the rater qualifications, expertise, and clinical training must also be mentioned.

In the methods section, there are five items: (1) explanation of sample size details (raters, subjects/objects, repeat observations), (2) sampling method description, (3) description of the rating process (time intervals, blinding, etc.), (4) statement on independence on the measurements/rating process, and (5) description of statistical analysis. The first two items are concerned with the explicit determination of sample size for population and/or raters as a part of the study design. This must be followed by the sampling method or plan, where, the terms like "random/consecutive/convenient" as used in the specific study must be explained. The statistical analysis is explained in the chapter on testing reliability and agreement (Chapter 9). The kappa or weighted kappa test must be stated with the choice of weighting-linear or quadratic with the reason for the same. In case intraclass correlation coefficient or other tests are used, it must be appropriately mentioned.

In the results, three items must be mentioned: (1) statement on the actual number of raters, subjects, and the number of observations (including repeat observations), (2) description of sample characteristics of raters and subjects, and (3) reporting of estimates of reliability/agreement with statistical uncertainty. The latter means that not only the statistical summary but also the confidence intervals must be stated as applicable. In the discussion, the practical relevance of the results must be mentioned. This means that not only grading as "poor" or "moderate" based on standard guidelines but also the meaning in terms of clinical application must be discussed. Finally, all the auxiliary materials such as detailed results, raw data, etc. could be provided as supplementary material.

6. Annexure 6: Proposed agenda for biostatistics for a health research workshop

Over the years, we conducted different workshops on biostatistics for health research and mentored researchers post-workshop till their publication. The need to write this book is primarily due to the participant feedbacks. While the book contains more details, it can be summarized in a workshop with hands-on exercises with the book as a reference manual. The workshop could be best conducted in an intensive 3-day session with at least one facilitator per five participants. For a 2-day session, survival analysis and multivariate and regression analysis must be skipped for advanced workshops after the 2-day basic workshop of other chapters (Table 12.3).

Table 12.3 Proposed agenda for biostatistics workshop.

Session	Topic	Chapter
Day 1		
1	Introduction to biostatistics	1
2	Data management and SPSS	2
3	Statistical tests of significance	3
4	Parametric tests	4
Day 2		
5	Nonparametric tests	5
6	Correlation	6
7	Testing for validity	8
8	Testing for reliability and agreements	9
Day 3		
9	Categorical variables	7
10	Survival analysis	10
11 + 12	Multivariate and regression analysis	11

References

Bossuyt, P. M., Reitsma, J. B., Bruns, D. E., Gatsonis, C. A., Glasziou, P. P., Irwig, L. M., Moher, D., Rennie, D., De Vet, H. C. W., & Lijmer, J. G. (2003). The STARD statement for reporting studies of diagnostic accuracy: Explanation and elaboration. *Clinical Chemistry, 49*(1), 7–18. https://doi.org/10.1373/49.1.7

Faizi, N., Kumar, A. M., & Kazmi, S. (2018). Omission of quality assurance during data entry in public health research from India: Is there an elephant in the room? *Indian Journal of Public Health, 62*(2), 150–152. https://doi.org/10.4103/ijph.IJPH_386_16

Harrington, D., D'Agostino, R. B., Gatsonis, C., Hogan, J. W., Hunter, D. J., Normand, S. L. T., Drazen, J. M., & Hamel, M. B. (2019). New guidelines for statistical reporting in the journal. *New England Journal of Medicine, 381*(3), 285–286. https://doi.org/10.1056/NEJMe1906559

Kottner, J., Audige, L., Brorson, S., Donner, A., Gajewski, B. J., Hróbjartsson, A., Roberts, C., Shoukri, M., & Streiner, D. L. (2011). Guidelines for reporting reliability and agreement studies (GRRAS) were proposed. *International Journal of Nursing Studies, 48*(6), 661–671. https://doi.org/10.1016/j.ijnurstu.2011.01.016

Lang, T. A. (2010). *How to write, publish, and present in the health sciences.* ACP Press.

Lang, T. A., & Altman, D. G. (2013). *5.7: Basic statistical reporting for articles published in clinical medical journals: The Statistical Analyses and Methods in the Published Literature, or SAMPL guidelines.*

Schriger, D. L., Arora, S., & Altman, D. G. (2006). The content of medical journal instructions for authors. *Annals of Emergency Medicine, 48*(6), 743-e4. https://doi.org/10.1016/j.annemergmed.2006.03.028

Index

'Note: Page numbers followed by "f" indicate figures, "t" indicate tables and "b" indicate boxes.'

Printed in the United States
by Baker & Taylor Publisher Services